BEYOND THE IMPASSE?
Scripture, Interpretation, and Theology in Baptist Life

BEYOND
The
IMPASSE?

SCRIPTURE, INTERPRETATION, & THEOLOGY in BAPTIST LIFE

Edited by
ROBISON B. JAMES
& DAVID S. DOCKERY

BROADMAN PRESS
NASHVILLE, TENNESSEE

© Copyright 1992 • Broadman Press
All Rights Reserved
4260-36
ISBN: 0-8054-6036-5
Dewey Decimal Classification: 220
Subject Heading: BIBLE // BAPTISTS - DOCTRINES
Library of Congress Catalog Number: 91-22661
Printed in the United States of America

Library of Congress Cataloging-in-Publication Data

Beyond the impasse? scripture, interpretation, and theology in
    Baptist life / edited by Robison B. James and David S. Dockery.
        p.   cm.
    Includes bibliographical references.
    ISBN 0-0854-6036-5
    1. Bible—Hermeneutics.   2. Baptists—Doctrines.   3. Southern
Baptist Convention—Doctrines.   I. James, Robison B., 1931–
II. Dockery, David S.
BS476.B48   1992
220.1'3—dc20   91-22661
                                                                CIP

With appreciation to

The Administration of
Samford University,
the Administration of
The Southern Baptist Theological Seminary,
the Office of the Chaplain of
The University of Richmond, and
The Virginia Baptist General Board

for hosting the conferences
that made this book possible

CONTENTS

Preface *Robison B. James* and *David S. Dockery*   **ix**

Part I: Present Challenges and New Directions

Chapter
1. A People of the Book and the Crisis of Biblical Authority   **17**
   David S. Dockery
2. Passing on the Biblical Tradition Intact:
   The Role of Historical Criticism   **40**
   Walter Harrelson
3. The Challenge of Recent Literary Approaches to the Bible   **64**
   John P. Newport
4. Has Theology a Future in the Southern Baptist Convention?
   Toward a Renewed Theological Framework   **91**
   R. Albert Mohler, Jr.
5. Beyond Old Habits and on to a New Land   **118**
   Robison B. James
6. Beyond the Impasse: Fidelity to the God Who Speaks   **149**
   Paige Patterson
7. Setting Our Feet in a Large Room   **169**
   Molly Truman Marshall
8. Conflict and Identity in the Southern Baptist Convention:
   The Quest for a New Consensus   **195**
   Timothy George

Part II: Dialogue and Further Reflections

Chapter
9. A Response by David S. Dockery   **217**
10. A Response by Walter Harrelson   **227**
11. A Response by John P. Newport   **232**
12. A Response by R. Albert Mohler, Jr.   **244**
13. A Response by Robison B. James   **255**
14. A Response by Paige Patterson   **278**
15. A Response by Molly Truman Marshall   **291**
16. A Response by Timothy George   **301**

Conclusion: Beyond the Impasse?   **310**
   Robison B. James and *David S. Dockery*

For Further Study   **315**

EDITORS' PREFACE

An impasse is a road with no exit, a dead end. In recent years, a situation of that kind has been created among a great many Baptists in this country.

The eight of us who have contributed to this volume explore the key biblical and theological issues that are tangled in the thick underbrush of that impasse. We offer in this volume some ways to grapple with and, so far as each of us thinks possible, to move *Beyond the Impasse* in Baptist life.

Since the two editors agreed to pursue this project in June 1989, they and the other contributors have engaged one another in discussions of the subjects treated in this book at professional meetings, in correspondence, and by telephone calls. The discussions also took place during two meetings of the Southern Baptist Convention (in 1989 and 1990) and during the meeting of the Cooperative Baptist Fellowship in 1991.

On one remarkable occasion, our entire group of eight got together. That was for a two-day dialogue, face-to-face, at Samford University, Birmingham, Alabama, in October 1990. We call this a "remarkable occasion" because the eight of us represent a very wide span of differences. Deliberately so.

In addition to these discussions within our group, we also "went on tour," so to speak, in the summer of 1990. Always preserving a balance of speakers, four of us delivered early versions of our chapters at the University of Richmond pastors' school in July 1990, and seven of us did the same thing the next month in Louisville, Kentucky, at The Southern Baptist Theological Seminary pastors' school.[1]

Partly because of these extensive interactions, any one of the chapters in this book will enhance the reader's understanding of the

others. In addition, the reader will discover that any of the chapters also makes complete sense when read on its own.

Thus the readers of this book have a great deal of freedom. They can read its chapters in any order they find most inviting. And yet—because of the extensive discussions that lie behind the book— the volume seems to us to vibrate with an interactive quality that makes it hang together as a whole.

In outline, the way the book works is as follows. Part I contains each contributor's "main chapter." The first four of these eight chapters are concerned with one major issue apiece. (1) David Dockery deals with biblical authority, (2) Walter Harrelson with historical criticism, (3) John Newport with literary criticism, and (4) Albert Mohler with theological method.

The other main chapters, five through eight, contain some amount of "response" to the first four chapters. The most clear-cut example is chapter seven. There Molly Truman Marshall devotes the first half of her chapter to a response to Newport, and then to Mohler. Only then does she launch into her own independent essay.

By contrast, Robison James, Paige Patterson, and Timothy George have written independent essays from the outset of their chapters (chapters five, six, and eight). Each of them has also built into his chapter a half dozen paragraphs, on average, of response to things said in chapters one through four.

That brings us to Part II of the book. Here the contributors' responses to each other become the whole story, of course. Even for these chapters, however (that is, for chapters nine through sixteen), the rule holds that a chapter can be understood as a self-standing unit.

The editors came to an agreement that it might be more fair than unfair if James, Patterson, Marshall, and George were given the chance to include "rejoinders" in their Part II chapters, that is, responses to the way the others had responded to them in the book.[2]

What is the book, then? At least selectively, it seems to us to be a theological buffet, and therewith a source of strength. We say "selectively" because not all readers are likely to pick the same entrees on our menu as "choice."

Is the book something more than a buffet, however? Could it also be some kind of denominational breakthrough?

The contributors answer that question with varying degrees of optimism or pessimism; and we editors believe we should not spoil their stories here, but let them tell those stories for themselves, including what we ourselves have written. We can say, however, that all of us seem to have our feet on the ground.

To show that our editorial feet are planted on the earth of real events, we take note here of some developments that have taken place since the book plan was adopted in 1989.

In May of 1991, moderate Southern Baptists organized the Cooperative Baptist Fellowship. It is not a new denomination on several important counts, but it is a structure within which one could develop. A few months later, a new Baptist seminary opened its doors in Richmond, Virginia. Though originally sponsored by the Southern Baptist Alliance, the new school is independent and had developed a financial tie with an additional body, the Fellowship, before it opened.

Meanwhile, conservative Southern Baptists increasingly gained control of significant leadership positions of the Southern Baptist Convention.

Against this backdrop, two events in the late spring of 1991 cast in relief the kind of differences with which this book deals. In May, a statement endorsed by the Fellowship's steering committee (though not adopted by the Fellowship) said, "We cannot claim more for the Bible than the Bible claims for itself. The Bible neither claims nor reveals inerrancy as a Christian teaching. Bible claims must be based on the Bible, not on human interpretations of the Bible."

The next month, in June 1991, Morris Chapman said in his presidential address to the Southern Baptist Convention, "When you refuse to believe the Bible to be God's perfect Word you have stripped away God's authority. All you have left is interpretation."

Nor is the Bible the only issue on which Baptist diversity is found. Differences exist concerning church-state issues, the role of women, and an array of ethical issues. And further events may (or may not) make these differences yet more salient, even before this book can appear.

As we look back on the origins of this book and the discussions and debates that have brought it into being, we are aware that the eight of us have learned from one other, sometimes even when we were most puzzled by another person's perspective. Though we have

sometimes felt that others should learn more from us than we from them, we hope we have been properly open and grateful for new insights, no matter where they have come from.

We have also come to know one another. That is always a good thing. We have experienced a *koinonia* or fellowship in Christ despite the differences that put us, in our practical lives, on paths that differ and sometimes conflict. There has often been frustration. But there has been appreciation, as well.

We hope our readers will sense that our attempts to communicate with each other, and to understand each other, have been genuine. And we hope this book may extend something of the same experience—including our candor with each other, our respect for each other, and our *un*willingness to abandon our principles—to wider circles of Baptist life.

We want to thank the administrations of Samford University and of The Southern Baptist Theological Seminary, and the Chaplains' Office of The University of Richmond for graciously hosting us during our visits to these campuses. We thank them for their support of our work. To our students and colleagues who have offered valuable suggestions concerning various parts of this book we offer our deepest appreciation. Finally, we all wish to thank our families who have given of their time so that this book could become a reality. Ultimately we offer praise and thanksgiving to our Lord Jesus Christ who has sustained us and enabled us through the lengthy process. May He help us all in days to come.

Soli Deo Gloria

Robison B. James
David S. Dockery
Advent 1991

Notes

1. Speaking and interacting in Richmond were Marshall, Mohler, James, and Patterson. The same four were in Louisville, plus also Dockery, Harrelson, and Newport.

2. Three of these contributors wrote final rejoinders, but the pressure of George's schedule was such that he was unable to exercise that option within these pages.

Admittedly there are other ways to look at it, but the reason this option was given is as follows. When Dockery, Harrelson, Newport, and Mohler started writing chapters nine through twelve, respectively, they were already responding to the way other contributors had responded to them. But this would not be the case for the other four authors. In chapters thirteen through sixteen, they would simply be responding to each other—*without* the chance to respond to others' responses to them—unless they could do a rejoinder.

PART I
Present Challenges and New Directions

1
A People of the Book and the
Crisis of Biblical Authority
*David S. Dockery**

The introduction of the new *The Baptist Hymnal* (1991) rightly describes the Southern Baptist people as "the people of the Book." The people of the Book have been embroiled in controversy centered around the nature, authority, and interpretation of the Bible since 1979.[1] In reality the present crisis of biblical authority can be traced to several issues prior to 1979. The two controversies over Ralph Elliott's *Message of Genesis* (1961) and *The Broadman Bible Commentary* (1969) set the stage for the current strife.[2] But perhaps we can point to something even more basic than these public controversies. In the early part of the 1950s two historic changes began to take place almost unknowingly in Southern Baptist life. The first was the introduction of historical-critical studies into the curriculum of Baptist seminaries and colleges. The result was a new and challenging way of reading and interpreting the Bible.

The other more wide-ranging shift was the movement to a program-oriented approach to ministry. This shift brought about a generation of leaders committed to programmatic expansion. Nothing typified this organizational and programmatic growth more than the "Million More in '54" campaign, which resulted in almost

David S. Dockery (Ph.D., University of Texas at Arlington) is General Editor of *The New American Commentary.* He has taught New Testament and Theology on the faculties at both Criswell College and The Southern Baptist Theological Seminary. He is the author of *The Doctrine of the Bible, Biblical Interpretation Then and Now,* as well as 35 articles. He is a contributor to *The New American Standard Study Bible, The Dictionary of Jesus and the Gospels, The Holman Bible Dictionary,* and other reference works. He served as consulting editor for the *Revell Bible Dictionary.* Dockery is the editor or co-editor of *New Testament Criticism and Interpretation, Southern Baptists and American Evangelicals, Baptist Theologians,* and *The People of God.* He is a member of the First Baptist Church, Hendersonville, Tennessee.

750,000 new Sunday School members in Southern Baptist churches. With this and other similar successful programs, a movement away from theological commitments to pragmatic ones, consciously or unconsciously, began to take place. I do not for one minute think it was a malicious attempt to undermine theology. The pragmatic outlook was what was central for a growing, successful denomination. Orthodoxy was understood in terms of "doing the right program" rather than articulating the right belief system. What resulted was a generation of people who had not become a "heterodox people" so much as an "a-theological" people. When controversies entered the public arena in 1961, 1969, and 1979 regarding matters related to biblical inspiration, authority, and interpretation, a theological foundation was lacking among many people to examine and evaluate such issues.

Even men and women who believed the biblical stories as reported, who affirmed the historical foundation of Holy Scripture, and who never doubted the miraculous claims of the Bible were confused by the use of such terms as "inerrant" and "infallibility." Since I believe that is still the case and since many people understand those terms only as labels for "denominational groups" within the SBC, I will articulate in this chapter what is meant by an evangelical view of the Bible by affirming its total truthfulness, complete reliability, and full authority for Christians today.

It would be naive to think that the issues being debated in the SBC are only being discussed in the SBC context, as though Southern Baptist theologians, pastors, and laypeople lived in a vacuum. Some of the trouble can be attributed to the cultural and sociological changes taking place among people who have functioned regionally and rather parochially, and now are attempting to come to grips with modernity. But that does not tell the whole story. In many ways the struggles in the SBC parallel debates taking place in Christianity at large. For example, the German scholar Wolfhart Pannenberg, commenting on "The Crisis of the Scripture Principle," notes that the development of historical research has led to the dissolution of the Scripture principle and thereby brought on the crisis in the foundations of evangelical theology which have become more and more acute.[3] Harvard theologian Gordon Kaufman observes that only in isolated places does the Bible have "anything like the kind of existential authority and significance which it once enjoyed throughout much of Western culture and certainly among believers.''[4] James Barr, almost twenty years ago, predicted that doubt about the status of the Bible may well come to be regarded as normal in the churches.[5] The developing concern over the inspiration and authority of the Bible in church and theology has greatly intensified during the past decade.[6] The controversy over the Bible is obviously not unique to Southern Baptists. The intensity of the controversy among Southern Baptists, however, is unrivaled in other Christian circles, thus creating a major impasse.

In this initial chapter I will seek to articulate a view of Scripture that balances its divine and human authorship, including what the Bible says about its own inspiration. This chapter will also investigate how a divinely inspired Bible could have been written by human authors. Because this volume is primarily concerned with issues addressed in Baptist life, I shall inquire concerning past and present models of biblical inspiration among representative Baptists. Finally, I shall affirm the importance of recognizing the Bible as inspired, inerrant, reliable, truthful, and authoritative.

The Bible's Testimony About Itself

"The Bible says" ends all questioning except the question, "What does the Bible say?" To even ask what does the Bible say about itself is, according to James Barr, an anachronistic question. Barr, with his characteristically powerful critique, writes:

> According to conservative arguments . . . the Bible "claims" to be divinely inspired. All this is nonsense. There is no "the Bible" that claims to be divinely inspired, there is no "it" that has a "view of itself." There is only this or that source, like 2 Timothy or 2 Peter which makes statements about certain other writings, these rather undefined. There is no such thing as "the Bible's view of itself" from which a fully authoritative answer to these questions can be obtained.[7]

The argument is extremely articulate, but not necessarily devastating. I would like to suggest that it is more than the citing of 2 Timothy 3:16 that informs our understanding of the nature of Scripture. It is rather a compounding of the biblical testimony coupled with the inward work of the Holy Spirit bearing witness by and with the written Word of God in our hearts.[8] Acknowledging these presuppositions, let us look at various ways Scripture speaks about itself.

Both testaments view the words of Scripture as God's own words. Just as the Old Testament treats the Mosaic law as God's words (1 Kings 22:8-16; Neh. 8; Ps. 119), so the Old Testament is viewed as a whole as "oracles of God" (Rom 3:2) written by men whom the Holy Spirit moved and taught (1 Pet. 1:10-12; 2 Pet. 1:20-21). Likewise Old Testament quotations or allusions are viewed not only as what Moses, David, Isaiah, or Jeremiah wrote, but as what they said through the Spirit (Mark 7:6; 12:36; Rom. 1:5,20; 11:9). In reference to the Old Testament, the New Testament adopts formulas like "God says" and the "Holy Spirit says" (Matt. 19:4; Acts 4:24-25; 13:47; 28:25; 2 Cor. 6:16; Heb. 1:5-13; 3:7; 10:15). Scripture and God are so closely joined together in the minds of the New Testament authors that they naturally could speak of Scripture doing what it records God as doing (Gal. 3:8; Rom. 9:17).

In keeping with New Testament practices, John's Gospel introduced statements or ideas from the Old Testament with the words, "it is written" (John 6:31; 8:17; 12:14; 15:25, etc.). Herman Ridderbos suggests that this phrase is employed in this Gospel to put "an end to all contradiction."[9] While this might be viewed as an overstatement by some, the authority resident in the appeal "it is written" is beyond dispute. Thus the Gospel's expression, "these are written" (John 20:31) intends to communicate the same authority present in John's message. Similarly, Pilate's words, "what I have written, I have written," (19:22) demonstrate the authoritative sense of *graphō* (to write).[10] The New Testament concept of faith is in accord with the divine character of the apostolic word (Rom. 1:5; 10:3; 16:26). The reference to the divine character of the apostolic word in its written and oral form deserves a response of faith and obedience. When Paul taught and commanded in Christ's name (2 Thess. 3:6), claiming Christ's authority because he was Christ's apostle (1 Cor. 14:37) and maintaining that both his words and ministry were Spirit-given (2:9-13), he was offering a pattern of inspiration that called for the same perspective toward the apostolic writings that the apostles had toward the Old Testament.

The Scripture, because of its divine content and origin, can be described as "sure" (2 Pet. 1:19), "trustworthy" (1 Tim. 1:15; 2 Tim. 2:11; Titus 3:8, NIV), "confirmed" (Heb. 2:3, NIV), and "eternal" (1 Pet. 1:24-25). Those who build their lives on Scripture "will not be disappointed" (Rom. 9:33, NASB; see also 1 Pet. 2:6). The Word was written for "instruction, . . . and . . . encouragement" (Rom. 15:4, NKJV), to lead to saving faith (2 Tim. 3:15), to guide people toward godliness (v. 16) and to equip believers for good works (v. 17). God's people will know and hear God's word (1 John 2:20,27; 4:6) which "cannot be broken" (John 10:35).[11]

Scripture's purpose is to place men and women in a right relationship with God and to enable believers to seek God's glory in all of life's activities. Scripture, however, is not just concerned with a person's spiritual needs, but also with humanity's nature, history, origin, and destination, their past and future. Thus the Bible teaches us to understand all of life *sub specie Dei*.[12] The Bible is not only a book of conversion but also a book of creation and redemptive history, and it is this perspective that best represents and defines the divine character of Scripture.

Central to Scripture is the unifying history of God's redeeming words and acts, of which the life and work of Jesus Christ serve as the ultimate focus. Yet, there are three linked levels at which God acts. The first is the public stage of history which included a series of redemptive events including predictions and explanations at various stages along the way. These acts and words emerged at a second level in, to use Calvin's description, written public records. These records included narrative, celebration, apocalyptic, letters, wisdom sayings, and historical explanation, all of which communicated God's ongoing work of grace. The third level is the human response and understanding of God's work as the Holy Spirit illuminates human hearts and minds to interpret the sacred writings.

Jesus Christ binds and unites together everything in Scripture— beginning and end, creation and redemption, humanity, the fall, history, and the future.[13] If this overriding unity is neglected, Scripture can become denatured, losing its "theological-christological definition" and become "abstracted from the peculiar nature and content of scripture."[14] Recognizing that there are numerous other passages that could be cited that address the Divine aspect of Scripture (e.g., Ps. 119; Luke 24:25-27; Heb. 1:1-2; 2 Pet. 3:16),[15] we have nevertheless offered a representative picture to show that Barr's critique is less than accurate. Yet he is correct to note that the primary witness to the Bible's own inspiration is found in 2 Timothy 3:16-17, "All Scripture is God-breathed and is useful for teaching, rebuking, correcting and training in righteousness, so that the person of God may be thoroughly equipped for every good work'' (author). Let us now look at this important passage and its witness to the Bible's inspiration.

The Divine Inspiration of Canonical Scripture

We must acknowledge that the approach of self-attestation is sometimes rejected on the grounds of circular reasoning. The dilemma involved in such as approach is obvious, however. Either the Bible has its starting point upon itself or upon some other foundation, which would be most inconsistent. Certainly there exists a place for additional testimony, but we maintain that Scripture's own claim must be given prior consideration. The argument for the indissoluble relation between ultimate Christ and penultimate Scripture is, of course, circular, but it is a salvific circle, a very viable circle, and certainly not a vicious circle. As with all points of theology, a consistent method would call for a theological statement in Scripture about itself to be considered prior to an examination of the phenomena in Scripture.[16]

The Bible affirms its own inspiration. The term ''inspiration'' (*theopneustos*) has a long heritage in the theological literature, but it is always used with further disclaimers and explanations. The biblical idea of inspiration, as used in 2 Timothy 3:16 should not be associated with illumination nor human genius. Neither does it mean ''a breathing into.'' The New Testament emphasis is that ''God breathed out'' what the biblical writers convey in their writings. The apostolic emphasis focuses on the divine initiative and divine source of Scripture.

Some contemporary New Testament scholars have suggested that 2 Timothy 3:16 does not refer to all of Scripture, a view that is indicated by the translation, ''every scripture inspired of God is also useful.''[17] Such a translation, however, is highly unlikely because it makes the translation of ''and/also'' (*kai*) quite awkward. It is most doubtful that the apostle would affirm that scripture has a second characteristic (''also'') before affirming its initial characteristic. I. Howard Marshall claims that this translation can be confidently rejected, since no New Testament author would have conceived of the possibility of a book being classified as Scripture and yet not being inspired of God.[18]

The grammatical construction of this passage evidences a predicate construction and calls for the more straightforward translation: "All [the whole of] scripture is inspired, . . ." as found in the *King James Version, New International Version, New American Standard Bible*, and the *New Revised Standard Version*.

H. Ridderbos says that the predicate significance of *theopneustos* (the inspiration clause) "is not in my opinion disputable."[19] G. Schrenk comments that this construction "obviously" refers to "every passage of scripture."[20] I recognize that some will differ with this conclusion, thereby affirming a limited inspiration for the so-called salvific parts. The problem with this approach is the difficulty in distinguishing the salvific parts from the nonsalvific ones. Certainly 2 Timothy 3:16 refers primarily to the Old Testament writings (*graphē*). All fifty usages of *graphē* ("Scripture") in the New Testament primarily refer to the Old Testament, though the entirety of canonical Scripture cannot be eliminated. The construction employed in verse 16 has a broader meaning that allows for the inclusion of all the New Testament writings as well. The anarthrous construction, *pas graphē* ("all scripture") can have a characteristic idea, so that the phrase can mean "all that has characteristics of canonical scripture."[21] In addition, *graphē* in such an inclusive fashion would yield a translation similar to "everything that takes on the character of scripture is inspired, . . ." thus including both Testaments, though verse 15 would suggest that the Old Testament is primarily what was intended by the apostle. Recognizing that all canonical Scripture is inspired, meaning all Scripture finds its source and initiative in God, we must ask how can an inspired Bible be written by human authors?

An Inspired Bible and Human Authors

To confess "all scripture is inspired" primarily points to the product of inspiration rather than the process. What is asserted is the activity of God throughout the entire process, so that the completed, final product ultimately comes from Him. The biblical concept of inspiration must be understood in broader terms than merely the time when the Spirit of God moves the human author to write.

Inspiration allows for the Spirit's activity without demanding that we understand all of the Spirit's working in the same way at all times and places. It is not beyond the understanding of inspiration advanced in this chapter to view God's Spirit revealing specific messages to the prophets (Jer. 1:1-9), guiding authors in research (Luke 1:1-4), prompting the poets' creativity (Proverbs), and adopting or adapting tradition or extra-canonical material (2 Peter 2). I. H. Marshall has summarized the variety and inclusiveness of inspiration saying that it encompasses

> . . . the collection of information from witnesses, the use of written sources, the writing up and editing of such information, the composition of spontaneous letters, the committing to writing of prophetic messages, the collecting of the various documents together, and so on. At the same time, however, on the divine level we can assert that the Spirit, who moved on the face of the waters of creation (Gen. 1:2), was active in the whole process, so that the Bible can be regarded as both the words of men and the Word of God.[22]

People who take seriously not only the divine aspect of Scripture, but also the human factors have used the term concursive inspiration to describe the activity of the Spirit with those of the human authors.[23] This approach readily affirms a plenary view of inspiration and yet takes seriously the circumstances of the human authors.

The tension produced by simultaneously asserting both aspects (divine/human) of Scripture can be best explained, or at least informed, by the spiritual characteristics of the biblical writers. These men of God had known God, learned from Him, and walked with Him for many years in their spiritual formation and pilgrimage. Through their unique backgrounds and experiences, God had prepared the biblical authors (and editors) for the sacred task of inscripturating the Word of God. Through their familial, educational, cultural, and social backgrounds God was preparing the writers and even shaping their unique vocabularies to pen Holy Scripture. Beyond these observations, further explanations regarding the "how" of inspiration result in speculation.[24]

The manner of inspiration is different in Luke's Gospel, the Proverbs, the Pauline Epistles, the Apocalypse, and the Ten Commandments.[25] The nature of inspiration is, however, the same throughout, even though some portions of Scripture may be more easily recognized as inspired Scripture. Yet, this distinction is due in part to the subject matter. The theological emphases of Romans or Ephesians differ from the historical accounts in Kings or Chronicles. The inspiration in such historical passages assumes the general characteristic of reliability that is brought to these records. Even though inspiration differs and is somehow less recognizable to the reader in some places, all canonical Scripture can be characterized as inspired (*pas graphē theopneustos*).

We must never forget that the biblical writers adopted the linguistic resources available to them as they wrote to specific people with particular needs at particular times.[26] An affirmation of the Bible's plenary inspiration does not neglect the human, the historical, nor the cultural elements in the writings. The human authors were not lifted out of their culture or removed from their contexts. The writers were functioning members, and most likely significant leaders, in the early communities of faith.[27] Thus they should not be seen as autonomous, abstract, or atemporal. They were people aware of God's presence and seeking God's leadership for the issues of their times.

Obviously, the writers were not unbiased historical observers but were people of faith. Whether or not they were fully aware that they were writing inspired Scripture, they did evidence an active God-consciousness. Thus the concursive action of Spirit and human authorship is shaped and informed by the writers' spirituality. The resulting canonical shape of the writings helps us understand that they are much more than mere ancient documents.[28] Therefore, they have an ongoing meaning and authority for contemporary believing communities far surpassing anything imagined by the initial penmen.[29]

We recognize the variety and diversity within the canonical witness.[30] The Holy Spirit is the one who, in a mystery for which the incarnation provides the only analogy, causes the verbal human witness to coincide with God's witness to Himself.

The Bible as a divine-human book is indeed a special book, but that means it must be treated both equal to and yet more than an ordinary book, not less than an ordinary book.[31] To deny that the Bible should be studied through the use of literary and critical methodologies seems to treat the Bible as less than human, less than historical, and less than literature. Viewing the Bible from the standpoint of concursive inspiration affirms the Bible as a literary work that is both human and historical and yet simultaneously the very word of God.[32] Having concluded that the Bible is a divine-human book, we affirm that inspiration applies to all of canonical Scripture (including the process, purpose, and ultimately the product) and assert that by the concursive action of God the Scriptures are, in their entirety, both the work of the Spirit and the work of human authors. Such a view of plenary inspiration is not only plausible, but necessarily important for a consistent evangelical affirmation of truth. This approach alone does justice to the theological teachings and the human aspects of the biblical text. From this brief overview we shall move our attention to a survey of representative Baptist views of inspiration to see how those who have wrestled with these questions in previous generations have articulated their beliefs.

Baptist Confessions and Biblical Inspiration

Traditionally Baptists have been cautious about the use of doctrinal confessions.[33] Yet Baptists have published numerous confessions of faith since the early years of the seventeenth century. It is our purpose to examine the statements regarding Holy Scripture in representative Baptist confessions from the seventeenth century to the present.[34]

Thomas Helwys' confession (1611) in Article 23 sets forth the following view on Scripture:[35]

> That the scriptures off the Old and New Testament are written for our instruction, 2 Tim. 3:16 and that we ought to search them for they testifie off CHRIST, Io. 5.39. And therefore to bee used withall reverence, as conteyning the Holie Word off God, which onelie is our direction in all thinges whatsoever.

The Standard Confession (1660-63) in Article 23 sets forth the characteristic General Baptist understanding of Scripture:

> That the holy Scriptures is the rule whereby Saints both in matters of Faith, and conversation are to be regulated, they being able to make men wise unto salvation, through Faith in Christ Jesus, profitable for Doctrine, for reproof, for instruction in righteousness, that the man of God may be perfect, thoroughly furnished unto all good works, 2 Tim. 3.15, 16, 17. John 20.31. Isa. 8.20.

The First London Confession (1644), a Calvinistic confession that predates the Westminster Confession, in Articles 7 and 8 states:

The Rule of this Knowledge, Faith, and Obedience, concerning the worship and service of God, and all other Christian duties, is not mans inventions, opinions, devices, lawes, constitutions, or traditions unwritten whatsoever, but onely the word of God contained in the Canonicall Scriptures.

In this written Word God hath plainly revealed whatsoever he hath thought needfull for us to know, beleeve, and acknowledge, touching the Nature and Office of Christ, in whom all the promises are Yea and Amen to the praise of God.

The Second London Confession (1677, 1689), basically following the wording and emphases of the Westminster Confession, contains ten articles on the Scriptures. In comparison to earlier Baptist confessions, there is a significant shift whereby the articles on Scripture are located in the first section of the document. In addition to articles on the canon (21), a denial of the authority in the apocrypha (3), statements on illumination (6), the original languages (8), and the perspicuity of Scripture in regards to salvation (7), it affirms:

1. The Holy Scripture is the only sufficient, certain, and infallible rule of all saving Knowledge, Faith, and Obedience.

4. The Authority of the Holy Scripture for which it ought to be believed dependeth not upon the testimony of any man, or Church; but wholly upon God (who is truth it self) the Author thereof; therefore it is to be received, because it is the Word of God.

5. We may be moved and induced by the testimony of the Church of God, to an high and reverent esteem of the Holy Scriptures . . . [and] it doth abundantly evidence it self to be the Word of God; yet, not withstanding, our full persuasion, and assurance of the infallible truth, and divine authority thereof, is from the inward work of the Holy Spirit, bearing witness by and with the Word in our Hearts.

9. The infallible rule of interpretation of Scripture is the Scripture it self: And therefore when there is a question about the true and full sense of any Scripture (which is not manifold but one) it must be searched by other places that speak more clearly.

10. The supream judge by which all controversies of Religion are to be determined, and all Decrees of Councels, opinions of antient Writers, Doctrines of men, and private Spirits, are to be exam-

ined, and in whose sentence we are to rest, can be no other but the Holy Scripture delivered by the Spirit, into which Scripture so delivered, our faith is finally resolved.

The Philadelphia Confession (1742), which so greatly influenced Baptists in America, followed the Second London Confession. At no place was the Philadelphia statement more influential than in Charleston, where the theological formation and development of Richard Furman, J. P. Boyce, and Basil Manly, among others, took place.[36]

The Orthodox Creed (1678), a General Baptist statement, contains a lengthy statement on sacred Scripture, which is positioned at the conclusion of the confession. Article 37 concludes by confessing the Scriptures "are given by the inspiration of God, to be the Rule of faith and life."

In 1833 the New Hampshire Confession, an altogether new document for Baptists in America, articulates a high view of Scripture with language that has been officially adopted by many other Baptist bodies.[37] Article 1 declares:

We believe that the Holy Bible was written by men divinely inspired, and is a perfect treasure of heavenly instruction; that it has God for its author, salvation for its end, and truth, without any mixture of error, for its matter; that it reveals the principles by which God will judge us; and therefore is, and shall remain to the end of the world, the true centre of Christian union, and the supreme standard by which all human conduct, creeds, and opinions should be tried.

Since 1845 the Southern Baptist Convention has approved only three documents that have served as confessions or statements of faith. These include the Abstract of Principles (1858), *The Baptist Faith and Message* (1925), and the revised *Baptist Faith and Message* (1963).

The Abstract of Principles maintains that the "Scriptures are given by inspiration of God, and are the only sufficient, certain and authoritative rule of all saving knowledge, faith and obedience." The two *Baptist Faith and Message* statements were born in the midst of controversy. The 1925 document responded to the evolution controversy and the 1963 statement developed in light of the Convention's rejection of Ralph Elliott's Genesis commentary.

Basically both adopted the wording of the New Hampshire Confession with minor changes. The 1925 statement, edited by E. Y. Mullins, inserted the adjective "religious" to modify the word *opinions*. The 1963 confession's description of inspired Scripture added the phrase, "and is the record of God's revelation of Himself to man." A hermeneutical guide was also provided, stating: "The criterion by which the Bible is to be interpreted is Jesus Christ."

Readily apparent is the confidence that Baptists have and have had in the Bible, its inspiration and authority. Yet the affirmations indicate developmental and contextual differences. The nuances and distinctions are worthy of notation, but all of the statements evidence a commitment to the Bible's truthfulness, reliability, and infallibility.

Theological development is to be expected,[38] though some would claim that any development of orthodox doctrine is corruption, deviation into heterodoxy, or heresy. But since any survey of historical theology, even one as brief and selective as the one in this section, recognizes some change, the challenge is to explain the development.[39]

Recognizing that there exists a smorgasbord of options[40] in Baptist life today on the matter of biblical inspiration, we must somehow differentiate orthodox doctrinal development from unorthodoxy, doctrinal corruption, or apostasy. We must make positive contributions to the theological task which, whether carried on in the arenas of academy, society, or church, must produce true statements about God and His relationship to His creation.

The purpose of raising this issue in this chapter is not to examine the subject in detail,[41] but only to suggest some guidelines for helping to distinguish and evaluate the differences among us. We must encourage proper theological method, including interaction and integration with such diverse sources as Scripture, tradition, experience, rhetoric, and philosophy including analytical and synthetic thinking.[42] Primarily development must result from improved exegetical study and hermeneutical procedure.[43] If, as suggested earlier in this chapter, an understanding of biblical inspiration and authority must be built on Scripture's own self-attestation, then the continuity in the development will arise from the Scripture, which is God's Word, rather than a past theological expression, which is a human formulation. This approach is also consistent with a commitment to *sola scriptura* and the Baptist belief of the priority of Scripture over tradition.

Models of Biblical Inspiration

A number of models have arisen in recent years attempting to articulate a view of biblical inspiration.[44] Space limitations prohibit an expanded survey, but a variety of views are present in Baptist life. Since all of these views are also represented in wider Christendom, examples will be offered from both Baptist and non-Baptist sources.

The dictation view places the emphasis on God's actual dictation of all words in Scripture to the human writers.[45]

The illumination view maintains little more than the Spirit's working within the human authors to raise their religious insight and express themselves with eloquent language.[46]

The existential view contends that the biblical writings only apparently or secondarily present descriptive statements about God and humankind. The view focuses on the reader's encounter with the text so the reader will perceive the existential possibilities of human being projected through it.[47]

The Neoorthodox view understands biblical inspiration as an ongoing work whereby the Bible can become a means of revelation to specific individuals or communities. This approach stresses the idea of ongoing inspiration more than the Spirit's work at the time of the Bible's composition.[48]

Feminist views begin with an acknowledgement that the Bible has been written, translated, canonized, and interpreted by males. An ongoing process of inspiration, illumination, and exegetical reconstruction allows women to enter again the center stage that they occupied during the days of Jesus' ministry.[49]

Views of the Radical (Liberation/Process) theologies involve a deemphasis on the Divine nature of Scripture and an elevation of the human aspect. While these theologies are diverse and difficult, if not impossible, to characterize, quite often inspiration, authority, and interpretation are immediately bound up together. As in radical feminist theologies, the Bible is read from a subjective, reader-oriented approach, a far-reaching hermeneutic of suspicion.[50]

The dynamic or sacramentalist view sees the work of the Spirit in directing the writer to the concepts he should have and then allowing great freedom for the human author to express this idea in his own style through his own personality in a way consistent with and characteristic of his own situation and context.[51] G. Berkouwer, D. Bloesch, P. Achtemeir have given this perspective a sacramentalist interpretation.[52] Contemporary explanations, such as W. Abraham, have expanded the view beyond the human author to see the place of the community in the Scripture's composition.[53]

The Plenary View has been initially explained in the first sections of this chapter. It seeks to view inspiration as extending to all (thus the adjective "plenary") portions of Holy Scripture, even beyond the direction of thoughts to the selection of words.[54]

From the different models and theologies surveyed, taking into account the Baptist articulations of Scripture and the importance of theological development, we shall move toward a model of biblical inspiration and authority for contemporary Baptist life.

Conclusion: Toward a Model of Biblical Inspiration for Contemporary Baptist Life

I would call for a doctrine of Scripture that is careful to maintain that the Bible's literary diversity is more than a historic accident or decorative device. This diversity is a vehicle for imaginative thought and creative expression about things difficult to grasp.

Commands, promises, parables, analogy, metaphor, symbol, and poetry cannot be forced into propositional forms without loss.[55] This is not a denial in any way of propositional revelation but a recognition that the Bible's literary diversity is so broad that it cannot all be seen in terms of propositions. Recognition of this literary diversity brings a healthy realization of the human aspect in Scripture, thus balancing the divine-human authorship of the Bible.

We need a model of inspiration that affirms that even words are inspired but is cognizant of contemporary linguistic theory that suggests that meaning is at the sentence level and beyond.[56] A model of inspiration articulated in this manner infers the complete dependability and truthfulness of Scripture. It maintains that what the Bible affirms is completely true and therefore normative for the contemporary church.[57] Our belief suggests that the purpose of divinely inspired teaching concerning God and matters relating to God and His creation (*sub specie Dei*) is normative for the contemporary church. When such matters are proclaimed and confessed in the twentieth century, however, mere repetition of early Christian beliefs may not be sufficient. A restatement that awakens modern readers to an awareness that the Bible speaks in relevant ways to contemporary issues in church and society is necessary. The resulting restatement may bring about doctrinal development that will need to be evaluated by means suggested earlier.[58]

We must now probe further and express the results of this view of inspiration. The primary purpose of this chapter is not to discuss the inerrancy of God's Word. Yet, because this issue has seemingly been at the center of the impasse in the Southern Baptist Convention, it must be addressed. While *inerrancy* is certainly a "red-flag" word among many and subject to continual misunderstanding among others, it remains an adequate term to describe the results of inspiration.

An affirmation of inerrancy is important primarily for theological and epistemological reasons. One's personal salvation is not dependent on a confession of biblical inerrancy. Nevertheless, such a confession is an important safeguard for the church to maintain consistent evangelical instruction and theological method which is needed for an orthodox statement in salvation matters. Thus we see that inerrancy, as a corollary of inspiration, is a foundational issue on which other theological building blocks are laid. Recognizing the importance of the issue we can now suggest a definition of inerrancy.

Inerrancy means:

> When all the facts are known, the Bible (in its autographs) properly interpreted in light of which culture and communication means had developed by the time of its composition will be shown to be completely true (and therefore not false) in all that it affirms, to the degree of precision intended by the author, in all matters relating to God and his creation.[59]

The definition is complex, but it seeks simultaneously to be faithful to the phenomena of Scripture as well as the theological affirmations in Scripture about the veracity of God.

While affirming the Bible's full authority, which means that its full message speaks prescriptively and normatively to us today, we still recognize the temporal and cultural distances that separate us and understand that certain teachings may be contextually limited (e.g. 1 Tim. 5:23; 1 Cor. 16:20; Eph. 6:5). Yet, because the Bible is divinely inspired, the underlying principles are normative and applicable for the contemporary church as well as the first century.

Moving Beyond the Impasse: What Must We do?

It would be naive to think that the only issue creating division among us today is the issue of Scripture. Many of our misunderstandings have been created by regional and cultural differences. Others have been fostered because we have very different understandings of the church, of education, of pastoral leadership, of church-state issues, and a variety of other matters. Yet, I think even with the other theological, philosophical, and methodological differences among us, there must be some confessional commonalities. We must maintain that we believe in a Trinitarian God. We must believe that Jesus is Lord—that He is fully God and fully human and has by His sacrificial work on the cross redeemed us from our sins; we must believe in the Holy Spirit who applies the benefits of salvation to us and brings life to the people of God. We must believe in salvation by grace through faith alone. We must believe in the resurrection from the dead and the return of our Lord for His people. These must be essentials of our faith. We can debate whether other matters need to be considered primary, secondary, or tertiary doctrines, but we cannot move forward without recognizing these theological parameters and affirming them as the core of biblical Christianity. To describe Christianity as ''biblical'' means we know these truths because they have been revealed to us today in Holy Scripture. It is in this sense that Baptists in the past, and hopefully in the future, can be called ''the people of the Book.''

We cannot give up the affirmation that the Bible is totally true and trustworthy because this foundational commitment serves these other primary affirmations of the Christian faith. A commitment to a completely truthful and fully authoritative Bible is the first step toward healing the deadly sickness in today's theological and ethical trends that threaten the very heart of the Christian faith and message.

When approaching the Bible, we recognize its authoritative and normative character that can enable us to discover truth and its implications for the answers to life's ultimate questions. We also can find guidance for godly living in our world. We want primarily to stress the truthful and trustworthy character of God's faithful revelation to humanity and believe it is impossible to move together in our ministry, missionary, and evangelistic efforts in our convention apart from this common affirmation. We need people who will proclaim the truthfulness and authority of God's Word while seeking to live under its authority.[60]

Contemporary Baptists need not only to affirm the Bible's inspiration, truthfulness, and normative nature, but we need to evidence our concern for these matters by careful theological reflection, faithful proclamation, repentance, and prayer. A confession that the Bible is fully inspired and totally truthful is necessary because it is the foundation that establishes the complete extent of Scripture's authority.[61] Baptists must choose to articulate a view of the Bible for the contemporary community that is faithful to historic Baptist positions that have characteristically confessed that the Bible is the written Word of God, is truthful, infallible, and is the only sufficient, certain, and authoritative rule of all saving knowledge, faith, and obedience. We can thus relate to one another in love and humility bringing about true fellowship and community resulting not only in orthodoxy but orthopraxy before a watching world. We thus commit ourselves wholeheartedly to the inspiration, truthfulness, and authority of Scripture and place our total trust and confidence in it.

Notes

1. See Bill Leonard, *God's Last and Only Hope* (Grand Rapids: Eerdmans, 1990); also David S. Dockery, "Holy Wars, Houses on Sand and Heresies: A Review of the Inerrancy Controversy in the Southern Baptist Convention," *Criswell Theological Review* 2 (1988): 391-402.

2. See H. Leon McBeth, *The Baptist Heritage* (Nashville: Broadman, 1987), 649, 680.

3. Wolfhart Pannenberg, *Basic Questions in Theology,* I (Philadelphia: Westminster, 1970), 6.

4. Gordon D. Kaufman, "What Shall We Do with the Bible?" *Interpretation* 25 (1971): 96.

5. James Barr, *The Bible in the Modern World* (London: SCM, 1973), 8.

6. See Mark A. Noll, "Evangelicals and the Study of the Bible," in *Evangelicalism and Modern America,* ed. George Marsden (Grand Rapids: Eerdmans, 1984), 198-99; also see D. A. Carson, "Recent Developments in the Doctrine of Scripture," in *Hermeneutics, Authority and Canon,* ed. D. A. Carson and John D. Woodbridge (Grand Rapids: Zondervan, 1986), 5-48; and John R. Muether, "Evangelicals and the Bible: A Bibliographic Postscript," in *Inerrancy and Hermeneutic,* ed. Harvie M. Conn (Grand Rapids: Baker, 1988), 253-64.

7. James Barr, *Fundamentalism* (London: SCM, 1977), 78.

8. Cf. John Calvin, *Institutes of the Christian Religion,* ed. J. T. McNeill (Philadelphia: Westminster, 1960), 1:75-80.

9. Herman Ridderbos, *Studies in Scripture and Its Authority* (Grand Rapids: Eerdmans, 1978), 21.

10. G. Schrenk, "*graphō,*" *TDNT,* 1:747.

11. I have amplified these descriptions in "The Divine-Human Authorship of Inspired Scripture" in *Authority and Interpretation: A Baptist Perspective,* ed. D. Garrett and R. Melick (Grand Rapids: Baker, 1986), 13-43; also see Sinclair B. Ferguson, "How Does the Bible Look at Itself?" in *Inerrancy and Hermeneutic,* 47-66.

12. Ridderbos, *Studies in Scripture and Its Authority,* 24.

13. A host of possible solutions have been offered to explain the unity in variety in Scripture. See the discussions in D. L. Baker, *Two Testaments: One Bible* (Downers Grove: InterVarsity, 1976).

14. Ridderbos, *Studies in Scripture and its Authority,* 25.

15. See the lengthy list provided by Wayne A. Grudem, "Scripture's Self-Attestation and the Problem of Formulating a Doctrine of Scripture," in *Scripture and Truth,* ed. D. A. Carson and J. D. Woodbridge (Grand Rapids: Zondervan, 1984), 19-59.

16. Further discussion on this particular issue will be given in a later chapter in this book by R. Albert Mohler. See also an evaluation of these two alternatives in James J. Grier, "The Self-Witness of the Bible," *Grace Theological Journal* 1 (1979): 71-76; and Dewey M. Beegle, *Scripture, Tradition and Infallibility* (Grand Rapids: Eerdmans, 1973).

17. Cf. Martin Dibelius and Hans Conzelmann, *The Pastoral Epistles,* trans. P. Buttolph and A. Yarbro (Philadelphia: Fortress, 1962), 120.

18. I. H. Marshall, *Biblical Inspiration* (Grand Rapids: Eerdmans, 1982), 25.

19. Ridderbos, *Studies in Scripture,* 27. Also see C. F. D. Moule, *An Idiom Book of New Testament Greek* (Cambridge: University Press, 1953), 95. Schrenk, "*graphō,*" TDNT 1:759.

20. Schrenk, "*graphō,*" TDNT 1:759; cf. M. Erickson, *Christian Theology* (Grand Rapids: Baker, 1984), 210-12.

21. It is highly probable that the apostle is not making a distinction in

his mind between the LXX and the MT in making this assertion. If that is the case, then all faithful translations, not just the autographs, could be described as inspired or at least virtually inspired. See Nigel Turner, *Syntax, A Grammar of New Testament Greek* (Edinburgh: T. & T. Clark, 1963), 3:199; also H. Kent, Jr., *The Pastoral Epistles* (Chicago: Moody, 1982), 281.

22. Marshall, *Biblical Inspiration,* 42-43.

23. I have detailed this position in "Divine-Human Authorship," 23-29. Also see the series of essays in *New Testament Criticism and Interpretation,* ed. David A. Black and David S. Dockery (Grand Rapids: Zondervan, 1991); George E. Ladd, *The New Testament and Criticism* (Grand Rapids: Eerdmans, 1967) and I. H. Marshall, ed., *New Testament Interpretation* (Grand Rapids: Eerdmans, 1977); Clark Pinnock, *The Scripture Principle* (San Francisco: Harper and Row, 1985); Gordon R. Lewis, "The Human Authorship of Inspired Scripture," in *Inerrancy,* ed. N. L. Geisler (Grand Rapids: Zondervan, 1979), 229-64; and Douglas Farrow, *The Word of Truth and Disputes About Words* (Winona Lake: Carpenter, 1986).

24. To reach this conclusion is certainly not to deny plenary inspiration and is in the best of Baptist tradition. See John A. Broadus, *Commentary on the Gospel of Matthew* (Philadelphia: American Baptist Publication Society, 1886), 58, who comments we should be cautious in theorizing as to verbal inspiration. This warning does not detract from Broadus's commitment to the full reliability of the Bible contrary to what E. V. McKnight tries to suggest in "A. T. Robertson: The Evangelical Middle" in *The Unfettered Word,* ed. Robison B. James (Waco: Word, 1987), 96. A full treatment of Broadus's views of Scripture, as well as those of Basil Manly and James Boyce can be found in Dwight Moody, "Theories of Inspiration" (Ph.D. diss., The Southern Baptist Theological Seminary, 1982). Also see Timothy George's treatment of these questions in *Baptist Theologians* (Nashville: Broadman, 1990).

25. It is possible that at points where the prophets utter, "Thus says the Lord, . . ." that dictation may be possible, though not probable. The Ten Commandments, however, are quite likely dictation material, but we cannot suggest this possibility for the rest of Scripture.

26. See the helpful insights regarding this matter in James A. Sanders, *Canon and Community* (Philadelphia: Fortress, 1984).

27. The writers are certainly time-related but *not* necessarily time-bound. See Eugene Nida, *Message and Mission* (New York: Harper, 1960), 85-90; Pinnock, *Scripture Principle,* 110-15.

28. Sanders, *Canon and Community,* 63.

29. Erickson, *Christian Theology,* 204-6.

30. Grant R. Osborne, "Genre Criticism—Sensus Literalis," *Trinity*

Journal 4 (1983): 1-27; Donald Guthrie, *New Testament Theology* (Downers Grove: InterVarsity, 1981), 49-59, 953-81; also the classic article on "The Psychology of Inspiration" in *Dictionary of the Apostolic Church,* ed. James Hastings (1915; reprint ed., Grand Rapids: Baker 1973).

31. See the discussion in Michael J. Christensen, *C. S. Lewis on Scripture* (London: Hodder and Stoughton, 1979).

32. Donald G. Bloesch, *Essentials of Evangelical Theology,* 2 vols. (San Francisco: Harper and Row, 1978), 1:67-81.

33. See Herschel Hobbs, "Southern Baptists and Confessionalism: A Comparison of the Origins and Contents of the 1925 and 1963 Confessions," *Review and Expositor* 76 (1979): 55.

34. Fuller treatments on this subject can be found in Thomas J. Nettles, "Creedalism, Confessionalism, and the Baptist Faith and Message" in *The Unfettered Word,* 138-54; William R. Estep, "Baptists and Authority: The Bible, Confessions, and Conscience in the Development of Baptist Identity," *Review and Expositor* 84 (1987): 600-02; William L. Lumpkin, "The Nature and Authority of Baptist Confessions of Faith," *Review and Expositor* 76 (1979): 35-42. Leonard, *God's Last and Only Hope,* 65-100; James Leo Garrett, Jr., "Biblical Authority According to Baptist Confessions of Faith," *Review and Expositor* 76 (1979): 43-54; idem, "Sources of Authority in Baptist Thought," *Baptist History and Heritage* 13 (1978): 47-49.

35. Citations from the confessions are found in William L. Lumpkin, *Baptist Confessions of Faith* (Philadelphia: Judson, 1959).

36. McBeth, *The Baptist Heritage,* 240-42, 440-42.

37. Cf. Mark A. Noll, "Confessions of Faith," *Evangelical Dictionary of Theology,* ed. W. Elwell (Grand Rapids: Baker, 1984), 262-66.

38. Cf. Peter Toon, *The Development of Doctrine in the Church* (Grand Rapids: Eerdmans, 1979); J. Pelikan, *Development of Christian Doctrine* (New Haven, Conn.: Yale, 1969); idem, *Historical Theology: Continuity and Change in Christian Doctrine* (London: Hutchinson, 1971).

39. See the helpful guidelines suggested by Craig A. Blaising, "Doctrinal Development in Orthodoxy," *Bibliotheca Sacra* 145 (1988): 133-40; also cf. J. J. Davis, *Foundations of Evangelical Theology* (Grand Rapids: Baker, 1984), 221-44.

40. See surveys in J. Leo Garrett, "The Teaching of Recent Southern Baptist Theologians on the Bible," in *Proceedings of the Conference on Biblical Inerrancy,* ed. Michael A. Smith (Nashville: Broadman, 1987), 289-315; 546-53. From a wider perspective, cf. D. K. McKim, *What Christians Believe About the Bible* (Nashville: Nelson, 1985).

41. I have treated the issue of development within the canonical text in "Pauline Pictures of the Spiritual Life: Contextual or Developmental," in

Scribes and Scriptures: Essays in Honor of H. J. Greenlee, ed. D. A. Black (Winona Lake: Eisenbrauns, 1992). Certainly the criteria would be applicable for the broader discussion in the area of historical theology.

42. Cf. Davis, *Foundations of Evangelical Theology;* Erickson, *Christian Theology,* 1:59-80; David L. Wolfe, *Epistemology: The Justification of Belief* (Downers Grove: InterVarsity, 1982); and Vern Poythress, *Symphonic Theology* (Grand Rapids: Zondervan, 1987).

43. See David S. Dockery, *Biblical Interpretation Then and Now* (Grand Rapids: Baker, 1992).

44. Cf. McKim, *What Christians Believe about the Bible*; David H. Kelsey, *The Use of Scripture in Recent Theology* (Phildelphia: Fortress, 1975); J. I. Packer, "Encountering Present-Day Views of Scripture," *Foundations of Biblical Authority*, ed. James M. Boice (Grand Rapids: Zondervan, 1978); Robert K. Johnson, ed. *The Use of the Bible in Theology: Evangelical Options* (Atlanta: John Knox, 1985); D. A. Carson, "Recent Developments in the Doctrine of Scripture," *Hermeneutics, Authority, and Canon* (Grand Rapids: Zondervan, 1986), 10-48; Dockery, "Divine-Human Authorship," 29-35.

45. E.g., John R. Rice, *Our God-Breathed Book the Bible* (Murfreesboro: Sword of the Lord, 1969).

46. E.g., L. H. DeWolf, *A Theology of the Living Church* (New York: Harper, 1960) 48-75.

47. E.g., R. Bultmann, *Kerygma and Myth*, ed. H. W. Bartsch (London: SCM, 1953); idem., *Jesus Christ and Mythology* (London: SCM, 1960); cf. John Macquarrie, *An Existentialist Theology: A Comparison of Heidegger and Bultmann* (London: SCM, 1955).

48. E.g., Karl Barth, *Church Dogmatics*, trans. G. W. Bromiley and ed. T. F. Torrance (Edinburgh: T. & T. Clark, 1956), 1:1, 51-335. A most helpful treatment can be seen in R. P. C. Hanson and A. T. Hanson, *The Bible Without Illusions* (London: SCM, 1989). The Hansons still advocate the Bible as normative for the church.

49. We must recognize there is not one feminist perspective. Broadly speaking we can identify three: (1) rejectionist or post-Christian; (2) reformist or liberation; and (3) loyalist or evangelical. Cf. P. Tribble, *God and the Rhetoric of Sexuality* (Philadelphia: Westminster, 1978); L. Russell, ed. *Feminist Interpretation of the Bible* (Philadelphia: Westminster, 1975); Elizabeth Schussler Fiorenza, *In Memory of Her: A Feminist Theological Reconstruction of Christian Origins* (New York: Crossroad, 1983); A. Mickelsen, *Women, Authority and the Bible* (Downers Grove: InterVarsity Press, 1986); A. Carr, "Is a Christian Feminist Theology Possible?" *Theological Studies* 43 (1982): 279-97.

50. See Jose Misguez Bonino, *Doing Theology in a Revolutionary Situation* (Philadelphia: Fortress, 1975), 86-105; Juan L. Segundo, *Libera-*

tion of Theology, trans. J. Drury (Maryknoll, N.Y.: Orbis, 1976); James H. Cone, *A Black Theology of Liberation* (Philadelphia: Lippncott, 1970).

51. J. Orr and E. Y. Mullins are representatives of this view, as was the influential Baptist theologian A. H. Strong, *Systematic Theology* (Westwood, N.J.: Revell, 1907).

52. Cf. G. C. Berkouwer, *Holy Scripture*, trans. and ed. Jack Rogers (Grand Rapids: Eerdmans, 1975); P. Achtemeier, *The Inspiration of Scripture* (Philadelphia: Westminster, 1980); Bloesch, *Essentials of Evangelical Theology*.

53. William J. Abraham, *The Divine Inspiration of Holy Scripture* (Oxford: Oxford University Press, 1981). Narrative theologians also adopt an approach to Scripture similar in many ways. E.g. Gabriel Fackre, *The Christian Story* (Grand Rapids: Eerdmans, 1978).

54. Cf. Erickson, *Christian Theology*, 199-220.

55. Cf. Kevin J. Van Hoozer, "The Semantics of Biblical Literature: Truth and Scripture's Diverse Literary Forms," *Hermeneutics, Authority and Canon*, 53-104; Arthur Holmes, "Ordinary Language Analysis and Theological Method," *Bulletin of the Evangelical Theological Society* 11 (1968): 33.

56. Cf. Peter Cotterell and Max Turner, *Linguistics and Biblical Interpretation* (Downers Grove: InterVarsity, 1989); Robert E. Longacre, *The Grammar of Discourse* (New York: Plenum, 1983); John Beekman and John Callow, *Translating the Word of God* (Grand Rapids: Zondervan, 1974).

57. This concept is superbly articulated by Paul D. Feinberg, "The Meaning of Inerrancy," *Inerrancy*, ed. N. L. Geisler (Grand Rapids: Zondervan, 1979), 267-304; cf. David S. Dockery, "The Inerrancy and Authority of Scripture: Affirmations and Clarifications," *Theological Educator* 37 (1988): 15-36. Rob James wrongly distinguishes between the inerrancy of the Bible and its truthfulness. See *The Unfettered Word*, 9-10. I would affirm that a statement about the Bible's truthfulness or reliability or dependability is the essence of the meaning of biblical inerrancy.

58. Cf. John Jefferson Davis, "Contextualization and the Nature of Theology," *The Necessity of Systematic Theology*, ed. J. J. Davis (Grand Rapids: Baker, 1980), 169-85; Pinnock, *Scripture Principle*, 210-21.

59. I have discussed this definition in some detail in "Divine-Human Authorship," 37-41; also, see chapters 4-6 in *The Doctrine of the Bible* (Nashville: Convention, 1991).

60. See Anthony Thiselton, "Truth," *NIDNTT* 3(1971): 874-902.

61. Geoffrey W. Bromiley, "Authority," *ISBE* 1 (1979): 364-71.

2
Passing on the Biblical Tradition Intact:
The Role of Historical Criticism
*Walter Harrelson**

My introduction to critical biblical scholarship began in the Lebanon Baptist Church, Funston, North Carolina, a country settlement in Brunswick County so small that it lost its post office during the Depression. The scholar who introduced me to the critical study of the Bible was my Aunt Zora; the setting was a Sunday School class of country boys who met together under Aunt Zora's tutelage for eight or nine years.

Aunt Zora taught us the Bible stories, concentrating on those from the Old Testament—or perhaps those were the ones I remember. She gave us vivid instances of God's guiding hand over the whole of history, of God's judgments and promises and how they came to fulfillment. But now and again, when the Bible depicted some extraordinarily cruel act of God against, say, the Canaanite population (Josh. 10:40-43; 11) or the Midianites (Num. 25; 31), Aunt Zora would say, "Well, children, that's what the Bible says, and it must be true. But you know, there's something wrong somewhere, for God is not like that."

---

*Walter Harrelson (Th.D., Union Theological Seminary) is Distinguished Professor of Hebrew Bible Emeritus, Vanderbilt Divinity School, where he also served as Dean. He has also taught at the Andover Newton Theological School and was Dean of the University of Chicago Divinity School. Harrelson has served as a co-editor and translator for the *New Revised Standard Version Bible* and as a contributing editor to the *Mercer Dictionary of the Bible*. His articles have appeared in numerous journals and reference works including *Encyclopaedia Britannica, Interpreter's Dictionary of the Bible*, and *The Hasting's Dictionary of the Bible*. He is the author of *Jeremiah: Prophet to the Nations, Interpreting the Old Testament, From Fertility Cult to Worship, The Ten Commandments and Human Rights, Sacred Times and Seasons*, and *The Messianic Hope in Judaism*. Harrelson is a member of First Baptist Church, Capitol Hill, in Nashville, Tennessee.

God is not like that. The Bible itself led Aunt Zora to a recognition that the biblical writers, who faithfully preserved the record of God's sacred teaching and saving deeds, sometimes must have misunderstood or slipped. God *could not have* commanded the Israelites to exterminate the entire population of Canaan or the wives and children of the Midianites who had led Israel into apostasy. Why? Because that is untrue to the character of the God of the Bible.

The thesis of this chapter is that historical criticism of the Bible helps the Christian community and its individual believers *to pass on the faith intact*, seeing to it that the biblical heritage, with all its complexity, variety, and integrity, does not die or atrophy. Already in biblical times, the equivalent of historical criticism was at work, as the community sifted its traditions and related them to changing circumstances and challenges. Under the guidance of the Holy Spirit, ancient Israel and the early Christian community devoted their best energies and thought to passing along this scriptural heritage. The result is our biblical canon, the Bible of today.

Historical criticism is not merely valuable; it is *indispensable* if the biblical heritage is to be passed along to the next generation. Of course, harm to faith can come from historical-critical study that is cynical about the Bible's truth or value, or arrogant about its scholarly claims, or indifferent to the religious community's basic concerns. On the other hand, harm to faith can also result from irresponsible attacks upon historical criticism by those who do not understand or care about its true character. But my thesis is that biblical faith has had no better ally through the centuries than historical criticism.

The term "historical criticism" covers many aspects of biblical research. It includes analysis of the literary sources, since the effort to unravel the strands of tradition and the various literary deposits aims at identifying the historical background and setting of these sources or traditions. Under historical criticism we also include form and genre studies, traditio-historical research, and the study of redactions. Moreover, historical criticism includes the study of the history of the biblical text, historical geography, and much of the work done by archaeologists of the ancient Near Eastern and eastern Mediterranean worlds, although there will be little emphasis upon these aspects of critical study in this chapter. Nor shall we include so-called "canonical" or sociological/anthropological approaches to the Bible or newer literary analyses of the Bible, though these must go hand in hand with much of the work of the historical critic. Our job is to address those features of historical criticism that have often been considered dangerous and damaging to faith, so that the positive gains—indeed, the indispensable value—of faithful historical criticism will be more clearly in view. Our purpose is not to refute the critics of historical criticism but to show its positive contributions to biblical interpretation and to faith itself. Baptists have taken the lead, in this country and abroad, in showing how historical criticism contributes positively to Christian faith. One needs only to mention William Rainey Harper and Edgar J. Goodspeed of the University of Chicago and H. H. Rowley of the University of Manchester or a host of earlier and contemporary scholars from Southern Baptist colleges and seminaries to make this point.

Historical Criticism on Which All Are Agreed

First, however, we should point out that there is widespread agreement on the value of some forms of historical criticism. All responsible biblical scholars practice historical criticism, for all of them want to know as much as they can know about the historical setting of the biblical narratives, the times and lives of the biblical personalities, and the historical worlds within which Israel's prophets spoke and the church's apostles and evangelists spoke and wrote. Above all, every Christian wants to know as much as possible about the world into which Jesus came, about those aspects of Jesus' parables and healings that a knowledge of the biblical world can reveal. Critical historical study, then, is of course appropriate and welcomed by most scholars, including those who criticize nonevangelical approaches to Scripture.

It will be useful to start by presenting a simple but very valuable diagram used by Professor John Barton in a recent book.[1]

This diagram serves the purpose of showing us graphically what is involved in historical and other forms of biblical criticism. The Bible is the text (no. 2 in the diagram), the text as it has been preserved to us as well as the original text that lies behind our present text. The historical events or theological ideas (no. 1) are that world of facts, events, and ideas that the Bible presents to us, a

1. Historical Events or Theological Ideas

↑↓

2. The Text

3. Author, or Authors,   **4. Reader**
   or Community

world also known to some considerable extent apart from the Bible
(through archaeological, historical, and geographical studies, and
by references from nonbiblical literature). The author or authors
must also include the community (no. 3), for in some critical study
it is not the individual writer who is of interest but the community
that preserves, shapes, and passes along the biblical story or tradition or poem or wisdom saying. And the reader (no. 4) includes the
addressee of the text in ancient times as well as the current reader or
hearer.

The value of this diagram is that right away it enables us to say
that our concern with historical criticism centers heavily upon the
author or authors or community (no. 3). We are, of course, much
interested in the world of fact and ideas that lies behind the Bible
(no. 1), but historical and literary-source criticism have the particular author or authors in view (no. 3). And the same is true of the
study of the way in which the text was transmitted and written down
into its present form. Even textual criticism and grammar, obviously
devoted to the text (no. 2), are concerned not with the text as such
but with the text of a particular book, with those responsible for
handing down that text or a translation of it, and with the processes
of transmitting and preserving the text.

Historical criticism does not work on the text of the Bible as a
whole but on its particular parts, seeking to understand the distinct
books and parts of books that are the object of study. We want to
understand the primeval history (Gen. 1—11) and for that reason
devote ourselves to an unraveling of what lies behind the stories of
creation, the flood, the tower; behind the genealogies, lists, and
theological judgments. Now, some of our concerns with Genesis
1—11 are not historical but literary and theological, not dependent,

or not heavily dependent, upon the historical background and setting of the material. But we count on historical criticism to help us compare other creation stories outside the Bible (the Babylonian creation story entitled "Enuma Elish," for example) with the biblical story, and to compare Genesis 1—2 with stories from other parts of the Bible (Job 26, or Ps. 104, for example). The same is true of the flood story. We have parallel accounts from Babylonian and other literatures (in the Babylonian Gilgamesh epic in particular), and we have other references to the flood in the Bible (Ps. 104, etc.). Historical criticism is of great value in tracing the background of the biblical stories. It enables us to discern how the accounts of creation and flood in the Bible differ from their counterparts in the literature of Israel's neighbors, and how these distinctive Israelite views were expressed over time in the life and literature of Israel.

Few would wish to dispute the value of historical criticism in offering such background. If, however, the historical critic were to claim that the continuing significance of Genesis 1—11 lay *only* in the identification of the comparative materials and the study of the biblical text in relation to the other texts, one would rightly protest. Genesis 1—11 is a *theological* affirmation about the origins of the universe and its peoples at God's initiatives. It must be studied and treated as a theological text. And that allows for various ways of interpreting its transcendent meaning, including the claim in faith that the one there called God or the *Lord* God was calling into being a meaningful world, a world with a meaning *given* to it, not just emerging from it. And whether or not one claims as historical fact the story of Adam and Eve, one cannot fail to see that the story of the first human pair is affirming that the *entire human race* has its origin in an act of the sovereign God, the Creator and Sovereign of all the peoples and families of the earth.

Similarly, historical criticism of the Psalms would be accepted by all responsible scholars as such criticism identifies and evaluates comparable psalms, hymns, and laments from the ancient Near Eastern world, as it studies the *forms* of psalms and seeks to identify the place of such forms or genres in the religious and cultic life of ancient Israel. Such psalm study, together with a study of the process of transmission of the Psalms, is of great value in enabling us to read and hear the Psalms as they were once read and heard in ancient Israel.

But if scholars should claim that the literary qualities and the theological weight of these biblical Psalms had been fully accounted for when the analytic and comparative work was done, we would rightly protest. Literature has to be studied as literature, and theological affirmations belong in the domain of theology. Baptist scholars, evangelical and nonevangelical, have usually made such distinctions, clearly seeing the purposes and the limitations of historical criticism. And they have recognized the value—for faith—of historical criticism.

Matters are a bit more complex when we address the question of a book that bears the name of a given prophet—say, Isaiah. But are they really as complex as we have sometimes made them out to be? Would not all responsible scholars want to know as much as can be known about the settings within which the prophet Isaiah spoke and acted? Clearly, they would and do. Thus the study of the background of the Book of Isaiah and the effort to place all of its oracles and narratives, its laments and oracles of salvation into appropriate temporal, cultural, and historical backgrounds, difficult as it is, should be welcomed by all.

Isaiah has been a storm ground of controversy through the centuries, since the materials found in the Book of Isaiah have been found by critical scholars to extend over a long period of time after Isaiah's death. The situation has materially changed, however, in recent years. Today there are responsible scholars who speak of the overall Isaiah-vision found in the sixty-six chapters, visions that do derive from different times and circumstances but all of which share a common general outlook and theological/literary direction.[2] In fact, some scholars are now claiming that the whole of Isaiah 1—33 can be placed in a historical context during the years of the prophet Isaiah (the latter eighth century B.C.E.).[3] Despite this changing situation, however, critical historical scholarship still operates on the principle that prophets do not customarily prophesy in advance about named kings who have not as yet been born (Isa. 44:28; 45:1; see also the prophecy of the coming of King Josiah to reform Israelite society [1 Kings 13:2-3]). It is not that such a thing is *impossible*; who would wish to say that God *could not* give Isaiah the name of Cyrus long before Cyrus had been born, or give the name of Josiah to a prophet of much earlier times? But the historical/critical question is, What would be the point of God's doing such a thing? Such a form of revelation seems not to accord with the Bible's customary portrayals of God's action in history or in the natural processes.[4]

At this point, the words of the evangelical New Testament scholar Bruce Metzger, in his 1971 presidential address to the Society of Biblical Literature,[5] carry special weight. Metzger argued that a pseudepigraphic writing (i.e., one attributed to an individual other than its actual author or authors), is no less inspired because of such an attribution. Did the ancient Israelites accept chapters 40—66 of Isaiah as inspired revelation because they were preserved in manuscripts that bear the name of Isaiah? Hardly. Did they give consideration to the question of whether all of the chapters stemmed from Isaiah? Was not their concern, rather, with the *authority* and the power and truth of these oracles?

In the massive Isaiah manuscript found at Qumran, a site near the northwest corner of the Dead Sea, there is a space left between chapters 33 and 34, as though the copyist knew of a tradition that the basic Isaiah tradition stopped with chapter 33. Chapter 34 is an anonymous oracle of judgment against Edom, chapter 35 is very much akin to the materials in 40—55, and chapters 36—39 are largely a lengthy, word-for-word excerpt from 2 Kings 18—20. There may be ancient support, therefore, for the notion that some, and perhaps many, did not claim Isaiah as author of all that was preserved under his name.

We can conclude, then, that there are uses of historical criticism that evangelical and nonevangelical scholars agree on substantially and practice regularly in their work. There are other aspects of historical criticism that pose difficulties for evangelical scholars, though ways may be found to manage such difficulties. But are there not points at which historical criticism and evangelical faith clash head on? That is our next topic.

Contested Uses of Historical Criticism

The Sources of the Pentateuch

Historical criticism met great resistance when it sought to show that the materials found in the first five books of the Hebrew Bible, the Pentateuch, were put together over a considerable period of time by a series of editors, using literary sources or traditions that had been produced at different times and places and for different purposes. The Documentary Hypothesis, as it was called, swept the field in biblical scholarship, but it was bitterly opposed by some evangelical scholars, particularly on the ground that the Gospels clearly suppose the materials in the Pentateuch to be from Moses. By contrast, for some time studies of the Pentateuch questioned whether *anything* in the first five books of the Bible stemmed from Moses or from his time.

That situation has changed markedly during recent decades. The Pentateuch is still considered to have been formed out of a number of distinct traditions, but these traditions preserve ancient materials reaching back, in many instances, to the times of early settlement in Canaan and to the time of Moses. The situation is much like that of the Book of Isaiah. Fundamental themes and views of God and the world, belonging to the early life of the tribes in Canaan and in the wilderness, have been elaborated, recast, and made to express particular views and outlooks of a later period. But the same historical/source criticism that first divided the Pentateuch into quite separate literary sources has, with later refinements and better perspectives, corrected the excesses of such literary source analysis. The Pentateuch materials reach back to the time of Moses and prior to Moses. They show us a living tradition that, because it was alive, continued to affect and challenge the lives of ancient Israelites. Under divine inspiration, the first five books of the Bible became *the* Torah par excellence for the Jewish people, and they are that to this day. And under divine inspiration, the Christian community also rightly looks to Moses as the great liberator and lawgiver, the great intercessor with God for a sinful people.

But what of Jesus' attribution of the Pentateuch, or parts of it, to Moses? The references are scattered throughout the Gospels and clearly indicate that in Jesus' day Moses was looked upon as the one through whom God's Torah was disclosed. Again, as in the case of Isaiah, one may simply respond by saying that the inspiration of the Pentateuch does not depend upon the material having all been written by the traditional author. Inspiration of anonymous material is as appropriate to claim as inspiration of material from a named author. Moreover, it is precisely a refined critical scholarship that today claims much more of the material to stem from Moses' time. The point is that we need to know the *process* by which our biblical material came to read as it now does, so that we can trace, to some extent, the actual course of God's revelatory dealings with Israel and with the church. Only historically oriented scholarship can enable us to trace that path. Again, Baptists the world over have had a large hand in critical work on the Pentateuch, and also in the newer studies that have shown the antiquity of much of the Pentateuch.

The Development of Israelite Religion

Critical scholarship has also been challenged for presenting a too simple picture of the evolution of Israelite religion. Such a challenge is in fact appropriate, although the fault lies not with historical scholarship as such but with the presuppositions of the scholars. Julius Wellhausen, one of the great historians of the religion of Israel and also a brilliant source critic, offered an all too familiar Christian perspective on Israelite religion in his famous *Prolegomena to the History of Israel*. For Wellhausen, the high ethical ideals of Israel's prophets represented the pinnacle of Israel's religion, to be reaffirmed and surpassed by Jesus. For Wellhausen, it was the postexilic period that saw the transformation of Israelite religion into a Judaism that was centered upon scrupulous observance of the Law, a Law that had become an oppressive burden laid upon the backs of the people by the religious establishment.

Wellhausen was criticized by evangelical scholars not so much for this picture of Judaism, which many evangelical (and liberal) Christian scholars shared. He was criticized for what seemed to be a lack of appreciation of divine revelation as such. When one can trace the course of the development of Israel's religion without much or any regard to the mystery of divine revelation, one may be suspected of not believing in revelation at all.

On this point there have been many false steps, within critical biblical scholarship and within evangelical scholarship. Recent generations of scholars have tended to locate biblical revelation too exclusively in external historical events, as though the factual details of biblical narratives and prophetic utterances were always the essential point. Both evangelical and nonevangelical scholars have made excessive claims along these lines. There is no doubt that for the biblical writers and collectors of tradition, the history of Israel and of the church was a history of life under God in the concreteness of the daily existence of the people and of its individuals. God entered their world, claiming their lives, and displaying the divine purposes through concrete events, including the language of the people.

But that did not mean that God's revelation in the lives of the people was centrally through historical events. Revelation in the Bible is fundamentally revelation through persons, with all the mystery of human personality and motivation and thought present in the revelation. God delivered slaves from Egypt, but many a slave saw no divine purpose in the deliverance, we may be sure. God called many an individual to speak against Israel's sin, but only a few prophets worked at the question of how to understand Israel's sin, how to speak effectively to sinners, and how to call the whole people to renewed acts of faith in God. Revelation happened through events in the inanimate world as well as in the world of human beings. But central to all events were men and women whom God touched and called to act in response to divine initiatives. The Bible itself contains earnest and poignant questionings of God's active guidance of Israel's history and of world history (Ps. 44; Eccl.).

This is what is wrong with many of the schemes by means of which both evangelical and nonevangelical scholars have reconstructed the religion of Israel. We have reason to be suspicious of theories of religious development such as Wellhausen used, theories that are evolutionary and offer a single standard of what is "authentic" or "healthy" religion. Was the postexilic period a time of serious religious decline, with the law becoming an oppressive burden upon the people? If the interpreter has no sympathy for a religion of absolute demand (as Wellhausen did not), and if the interpreter ignores much of the literature produced during the postexilic period (as Wellhausen did), then the results will surely be unreliable. Psalms 1, 19, and 119 show clearly what a treasure, what a mystical presence, God's Torah was for some in postexilic Israel. And other literature from postexilic times sharply challenges the outlook of Ezra and Nehemiah with regard to mixed marriages and the relation of Israel to foreign peoples (the Books of Ruth and Jonah, though Ruth may belong to a period earlier than the return from exile). Some of the most openhearted of biblical texts belong to the period after the return from Babylonian exile, when God's Torah was becoming more and more a reality to be applied to all features and facets of the lives of the people. Look, for example, at Zechariah 2:1-12, Isaiah 35:1-10, Zechariah 14:16-21, Isaiah 19:23-25.[6] These texts, and many more from the period after the return from exile, show that there is a universalizing tendency in

Israelite religion that is just as powerful as any tendency of the people to turn in upon themselves.

It is right, therefore, to be suspicious of facile reconstructions of Israelite religion along evolutionary lines or reconstructions that fail to give sufficient attention to the personal initiatives of the individuals and groups involved as bearers and interpreters of that religion. On this point, however, we have to acknowledge that both evangelical and nonevangelical scholars have often gone astray, and that historical criticism is indispensable if we are not to be imprisoned in their mistakes or in others just as serious.

Inaccuracies in the Record

But what are we to do with what seem clearly to be inaccuracies in the biblical record? Inaccuracies of a factual sort seem to have caused much more trouble than inaccuracies in the perception of the claims and demands of God, though the latter are the ones that have actually done the greater damage, by far, to religious faith.

First, we should point out that the biblical record is remarkably well preserved textually, and all scholars may well claim that the divine Spirit is involved in the preservation of a faithful biblical record. But there are the little inaccuracies at points that seem really not to matter at all. The Gospel of Matthew (27:9-10) refers to Jeremiah when apparently Zechariah was intended, although there are references in Jeremiah to which one can point. The order of persons named in Acts 5:33-39 seems to be historically erroneous: Judas the Galilean appeared before Theudas. Some cities destroyed by Joshua seem not to have been in existence as walled towns at the time normally assigned for Joshua's battles.

Efforts to show that Genesis 1—11 contain a strictly historical account of the development of life on the planet and of a great flood that covered the entire surface of earth are, in my view, misguided. We shall attempt to show in the next section what power and truth are contained in these materials about God as the Creator of heaven and earth, power and truth that do not derive from their being historical records of the creation.

Biblical history can be reconstructed today to a considerable extent, and much of the material of the Bible can be set into particular historical contexts. This is a remarkable achievement of critical scholarship, and it tends to show overwhelmingly how faithful a record we have of the life of ancient Israel and of the early church, how accurate the biblical record is, how well preserved is its text, and how overwhelmingly profound its portrayal of the meaning of the life of humankind under God. Baptist scholarship has made a significant and commendable contribution here.

The Value of Historical Criticism: Passing on the Tradition Intact

Why, then, should historical criticism have been singled out as so damaging to faith? The problem lies, I believe, in the attitude of interpreters toward the notion of historical change. Historical critics are convinced that in early Israelite life there were understandings of God and the world, of sin and redemption, of God's justice and love, and the like, that changed over time. But how can eternal truths change and still be eternal? One's response to this question is crucial. More and more I have become convinced that a religious community's greatest challenge is to find ways to pass along to the next generation those religious understandings and disclosures that support and animate the community's religious existence. How *can* our religious faith, which was passed along to us even as it was claimed by us through our own act of personal faith and commitment, be passed along *intact* to our children? This is the central question faced by all religious leaders. It takes a special form within Christian communities like our own free church community, for it is the *biblical* heritage that is, first and last, central for us. But how can traditions be passed along intact?

A good analogy is to be found in the field of Bible translation. How can the sacred story be translated into the next language of the believing community? The early Christians knew the Old Testament largely in the prevailing Greek translations that had been made of it, as we can see from the quotations of the Old Testament found in the New. Often in recent years we have heard how much was lost in that process of rendering the Hebraic world of ancient Israel into the Hellenistic world of Greek speakers of Jesus' day. But the problem is just as real in translating the Hebrew into Aramaic, another Semitic language with the basic characteristics of Hebrew, or into any language. It is not the character of the language into which one translates but the nature of the translation process itself that is our analogy.

I have often quoted the saying attributed to Jehuda ben Ilai (third century C.E.) about the translation of the Scriptures into Aramaic: "One who translates literally, lies; one who adds anything to the text, blasphemes." Here we have the Scylla and Charybdis of the Bible translator, and (I believe) of the one who passes along the biblical tradition faithfully. It must not be done literally, as though the social world from which our tradition has come to us is itself the social world of our children. But it must not be adapted to the new world for the sake of its becoming acceptable, for if that happens, then it is not any longer itself. So we sail our course between lying and blaspheming—a perilous journey indeed!

And that is where historical criticism comes to our aid. We need to understand the language and the idioms, the customs, the basic ideas, the prejudices and the special leanings of the persons responsible for the document we translate—in this case, the Bible. Of course, we cannot know all that we wish to know, but we have to keep studying, digging, reevaluating, searching for the best possible meaning. And then we have to find in our own language and culture the nearest equivalent for the thought and the idioms of that ancient world, rendering the *meaning* of the text into an *appropriate and equivalent form*, to the extent that that is possible.

But how can we possibly do that if we hold the biblical text at a distance from our own world, from its thought-forms, from its customs, from its prejudices, from its special insights? There will be sufficient clash, at best, as this biblical heritage is passed on, but if it is to be passed on *intact*, it has to enter so deeply into the contemporary world that it undergoes small, subtle, but real changes, *precisely in order to be intact*. If the tradition is held at a safe distance from our world, protected from the "acids of modernity," then it is likely to be a foreign body, an alien set of beliefs, that we may of course pass on to our children and help or compel them to accept. But it will not have sufficiently entered into the thought and images and styles of their (and our) world that it really is *the biblical tradition itself* that we pass along. In such a case, we are passing along our parents' or perhaps our own version of that tradition that did address the earlier world but hardly speaks to the current world at all. Thus, the tradition is not *intact*, because the tradition is no longer alive. It is more fossil than living religious witness.

To be sure, this analogy from translation theory and practice is an analogy. We are not translating the Christian faith into an entirely new language for an entirely new world. The continuities are many, and they are real, between these "worlds." And we have long and expert experience in passing the tradition on to the next generation. It is a part of our very lives, our hymnody, our ethics, our world of thought, imagery, feeling, and prayer. Even so, in particular ways, we can find ourselves between "lying" and "blasphemy" as we try faithfully to interpret our Scriptures for the contemporary world.

Historical criticism, then, is not simply an aid to us in clarifying the historical settings of biblical texts, showing us the course of the development of biblical religion. Historical criticism is our *best instrument* in the faithful passing along of the central core of the biblical heritage.

Historical criticism also is of great importance in showing us the *dominant themes and ideas* of our biblical heritage. The Bible has a mysterious way of helping its readers to confront what are its central affirmations. For example, Exodus 34:6-7, a text telling how the very inner character of God is *mercy*, is quoted over and over again in later texts, including the apocryphal writings (see 2 Esdras 7:62 to 8:36, for example). Historical criticism, along with literary and sociological and theological studies, helps us to spot these central affirmations, enabling us to see that there were certain *core biblical traditions* that biblical authors turned to and passed along time after time. Think of the prominence of the Exodus tradition and its portrayal of a liberating God. Think of the repeated references to God's gift of the land of Canaan, a land that is *God's* to give but is being granted to a faithful Israel in trust. Think of those texts that entwine divine justice and divine mercy, never playing one off against the other but always showing the love and mercy that are expressed in the very heart of God's just demands. Think of the theme "promise on the way to fulfillment," which animates all of biblical eschatology and much of biblical history. Here too, passing on the tradition is helped by historical criticism that can offer clues to each generation as to what stands close to the center of biblical faith and what lies more toward its periphery.

This is not a mere picking and choosing of those biblical themes that we like, for it is the biblical tradition itself, critically reviewed and clarified, that directs us more and more toward the center.[7] The Bible, under the Spirit's tutelage, guides all readers over and again toward its central affirmations, and historical criticism serves to help it do so. And once again, the Baptist community through the ages

has seen this quality and character of the Bible and has based its life
and faith squarely upon these central affirmations.

Examples of Historical Criticism at Work

For the remainder of this chapter I want to offer two quite
different pictures of how historical criticism helps us with biblical
texts. I am going to use texts familiar to me, attempting to show that
historical criticism not only does not destroy biblical faith or erode
it, but enhances and strengthens and deepens that faith. The first is
an examination of how the Book of Isaiah looks when viewed as the
product of a long period of *faithful* passing along of the basic
theology of the prophet Isaiah, and the second is a look at several
biblical passages dealing with God's creation of the universe.

The Isaiah Tradition and Faith

Our first example takes us once again to the Isaiah tradition.
We choose Isaiah because of the revelatory power and truth that
come through in these sixty-six chapters. Historical criticism finds
three major units, as we noted above: chapters 1—33 (or 1—39,
including chapters 34—35 and with the additions from 2 Kings),
40—55, and 56—66. How do these parts relate to one another?

The answer can be given in literary terms, to some extent. One
may also deal with the sociological reality of a community
associated with Isaiah's name and seek through sociological means
to attempt to identify the character of the community. But many
aspects of the answer can best be addressed through historical
criticism. One wishes to find a context for these several oracles, a
historical/social/religious context. In some instances, the tradition
gives at least a partial answer itself: Isaiah 7:1 to 9:7 belongs to
the time of the Syro-Ephraimitic War (734-32 B.C.E.), while
Isaiah 22 probably reflects Sennacherib's siege of Jerusalem in
701 B.C.E. But it is often much more difficult to identify the
setting of certain oracles, some of which refer to events not
otherwise known (Isa. 21). Even so, the three major parts of the
book can be roughly identified: Chapters 1—33 belong to the
period before the Babylonian exile; chapters 34—35 and 40—55
to the time of exile; and chapters 56—66 to the time after the
return from exile.

In terms of faith, this threefold division is of great importance. While some of Isaiah's promises of a day of consummation may have been recast by the later Isaiah traditionists,[8] the present text of these promises makes it clear that Isaiah was looking for a true, just, and faithful monarch related to the line of David. He was certainly not uncritical of the monarchs who were David's descendants (see Isa. 7:1-17!). But he believed in the kingship and believed that God would restore faithful rulers to guide Israel in the last days.

No such confidence in Israel's kings shows up in chapters 40—55. God's agent for deliverance of Israel is Servant Israel, or some representative of Servant Israel, punished double for its sins, awaiting redemption, and on the threshold of being redeemed. God will be faithful to the promise made to David (Isa. 55:1-5), but not by raising up another descendant of David's line to sit on the throne. Zion is much more important than some descendant of David. And *God* is Israel's true Redeemer.

In Isaiah 56—66 too there is little sign of a Davidic ruler of the Isaiah sort. What counts now is fidelity to God's righteous will, acts of mercy and faithfulness in daily life, and confident trust in the coming day of consummation. The influence of the themes of Isaiah 40—55 is great upon Isaiah 56—66, and the entire collection breathes the same hope in God that animates 40—55.

What holds the three parts of the Book of Isaiah together? In addition to the literary and the theological themes, we have to say that Israel's history under God holds them together. The message of Isaiah of Jerusalem fits the times within which the message was delivered. Prophetic judgments and promises address people in the concreteness of their historical existence, and historical criticism helps us to rediscover that concrete world addressed by the prophet. The message of Isaiah 40—55 fits the needs of a people in exile, about to lose heart, fearful that there will be no deliverance. Was Jeremiah's promise of a return within seventy years (Jer. 29) an illusion? The prophet says no, and seeks to kindle faith and hope in a despairing people. The message of Isaiah 56—66 also fits the needs of a people in Judah, struggling to make a new life for themselves under very difficult circumstances. The message here is intended to encourage those who are suffering at the hands of oppressors from within their own community, but it is intended also to challenge wrongdoers and evoke a fresh commitment of faith from them.

Consider what it would mean to treat all of these sixty-six chapters as coming from the last half of the eighth century B.C.E. The prophet, under such circumstances, would be foretelling needs within Israel that had not arisen, would be offering a message to people as yet unborn. But if disciples of Isaiah of Jerusalem kept his message alive and thriving, developed the prophet's themes in new circumstances, and claimed that heritage for themselves in their changed situation, then surely they were keeping the prophetic word alive, powerful, and true—or, to look at the matter from the other side, the prophetic word was demonstrating its truth and exercising its power through their labor. In short, Isaiah's disciples were doing just what we suggested that each generation has to do. To pass the tradition on intact, we have to let it undergo such transformations as will make it genuinely address the new situations, thereby being maintained in its integrity and truth and power.

Historical Criticism and Creation

What does historical criticism contribute to a faithful reading of the Hebrew Bible's teaching about God as Creator of heaven and earth? Let us look at several of the biblical portrayals of the creation and reflect on their cumulative impact for faith. Note that we are not talking about some evolutionary development of notions of creation, as though the thought begins in primitive naivete, moves on to tribal understandings, to those of the kingship, of the prophets, of the exilic thinkers, of the wisdom writers of late times, etc. The point is that the several understandings of creation gain contour and depth perspective when they are set in their own particular world of thought, feeling, and purpose. The most profound view in some respects will, as it turns out, be the earliest, but it need not have been so. And all—*every one*—of these views of creation contribute to the whole picture, and all—*every one*—show the mark of divine revelation.

We will take them as they come in the present order of our Christian Bible: Genesis 1; Genesis 2; Job 26; Psalm 8; Psalm 104; Proverbs 8; Isaiah 40—55. We can do no more than characterize each of these by means of a few observations.

Note that all of them presuppose an older view; none is our "initial" or "first" story of the creation, for historical criticism makes it clear that each of the authors builds upon traditions that are already present in the author's community.

Genesis 1.—Here the author seeks to correct misunderstandings and to lay out the central teachings that the community should respect with regard to creation. God is the sovereign and authoritative author of all that has being, for God called into being, by the spoken Word, the entire universe. Before there were sun and moon and stars, God had already created light. One must not suppose, therefore, that God *depends* upon sun and moon and stars to give light to the creation. God created human beings as the last act of creation, giving them responsibility for the care of the created earth and its inhabitants, though God shares in that responsibility. Human beings, male and female, constitute humankind. They exist not through procreation, for God spoke them into being. They exist for more than procreation, therefore, but they are to bear children and fill the earth. God rests on the Sabbath Day and thereby sanctifies rest as well as labor. Human beings are made for both.

This priestly tradition almost surely drew upon many sources, including the old Babylonian creation story, Enuma Elish. But Genesis 1 is not to be played off against other stories of the creation; it is rather to be seen as clearing up error, upholding the authority and the sovereign freedom of the Creator. The questions that it does not answer are, by their omission, inferred not to be of most importance. What counts immensely for the priestly community that produced Genesis 1 is God's utter control of the processes by which the world was brought into being. By contrast with what we see in nonbiblical accounts, in Genesis 1 there is no conflict within the heavens, nor are earth and its creatures created only to serve the gods. There are no demonic powers lurking in God's world to undo the creation or to pounce upon the unsuspecting. God's creation is secure, and it is also good.

There are two kinds of reality portrayed here: there is God, and there are the things and the beings that God created. No other kinds of being exist in the entire creation. There is no dualism, there is no devil, there is no positive evil, no fundamental malevolence in the creation—none, that is, outside of God's sovereign control. If human beings will live with God, faithful to God's demands, claiming their place in God's good creation, all will go well with them.

This priestly tradition with which the Bible opens knows of alternative ways to speak of the creation. Indeed, below the surface and barely visible are other strands: God addresses the earth and calls on it to bring forth vegetation and herbage, and later, earth's animal life. Earth has a bit part in the creation, though it is still the commanding divine Word that gets earth started as cocreator. And human beings are also cocreators, sharing in the gifts and powers of the Creator as those who people the earth and see to its needs in God's behalf. References to the plurality in the Godhead ("Let *us* make humankind" (Gen. 1:26, NRSV, author's italics; see also 3:22 and 11:7) also show that an older view of the heavenly realm, with God's heavenly servants having a hand in the creation, must have been known to our priestly community.

But only historical criticism and the comparative study of the notions of creation among the religions of the world will enable one to see this story in its full grandeur. The priests are saying "No!" to ways of understanding creation that they consider dangerous. Such views are dangerous, and the priests themselves are rightly doing historical criticism on the traditions available to them.

Genesis 2.—The same can be said of Genesis 2. It is generally taken to be an older tradition, belonging to the early narratives of the Books of Genesis, Exodus, and Numbers. But Genesis 2:4*b*-6 opens with traces of an even older view of creation (speaking of the time "before" the LORD God began the process, when no rain fell and no herbage had developed). This older material is mere background as the narrator unfolds the magnificent account of the Lord God forming the first human pair, intimately and with the loving hands of an artist, from the material of earth, watered by a strange "mist" or "flood" (v. 6, NEB).

In this narrative, God works to shape and arrange the realities of earth in accordance with the needs of the first human pair. God is partner and companion of the first human pair, interested in their work and discoveries, watching to see if they will be both inventive in dealing with earth's needs and at the same time faithful to the divine prohibition ("[do not] eat from the fruit of the tree of knowledge of good and evil," Gen. 2:16, NIV).

In both stories, the human community is the center of attention. In the first story, however, the priests want to make sure that the people do not worship the gods of the land of Canaan and do not miss the sovereign grandeur of a God who "spoke" the world into existence, a world utterly good, and then rested on the Sabbath Day, as all must do. In the second story (Gen. 2) the narrator-theologian wants the community to recognize God's intimate connection with all human beings as their Creator/Shaper. Here is a picture of the creation like that portrayed in Psalm 139. God works in the divine workshop, framing, knitting together the very substance of the human self. Human beings are made for one another; male and female each complete the existence of the other. The companionship in the Garden is shared by God daily. All is harmony and life is rich and full. Only a single command provides the limits appointed for the first human pair. And the entire human race, which (according to Gen. 2 and the following chapters) derives directly from this first human pair, will also live under the gracious guidance of God the Creator, and under the divine commands that will from time to time be given by God.

Poetic texts on creation.—In Job 26, the poet wishes to make an entirely different point. Job's friends suppose that they have wisdom and can explain to Job the mystery of evil in the world. But Job is confronted with a wisdom and a Mystery entirely beyond his fathoming. He speaks of a creation that quakes before its Creator, before One who has stretched out the north over the void, who hangs the earth upon nothing! (v. 7). God is One whose might and mysterious doings are only barely hinted at in what the human eye can see: these are no more than "the outskirts of [God's] ways" (v. 14, NKJV).

Psalm 8 presents quite a different picture. Here it is the creation of the human self and the extraordinary responsibility placed upon the human self that get the emphasis. God's "name" is exalted above the heavens, says the psalmist, and who is it that can name God? Only the human being can pronounce God's name, through the mystery of human speech, speech already adumbrated in the babbling of babes and infants. And this speaking being has been charged by God with responsibility for the entire creation, under God's oversight, of course. This psalm shows dependence upon Genesis 1, but the psalmist's concerns are not for correcting error (as the priests wanted to do in Gen. 1), but for seeing that the human community fulfills its extraordinary mandate from God in caring for the creation.

Psalm 104 is a lengthy and marvelous portrayal of the order and appropriateness of all God's creation, a creation that exists not only for human beings. Plants and animals, mountains and streams, sea and dry land, even the rocks serve their appointed ends, all ordered and secure, and yet at every instant entirely dependent upon God's sustaining presence. God provides food for all, and breath of life. Should God withdraw the divine breath, all living things perish. Here it is as though the psalmist wants to be sure that people do not misunderstand the mandate of Genesis 1 to subdue the earth, or the praise of humankind found in Psalm 8.

A texture of texts about creation has been woven by Israel's poets, each contributing facets to the understanding, and all requiring investigation as to their historical relations and the ways in which they should be related chronologically. Historical criticism does not adequately answer our questions about these creation texts, for they are literature, magnificent and inspired literature. But they also belong in relationship to one another and they show changing perspectives on the meaning of creation.

Wisdom texts.—Proverbs 8:22-31 presents the creation as carried through in the presence of wisdom, the first of God's creative acts. It is clear that wisdom is itself a creation of God, not some independent divine entity. But wisdom takes delight in all that God has made, applauds the mysteries of the creation, and may indeed have a hand in the actual creative process, leaving its traces on the whole of the creation. In Sirach (Ch. 24) and The Wisdom of Solomon (ch. 7—8)—two apocryphal texts accepted as Scripture by early Christians—wisdom has an even closer relation to the created world. In Sirach, wisdom is like a mist that comes from God, overshadowing and touching the totality of the creation. Wisdom shares in the divine glory and honor, sharing too in the divine secrets. And wisdom has found lodging in all peoples, but has made her abode, at God's direction, with Israel, the people of God. It is God's gift of Torah that has planted cosmic wisdom in the world, fully and firmly. Wisdom, and therefore Torah, bring the reality of God into the historical world.

In the Wisdom of Solomon, wisdom is a reality that pervades the totality of the creation. God's presence through wisdom is not absent from any facet of the creation.

Without the results of historical criticism in bringing these creation texts into relation with one another, how could one possibly understand the background and import of such critical New Testament texts as John 1:1-14 or Colossians 1:15-20?

Isaiah 40—55.—These chapters bring special emphasis to God's act as Creator. The prophet is particularly concerned with the relation of creation and new creation. God the Creator is God the

Redeemer. God has the *power* to redeem exiled Israel, for God is the Creator of the ends of the earth; nothing is too difficult for God. Before the true God, the idols are nothing, impotent, for there is one God and one God only. But God has the *intention* to redeem exiled Israel, for the entire history of Israel is a history of redemption, going back to the time of Abraham. And God's new creation is already breaking out, for the signs are everywhere for eyes of faith to see.

There are many more creation texts that could be reviewed, but these should suffice to make the point. Historical criticism is indispensable in identifying biblical themes and motifs, studying them in their respective contexts, and seeking to relate them to one another. Creation texts are also literature and have to be studied as literature. But if one wishes to know what ancient Israel thought about creation, historical critical work on the creation texts is a first and essential operation. And once again we must say: passing on the creation tradition *intact* is much more faithfully done with the aid of historical criticism. Indeed, can the creation tradition be passed along intact *without* historical criticism?

Conclusion

The value of historical criticism for faith, then, is that it contributes toward keeping faith pointed, alive, and relevant to ever-changing circumstances. Those who interpret the Bible for contemporary readers will want to know about the ancient readers and hearers, and thus they will want to have the results of historical criticism. Those who are concerned to hear the text only, without regard to authorship and transmission of the text through the centuries, may be able to get along without historical criticism, but they may miss much in the very texts that they revere. And those who are content simply to affirm the literal and historical and factual truth of the entire Bible, without regard to time and circumstance or the purpose of the Bible's authors and transmitters of tradition, run the risk of doing the very last thing that they wish to do: making the Bible irrelevant to the needs and concerns of contemporary men, women, and children, or imposing upon them a mistaken notion of what the Bible makes central in faith and in life.

Historical criticism needs believing faith. Historical criticism, rightly carried through, helps to clear the ground for an informed faith. Our Baptist heritage, a biblical heritage through and through, is and must be centrally committed to passing along that tradition *intact* to the succeeding generations. And for that reason, historical criticism is not just a good thing; it is *indispensable*.

At this time in our Baptist history, faithful historical-critical approaches to the Scripture can help us to move beyond the impasse that we confront. It can do so by showing evangelicals and nonevangelicals alike the critical necessity of passing on intact the truth and power of the Bible.

Historical criticism must help evangelicals see, if they do not see already, that if the tradition is to reach the next generation as a living and powerful truth, it must confront the real world in which we live. That means criticism of the Bible, but reverent criticism, and it means deep and soul-searching wrestlings with contemporary life and culture, too.

But historical criticism must help nonevangelicals see, if they do not already see, that the concern of faithful evangelicals is precisely *to pass this biblical tradition on intact*. Nonevangelicals may underestimate the difficulty of this task, may be too ready to adapt the biblical message and story to new, more palatable ways of presentation. And they may be too quick to impugn the motives of evangelicals.

How will we know when we have gone beyond the current impasse? We will know not only because conflicts will have subsided and civility will have returned. We will know because there will be a new spirit of collaboration among those charged to receive, in the Spirit, this biblical message, and, by the same Spirit, to pass it on to our world—faithfully, with joy and passion, and with critical discernment. Historical criticism has a major place in this urgent undertaking.

Notes

1. John Barton, *Reading the Old Testament. Method in Biblical Study* (Philadelphia: Westminster, 1984), 201.

2. See John D. W. Watts, *Isaiah 1—33* and *Isaiah 34—66* (Waco: Word, 1985, 1987).

3. See John H. Hayes and Stuart A. Irvine, *Isaiah, The Eighth*

Century Prophet: His Times and His Preaching (Nashville: Abingdon, 1987).

4. None of the numerous Old Testament references that Christian faith sees pointing to Jesus refers to Him by name as Jesus of Nazareth. The same lack of names is encountered where types and figures of things to come are found in the Bible.

5. Bruce M. Metzger, "Literary Forgeries and Canonical Pseudepigrapha," *Journal of Biblical Literature* 91 (1972): 21-22.

6. Isaiah 35:1-10 seems closely akin to the materials in Isaiah 40—55, describing a return from exile that will show God's blessing and favor upon the weak, the ill, the disfigured, and even the leprous, it seems. Isaiah 19 is a very complex chapter, difficult to date, but its closing verses are generally believed to come from the exilic or early postexilic period. For a contrasting view, see John H. Hayes and Stuart A. Irvine, *Isaiah*, 226.

7. See my essay, "Life, Faith, and the Emergence of Tradition," in Douglas A. Knight, ed., *Tradition and Theology in the Old Testament* (Philadelphia: Fortress, 1977), 11-30. The volume has recently been reprinted by Sheffield University Press (1990).

8. Here it may be well to recall what we discussed earlier in this chapter, namely, that the divine inspiration of some part of Scripture does not depend upon its being written by this or that human author. If some part of the Bible was preserved and recast over a period of time by a series of persons—for example, by the "Isaiah traditionists"—that does not in any way deny that this part of the Bible is inspired. The inspiring Spirit can work through a community of persons over the course of years just as effectively as the Spirit can work through a single author in a short period of time.

3
The Challenge of Recent Literary Approaches to the Bible
*John P. Newport**

Diverse perspectives on recent literary approaches to the Bible constitute one aspect of the Southern Baptist impasse. According to some fundamental-conservatives the wholesale adoption of recent literary approaches tends to undercut the historicity of the Bible and thus undermines its infallibility. The moderate-conservatives respond by stating that literary approaches do not necessarily undermine the Bible's reliability. Rather, they can help us to better understand the Bible and, in many cases, disclose new and relevant meanings of the Bible for contemporary persons.

One way beyond the impasse would involve a critical use of recent literary approaches within the context of evangelical presuppositions. Such an approach would result in a better understanding of biblical intent and significance.[1] For example, Mark Ellingsen contends that the narrative approach can do much to enliven and enhance the evangelical view of the Bible.[2]

Biblical studies have had contact with secular literary studies for centuries. Genuine interaction has been sporadic, however. That fact lends added interest to certain recent developments.

John P. Newport (Ph.D., Edinburgh) is Special Consultant to the President for Academic Research, Southwestern Baptist Theological Seminary, where he also has served as Provost and Professor of Philosophy of Religion. He also served on the faculties at New Orleans Baptist Seminary, Baylor University, and Rice University. In addition to his numerous lectureships, Newport has written many articles for numerous journals and reference works such as *Encyclopedia of Southern Baptists* and *The Broadman Bible Commentary*. He has written ten books including *Theology and Contemporary Art Forms*, *Why Christians Fight over the Bible*, *Christ and the New Consciousness*, *Nineteenth Century Devotional Thought*, *Paul Tillich*, *What Is Christian Doctrine*, *The Lion and the Lamb*, and *Life's Ultimate Questions*.

Within the last two decades, biblical students have begun to employ the concepts and tools of literary analysis in a sustained fashion. On the one hand, biblical scholars have turned to literary study (Polzin, Detweiler, Crossan, Via, McKnight). And, on the other hand, an increasing number of literary scholars have turned to the Bible as an object of study (Alter, Kermode, Ryken, Frye).

Such interests have led to the rise of a number of literary approaches, or to a number of forms of "literary criticism," as these approaches are most commonly called. Although these approaches are able to make important contributions to our understanding of the Bible, as will be pointed out later, it may be well to begin with a note of caution.[3]

The Traditional Evangelical Approach

Many of the forms of literary criticism that have come to prominence since mid-century have an "aesthetic" character (to be explained shortly) that is at odds with some basic features of traditional evangelical hermeneutics. In evangelical commentaries on the Bible, for example, the goal has been to reconstruct and represent the author's intention. This goal determines the method used: a study of the grammar of the language and the original situation of the author.[4] J. I. Packer writes:

> So the first task is always to get into the writer's mind by grammatico-historical exegesis of the most thoroughgoing and disciplined kind, using all the tools provided by linguistic, historical, logical, and semantic study for the purpose.[5]

For the traditional evangelical, meaning is held to be objectively real, independent of the mind's perception of it, waiting to be uncovered. Without a discernible norm for meaning, there would be no validity in interpretation, only relativism. The view that the author is the locus of the meaning of a text provides theoretical stability to interpretation.[6]

Philosophical Roots of "Aesthetic Criticism"

The "aesthetic" orientation that goes beyond these evangelical assumptions can be understood best in terms of its philosophical roots. Only the briefest sketch will be attempted.

Kant

German philosopher Immanuel Kant (1724-1804) stated that what we know is relative to the categories or channels through which knowledge comes to us through the knowing process. In relation to aesthetics, he developed this method in his *Critique of Judgment*. Through creative imagination the mind constructs order or purposiveness. Aesthetic judgments go beyond the limits of our actual experience of the world and construct a world "as if" it had purpose and beauty. Kant's aesthetic theory favors the creative imagination and accords a special status to "feeling" and poetry. This same emphasis can be traced through the history of German Idealism and Romanticism to the present.[7]

German Idealism

According to Friedrich von Schiller, human beings are unique for only they can experience beauty. This is the argument of his letters *On the Aesthetic Education of Man*. It is in the aesthetic sphere that the creative impulse builds "a joyous realm of play" transcending both the rational and pragmatic realms.[8]

Northrop Frye, the Canadian literary critic and author of *Anatomy of Criticism: Four Essays* (New York: Atheneum, 1967) works in the tradition of Kant and Schiller. He insists that literature is an autonomous realm that alone provides the vision which can free us from the oppressive dimensions of our environment.[9]

Romanticism

In the Romanticism of the late 1790s and the early 1800s, the aesthetic realm was predominant in a way that would not be equaled until the mid-twentieth century. For Coleridge, the poet's imagination is the most important channel for perceiving cognitive meaningfulness, and symbols are its privileged product. By creating an awareness of purpose, art and poetry make us feel that we belong in the world.[10]

In our present era Paul Ricoeur, the French phenomenologist, belongs in the Romantic tradition. Ricoeur says that poetic discourse expresses modes of being that ordinary vision obscures or represses.[11]

Jacques Derrida

Derrida is a French philosopher heavily influenced by Nietzsche and Heidegger. The result of Derrida's "deconstruction" of philosophy is that philosophy comes to resemble literature. There are no facts, no truth, only interpretations. In Derrida there is no interest in the author or his intention.[12]

What began with Kant's positing an autonomous realm of beauty has now expanded to include all of life. The world is a textual labyrinth whose signs may, as Wittgenstein noted earlier, have some kind of family resemblance, but never refer to anything outside the sign system. People are thus invited playfully to interpret the text. There is no way to distinguish exegesis from eisegesis.[13] For this reason Robert Detweiler could say that Derrida "poses perhaps the greatest contemporary threat to traditional biblical scholarship.[14]

C. Hayden White

An example of the aesthetic approach to history is found in the work of C. Hayden White. His basic philosophy is that historical narratives are verbal fictions which make sense of experience in the same way as do novels and other fictional models. Fiction and history belong to the same class of narrative structure. In both history and fiction, human consciousness "colonizes the world" by imposing meaningful forms.[15]

Recent Major Developments in Literary Criticism

The developments in philosophy outlined above have had their largest application in the sphere of literary studies. However, each philosophical development has in some measure found biblical scholars who have adapted its principles to biblical studies.

"New Criticism" or Formalism

New Criticism describes a general trend in literary theory that became dominant in the middle of this century. Cleanth Brooks,

Robert Penn Warren, and W. K. Wimsatt in the United States and F. R. Leavis in Britain are a few of the prominent scholars usually associated with this movement.

The primary tenet of New Criticism is that the literary work or text is deemed self-sufficient; the author's intention and background are secondary or even irrelevant. New Critics speak of the literary text as an artifact or verbal icon. Both of these metaphors express the self-sufficiency of the literary work. These critics require (indeed must restrict themselves to) only the text and do not use outside, or extrinsic factors in their interpretations.[16]

For the New Critics, meaning is the sense the words bear in their immediate verbal context. Literature is an independent and self-sufficient kingdom. Cleanth Brooks characterizes any attempt to separate the meaning of a text from its form as the "heresy of paraphrase."[17] Poetic insight cannot be captured in prose and translated into propositional language. Literature is here freed from any responsibility to assert meaning or to describe the world; it does not have to be "about" anything. This stance has been used by M. Weiss to justify his rejection of external approaches to the meaning of a passage of Scripture, and his insistence upon reading the text "closely."[18]

This process is called synchronic analysis. It involves viewing a text as a chronological unit apart from its historical development or references. For example, in this perspective the Gospels are not windows through which one can look at the historical processes out of which they arose. Rather, the Gospels are viewed as mirrors in which one can see a self-contained textual world.

The synchronic exegete concentrates on the Gospel itself, on the narrative world that the author has constructed within the text. This narration itself is what is signified and should be the interpretative focus.[19]

Structuralism

By comparison with the New Criticism, structuralism adds some fresh elements. For example, it sees language as a constant that makes cross-cultural comparisons possible.

Even so, structuralism also holds many concepts in common with New Criticism. There is a focus on the text as it stands rather than on the author's intention and historical context. Interest is also expressed in literary form, paradigm, and genre.

The ultimate goal of structuralist critics is to make the tacit "grammar" of literature, its underlying structure, explicit. The "author" or "subject" is not the primary determiner of meaning; meaning is rather determined by the conventions or "codes" within a given cultural context which are reflected in the form of the text. The unconscious constraints of linguistic convention, not the author's conscious intent, are the real determiners of meaning.[20]

The author of a text as a human being and a member of a given social culture will passively assimilate a variety of structures capable of bearing meanings. In the composition of a text, these structures will be utilized, normally in an unconscious way. This is true because these deep structural patterns are found in all linguistic expressions and literary works.

Every Russian folk tale, for example, begins with an initial sequence where the social order is somehow disrupted. The rest of the narrative consists in attempts to reestablish the social order. The final correlated sequence shows the social order eventually being reestablished, and then life continuing as normal.

These same patterns can be seen in the parable of the good Samaritan: the wounded man, the ideal and false religious persons, the robbers, the kingdom of heaven and the threat of evil all fit together to constitute a deep mythological structure beneath the surface of the parable.[21]

In the end the author, the conscious "subject," is overshadowed by the literary codes that are held to be the real determiners of meaning. Cut off from any individual author, the text is implicated in a structure of cultural conventions. The meaning of a text is therefore essentially a reflection of the textual medium, its type of literature, and its place in the larger literary code.[22]

Structuralists maintain that, like computers, the human brain perceives and processes data according to the binarian principle of oppositions, or antithetical thinking. They are therefore committed to a functional method of trying to synthesize the opposing tensions in any given literary form.

Because of these structures, structuralist critics concentrate on "correct" reading or "literary competence." This does not mean reconstructing the author's intention but using the requisite conventions so that the text makes sense. John Barton has made an incisive critique of this tendency of structuralism:

If taken to their logical conclusions these principles produce a theory of literature which is both determinist—so much so, that the author has no control at all over the meaning of his own work—and also wholly conventionalist, in the sense that "meaning" has no existence outside the arbitrary conventions of human society and its aesthetic systems.

He concludes that this model leads inevitably to relativism, for "meaning" must change whenever society changes.[23]

Reader-Response Approach or Post-Structuralism

Beginning in the late 1960s and becoming more prominent in the early 1970s the proponents of the reader-response approach stressed the reciprocal relation between the text and the reader. This is opposed to earlier emphases on the autonomy of the text and structuralism.

Wolfgang Iser is one of the foremost scholars studying secular literature with this methodology. According to Iser, the historical-critical method can discover much of the history behind the text and the intention of the author. Structuralism can analyze cultural codes and the narrative and mythical structures that comprise the text. Ultimately, however, the basic meaning of the text is supplied by the reader.[24]

The point of departure for reader-response criticism is the affirmation that a literary work is a bipolar entity. Every truly literary work has both an artistic pole and an aesthetic pole. The artistic pole is the creation of the author. The aesthetic pole is the work of the reader. Without this aesthetic dimension, a literary work is simply a potentiality. By actually reading it, participating with it aesthetically, the text comes into being, becomes real, has meaning, and realizes its purpose.[25]

Authors deliberately create artistic works that will involve the activity of the reader. They tantalize, tease, challenge, provoke, and invite the reader to get into the text and participate. The author intentionally leaves gaps in the information, and the reader is then stimulated to fill in the missing parts, at least tentatively, in order to make sense out of the composition.[26]

Much of the philosophical background for reader-response criticism is found in the writings of the German philosopher Hans-George Gadamer, author of *Truth and Method*. According to

Gadamer, the meaning of any text is codetermined by the horizons of the author and the interpreter. Understanding a text involves a "fusion of horizons" between past and present. Gadamer believes that it is impossible simply to reduplicate the original author's view, because our contemporary perspective is always fused with the text in any act of interpretation. This means that in Gadamer's hermeneutics the intent of the author cannot be decisive for determining the meaning of the text for a given reader.[27]

From the Enlightenment perspective the disinterested reader is supposedly free of the constraining prejudgments of history. But those prejudgments are the very things that Gadamer believes the interpreters of texts and history cannot and need not avoid because they are an integral aspect for any creative or constructive interpretation. The prejudgments of the individual, far more than his judgments, constitute the historical reality of his being. Proclaiming his deep indebtedness to Heidegger, Gadamer stresses the way in which all reading and understanding begin with the interpreter in some way already "interested in that which he or she is trying to comprehend." The idea of a disinterested interpretation of a literary text becomes an impossible one for hermeneutical theory.[28]

The reader expands the horizon of the text by appropriating it in a particular historical situation. The text, in turn, questions its readers by challenging and enlarging the structures they have brought to it. As they encounter alien elements questioning them through the text, the readers are forced to revise their assumptions. And out of this process comes the fusion of horizons.[29]

Liberation and Feminist Interpreters

The most frequent appeal for a reader-response theory in biblical studies comes from those who might be called "ideological readers." This term refers to those who read the Scriptures with a definite, usually political or ethical, agenda. The two most prominent types of ideological readers today are liberation theologians and feminist scholars. African-American theologians could also be included in this category.

Liberation theologians read the text, attending primarily to what they perceive are the needs of their contemporary society. Many do this from the perspective of the modern political philosophy of Marxism. Such a reading will bring certain elements of the text into prominence, in particular, those texts concerning the liberation of the oppressed. The exodus, which is certainly a major biblical theme, takes on even larger proportions in the writings of theologians of liberation. In this connection the work of N. Gottwald is noteworthy.[30]

There are many differences among biblical scholars who are classified as *feminists*. Some wish simply to explore the biblical characters, books, and themes that are relevant to the situation of the modern woman. Other feminist scholars want to read the whole text from a female perspective to see what difference it makes if the reader is a woman rather than a man. Still others wish to read the Bible as women in order to "explode the myth of patriarchy." They seek to show the innate prejudice of the Scriptures against women and to expose the Bible as a potential or possible tool of oppression. All three types of feminists are united in the sense that they approach the text with a definite social objective in view. Some appear to utilize reader-response theory in order to give a methodological justification for allowing a reader's personal convictions to play a greater role in interpretation.[31]

Other feminists accept the Bible as only one among four sources of authority which include experience, tradition, biblical witness, and intellectual research. In principle, for these feminists tradition, historical research, and experience have authority equal to Scripture. In practice, they do not give tradition this parity. From their perspective, patriarchy has tended to dominate the history of theology. This means that feminists believe that they can use only selective and radical reinterpretations of their heritage. Experience, therefore, refers not to human experience in general, but the experience of oppressed women struggling for liberation in concert with others of marginal race, class, or status.[32]

Narrative Criticism

A highly developed methodology for studying biblical narratives from the perspective of reader involvement has been taken over from secular literary critics and is usually referred to as narrative criticism. For example, the gospels are seen as macronarratives which contain micronarratives. In the past, literary aspects of Gospel narratives were subordinated to dogmatic and historical interests. Since the late 1960s, however, literary aspects of narrative have increasingly become the center of interest.[33] The Gospels as they stand in their story form, rather than their sources, historical background, or theological themes, are the subject of study.[34]

Narrative criticism distinguishes the various readers of a literary work. The *real* reader is the actual flesh and blood person who picks up the text and reads. The *implied* reader is the existential role the real reader assumes as he or she becomes involved with the text, a role that involves assuming certain presuppositions, values, insights and challenges implied by the text. It is only by assuming the role demanded by the text that the real reader is able to make sense out of the text or, in the terminology of narrative criticism, to actualize what is merely potential in the text.[35]

One of the things that narrative critics have done is to focus on the *narrator* who is discernible in each of the Gospels, or at least in the major narrative passages. The historical processes leading up to the formation of the Gospel of Mark may have been long and complex, but the final work is integrated around a unified narrative motif. One can similarly discover a narrator, or narrators, for each of the other three Gospels. One thing that can be noticed is that the point of view of the narrator, the point of view from which the narrator tells the story, differs considerably among the Gospels. For example, the overall perspective from which the Gospel of Mark is told is very clearly the imminence, the immediacy, or the "about-to-appearness" of Jesus. The perspective from which the Gospel of Matthew is told is very clearly from the vantage point of the absolute authority of the Father.[36]

The narrator plays a pivotal role in shaping the reaction of the reader to the passage he or she is reading. The narrator achieves this response in a variety of ways, ranging from presenting and withholding information from the reader, to explicit commentary.

Third-person narrative refers to all the characters impersonally, and in this mode the narrator may assume the literary stance of omniscience and omnipresence. Most narrative in the Bible is in the third person, a feature of biblical narrative that reinforces the impression of evangelicals that the Bible is divinely inspired and can even evoke that impression in other readers as well.[37]

Rhoads and Michie, for example, describe such a narrator and point of view in the Gospel of Mark:

> The narrator does not figure in the events of the story; speaks in the
> third person; is not bound by time or space in the telling of the story;

is an implied invisible presence in every scene, capable of being anywhere to "recount" the action; displays full omniscience by narrating the thoughts, feelings, or sensory experiences of many characters; often turns from the story to give direct "asides" to the reader, explaining a custom or translating a word or commenting on the story; and narrates the story from one overarching ideological point of view.[38]

This description surely applies to most biblical narrative. The voice of the narrator is often the authoritative guide, directing the reader in his or her analysis and response to the events and characters of the story.

Just as there is, in each of the Gospels, a narrator, so also each Gospel has its *narratee.* Usually the narratee is unmentioned, unnamed, and almost invisible except in the Gospel of Luke. Theophilus is the narratee in the Gospel of Luke, he is named at the beginning and is the person to whom the book is addressed. The characterization of Theophilus as "lover of God" should influence how one responds to the style and story which the narrator unfolds.[39]

An interesting book to which to apply the concept of the narratee is Nahum. The original readers were no doubt Judeans. The implied readers were faithful Judeans who desired the destruction of Nineveh. The narratees, however, are the Ninevites. It is doubtful whether the Ninevites ever read the book, but the narrator addresses the book to them, and the reader sensing this will be better able to appreciate the message of the book through these literary nuances.[40]

Narrative critics are thus concerned with how an author has utilized a set of values and concerns in creating a narrative work. This telling of a story by a narrator to a narratee is observed by an implied reader who is challenged to put the story world together. To the extent that the real reader assumes the role expected of the implied reader, he or she will receive what the text is supposed to give.

For example, for a real reader to be able to assume the role of the implied reader of Matthew's Gospel, that person must regard him or herself as a member of the believing community presupposed by Matthew's Gospel. Matthew was relating Christ to the Jews in light of the Old Testament. Why does Matthew choose to report the sermon as taking place on a mountain? The answer comes as we recognize that Matthew repeatedly draws analogies between the life of Jesus and the Old Testament exodus, wilderness wanderings, and conquest. In Matthew's account, after Jesus returns from forty days in the wilderness, He "ascends the mountain" where He presents His interpretation of the law of God. Jesus' preaching on the law on the mount is therefore deliberately compared to Moses receiving the law on Mount Sinai.[41]

Deconstructionism

One of the areas of literary studies which became prominent in the 1980s is deconstruction. It came as the "new wave" from France. Like the previous imports (existentialism, structuralism), deconstruction has brought strong reactions, both positive and negative, from English and American scholars.[42]

Deconstruction is most closely associated with Jacques Derrida. His first major writings appeared in 1967, but his major influence came in the 1970s and continues in the 1980s and early 1990s. Derrida is part philosopher and part literary critic.

Derrida argues for the priority of writing over speech. He believes that writing is a clearer illustration of what characterizes all language acts: the slippage between sign and referent, signifier and signified. Derrida's extreme language skepticism calls into question the act of literary communication. A clear-cut meaning is never established; the pun becomes the favored interpretive device.[43]

The New Testament scholar John Dominic Crossan has been active in bringing Derrida's thought to bear on issues of interpretation. This influence is most readily seen in his book *Cliffs of Fall: Paradox and Polyvalence in the Parables of Jesus* (1980), in which he analyzes the parables from a Derridean perspective. He finds that the metaphoricity of the parable has a "void of meaning at its core. . . . it can mean so many things and generate so many differing interpretations because it has no fixed, univocal or absolute meaning to begin with." Instead of searching for the meaning of the parable, Crossan plays (a favorite metaphor of deconstructive method) with the word of the text.[44] For Crossan, the Bible, like other works of literature, always deconstructs itself.

Perhaps the most explicit deconstructive study of Old Testament texts is found in Peter Miscall's *The Workings of Old Testament Narrative*. Miscall concludes that to attempt to pin down a single meaning of the text is misguided and argues that most exegetical issues are undecidable. He argues that the type of ambiguity he demonstrates about David in 1 Samuel 17 is the result of the nature of literary communication (the slippage of signifier and signified).[45]

Weaknesses and Pitfalls of the Literary Approaches

Before we note the possible contributions of these literary approaches, it will be important to note some of their weaknesses.

When the Bible is seen primarily as an aesthetic object, it tends to be cut off from its original situation in history and from the authority of its author.—Much of the growing interest in literary-critical exegesis, as well as modern theology's preoccupation with categories such as metaphor, story, narrative, art, and the imagination, derives from an approach to the text as aesthetic object. This aesthetic bias is often accompanied by an increasing skepticism about what can be known and referred to, and from a desire to preserve literature in a realm of its own.

The more problematic side of the aesthetic emphasis is seen in its tendency to make the author and history irrelevant for interpretive purposes. To dissociate the work from its original context and author is to set it adrift, allowing it to have as many meanings as there are interpreters.[46]

It is not surprising that an aesthetic approach should turn first to Jesus' parables, given their explicit fictional status and strange power. As extended metaphors, the parables cannot be reduced to a single "point." The parables renew our religious imagination, force us to view the world in a new manner, and compel us to make a choice between the old and the new way. The trouble comes when the parables are taken to be paradigmatic for *all* biblical literature. In this connection, it is significant that in Paul Ricoeur's 115-page study entitled "Biblical Hermeneutics" the focus is almost entirely on only one of the biblical literary genres: the parable.[47]

One major literary voice that has defended authorial intent is E. D. Hirsch. He posits an author-centered interpretive method that seeks to arrive at the author's intent. This approach, Hirsch believes, provides an anchor of determinant meaning in the sea of relativity introduced by other theories. Although Hirsch's views have not been widely accepted by his fellow literary theorists, his emphasis provides a needed counterbalance to many of the trends in secular theory.[48]

Hirsch also argues that Gadamer overstates the influence of the interpreter's context on the perception of meaning. Gadamer exaggerates a difficulty into an impossibility. It is difficult to bracket out a person's cultural categories in interpreting an ancient text. However, the work of biblical and literary scholars, Bible translators, anthropologists, and archaeologists demonstrates that it is possible to transcend imaginatively one's own categories with some degree of success and identify sympathetically with the categories of a different culture. The text can be seen as having a meaning (the original author's) irrespective of the various perspectives from which the interpreters may be viewing it.

Hirsch further points out that Gadamer has confused *meaning* and *significance*. The meaning of the text is that intended by the author, and is thus a determinate entity. Significance, on the other hand, which involves the value or impact of a text in relation to the interpreter, will vary from context to context. Paul's concept of justification by faith meant exactly what Paul intended for it to mean, no more and no less. The contemporary significance of that concept for psychology or the health professions, for example, may well transcend what Paul consciously intended. New contexts lead to new significance for an original meaning. The same point could be made by saying that an original, determinate meaning may have various *applications* in different cultural contexts.[49]

The various literary approaches tend to lead to one-sided, distorted results.—Every major movement in literary theory of the past forty years is mirrored in the work of biblical scholars: New Criticism (Weiss); Northrup Frye's archetypal approach to literature (Frye himself, Ryken); phenomenology (Detweiler, Ricoeur); structuralism (Jobling, Polzin, Patte); Marxism (Gottwald, liberation theologians); feminism (Trible, Reuther, Fiorenza); deconstruction (Crossan, Miscall).

Each of these movements has some truth which we will note later. But in each case the secular theory tends to lead to a new imbalance. New Criticism rightly attacked certain cases of appealing to the author's intention for the meaning of a text, but it went too far in restricting the interpreter to the text alone, the text as artifact, leaving both author and reader out of the picture. Marxist and feminist readings have a tendency to distort the text by insisting that their themes are the primary interpretive grids. And deconstructionists use their insight into the slippage between sign and object to attack theology or any type of literary communication.[50]

As against these one-sided results, Robert K. Johnston has shown that it is possible to combine the better features of these approaches so as to give an appropriately balanced emphasis to author, text, reader, and the spiritual reality or worldview that is presented in the biblical text.[51]

The literary or aesthetic approach tends to deny referential function to the biblical text.—Recognition of the literary characteristics of the Bible has led some scholars to equate the Bible and literature. This leads to the corollary that the Bible as a literary text does not refer outside of itself and, in particular, makes limited reference to history. This position leads on the part of some to a complete or substantial denial of a historical approach to the text, which most often takes the form of denying or denigrating traditional historical-critical methods.[52]

The following quotations represent the views of some who adopt the literary approach: "Above all, we must keep in mind that narrative is a form of representation. Abraham in Genesis is not a real person any more than the painting of an apple is real fruit." "When viewed as a literary achievement the statements in Mark's narrative, rather than being a representation of historical events, refer to the people, places, and events in the story."[53] For these authors, the truth of the biblical story of Jesus is independent of any historical information. Biblical narrative is history-like and not true history with an ostensive, or external, reference. For example, the Old Testament is largely "historicized fiction," or fictional history.[54]

A well-known literary critical work is Hans Frei's *The Eclipse of Biblical Narrative*. Frei says that the literal meaning of the Gospel narratives is its narrative shape. Frei laments that the meaning of the Gospel narratives has come to be associated with something other than the narratives themselves, namely, an external history.[55] John Barton observes: "In Frei's book we have a non-referential theory of biblical narrative texts, which is closely akin to the New Critical theory of literature in general as non-referential."[56]

While interpreters who hold to an authoritative Bible might in some respects be glad to see the end of certain types of negative historical criticism, they have a high stake in the question of history. To identify Genesis simply as a work of literature, for example, is to move it out of the realm of history and of revelation. This characterizes some, if not most, of the literary approaches to the study of the Old Testament. On the one hand, Genesis is not reducible to a work of fiction. However, this does not prevent us from applying a literary approach because Genesis does possess literary qualities.[57]

Possible Contributions of Recent Literary Approaches

While the Bible is more than just narrative literature, it is also a literary creation. Thus a literary approach can help us as we seek a proper understanding of the Bible.

Literary theory helps us understand the conventions of biblical literature.—The literary text is an act of communication from writer to reader. The text is the message. For it to communicate, the sender and receiver have to speak the same language. The writer, through the use of conventional forms, sends signals to the readers to tell them how they are to take the message.

A literary approach explores and makes explicit the conventions of biblical literature in order to understand the message it intends to carry. It is significant to discover that Deuteronomy is in the form of a treaty and that repetition is not necessarily a sign of multiple sources but a literary device.

In ordinary reading we recognize much of this information automatically. We passively let the narrator shape our interpretation of the event being reported to us and we make an unconscious genre identification. As interpreters of a text, however, it is important to make these conventions explicit. This is even more urgent in regard to the Bible, since it is an ancient text and the conventions it employs are often not the ones we customarily use.[58]

Some evangelicals hold views close to the "early" Wittgenstein's picture theory of reality. This view seems to entail regarding the literary form not only as dispensable packaging but as an actual hindrance to the perception of meaning. The search for transparent propositions seems to involve a disparaging of and cavalier attitude toward the everyday forms of language and literature. The "early" Wittgenstein *Tractatus* distrusted ordinary sentences because they disguised the proposition.[59]

In his later work (*Philosophical Investigations*), Wittgenstein was interested above all in describing the everyday forms and uses of language and in watching how they were employed in various contexts (language games). This is in contrast to tinkering with sentences and translating them into a standard propositional form. Evangelicals should utilize literary insights and develop a model of biblical revelation that will preserve the substance of "propositional" revelation (i.e., the emphasis on verbal, cognitive communication) while at the same time allowing for greater appreciation of the "ordinary" language of Scripture and its diverse literary forms.[60]

The "Chicago Statement on Biblical Hermeneutics" explicitly addressed this issue:

> ARTICLE X: WE AFFIRM that Scripture communicates God's truth to us verbally through a wide variety of literary forms.

> ARTICLE XIII: WE AFFIRM that awareness of the literary categories, formal and stylistic, of the various parts of Scripture is essential for proper exegesis, and hence we value genre criticism as one of the many disciplines of Biblical study.[61]

The earlier "Chicago Statement on Biblical Inerrancy" handles Scripture's diverse literary forms quite successfully:

> So history must be treated as history, poetry as poetry, hyperbole and metaphor as hyperbole and metaphor, generalization and approximation as what they are, and so forth.[62]

The Bible obviously is a literary and oratorical book. God apparently allowed the biblical writers to use the literary forms of the biblical times as their mediums of expression. The well-known conservative author, James Orr, saw nothing contrary to a strong doctrine of inspiration in accepting Job as a poetically edited drama. Orr even suggested the possibility of pseudonymity where some unknown author affixes the name of some important or famous person to his composition. If a biblical author had ascribed his name to a book in order to deceive, then such an act would be offensive. However, if pseudonymity were a recognized literary form in the culture of the biblical writer, then Orr affirms that we must be ready to accept this as a proper form of special revelation.[63] The conservative scholar, E. J. Young, suggests that Ecclesiastes was pseudonymous. "The author of the book, then, was one who lived in the post-exilic period and who placed his words in the mouth of Solomon, thus employing a literary device for conveying his message."[64] Other literary forms such as expanded and contracted speeches were obviously used, says Orr.[65] Is not Ramm correct in affirming that the Bible was brought to concrete expression in the literary and oratorical forms current at the time of its entry into the world?[66]

The literary approach stresses whole texts or the organic unity of the text.—Evangelicals commonly tend to atomize the text and to focus attention on a word or a few verses. The literary approach asks the question of the force of the whole. For this reason many evangelical scholars have recognized that the literary approach can serve a corrective role in their hermeneutics.[67] For example, all portions of the book must command the reader's attention if the whole book is rightly to be understood.

A correlative contribution of narrative and canonical approaches is the high-value they place on human language and its adequacy for communicating divine revelation. This commitment is especially evident when one considers the claim of Hans Frei that the written text is actually God's linguistic presence to His people.[68]

It should also be noted that the narrative idea that the biblical text functions like a realistic novel in overwhelming and transforming our reality suggests promising avenues for proclamation of the gospel.[69]

The literary approach calls attention to the importance of the reader's pre-understanding and cultural background.—The reader-response approach recognizes the role of readers and their predisposition as they approach the text. One of the goals of the traditional historical-grammatical exegesis is to answer the question, How did the original readers understand the passage? This question is valid and must be answered. But twentieth-century men and women are readers, too. We are distanced from the text in a way that the original readers were not. The goal of the contemporary reader is to understand the text by means of its ancient conventions, but such a reader approaches the text through a new grid of questions that are evoked by the situation of modern society and culture.[70]

Evangelicals (and others who are committed to the authority of Scripture) affirm that the text imposes restrictions on possible interpretations. However, we must recognize that the readers' backgrounds and their interests will lead them to attend to certain parts of the Bible's message more than other parts. We should recognize the importance of contextualization and multiperspectival approaches to the text.

We also must note the value of what might be called ideological readers, even when they tend to be unbalanced. Feminists and liberation theologians, for example, read the Bible with colored glasses, which often leads to distortion. However, such readers do bring out important issues and themes that other, less interested, readers miss. In fact, in many respects the church down through its history has fallen behind the beginnings of equality of the sexes that we find with Jesus and earliest Christianity. Thus theological feminism has indisputable elements of truth.[71]

Evangelicals should remember that the Bible has been used to oppose freedom for slaves. Appeals to divine authority of this kind amount to using the Bible, however unwittingly and sincerely, as an instrument of power and domination for social or religious control. For some it is a very short step to move from calling the Bible the Word of God to calling the preacher's personal gloss on the text the word of God.[72]

Because of this possibility, certain interpretations of the Bible are described by some as an ideological smokescreen for the power interests of a group of aging middle-class, white, Anglo-Saxon, North Atlantic/North American males. Here is a postmodern challenge of major proportions.

We must have a self-critical stance toward our tendencies to intrude our own agenda into our exposition of the Scriptures. We need to practice what Paul Ricoeur and others have called "a hermeneutics of suspicion."[73] We may mistake purely human concerns about the ordering of human lives for "religious" ones, or for divine commands. Long before Freud, the biblical writers called attention to this same capacity for very deep self-deception through their language about the deceitfulness and wickedness of the human heart. Hence, there is also the need for suspicion about the possibility of fallibility in one's own interpretation of Scripture. Our own interpretations should remain the object of suspicion and critical evaluation. How to give substance to this goal is one aspect of the study of hermeneutics.

Evangelicals thus should agree with Heidegger and Gadamer to the extent that interpreters often impose conceptual grids on a text like the Bible without due reflection. A person's particular context tends to shape the understanding and interpretation of the message of the Bible. However, the horizon of the hearer is not the decisive, let alone the only, maker of meaning. In this respect reader-response theory in its more radical forms claims too much. But neither is meaning a mere "item" to be handed over as if it were a physical object borrowed from Newton's universe. Every Christian pastor and evangelist understands something of what Heidegger meant when he spoke of language bearing meaning within the horizon of time.

The literary approach calls attention to the creative role that the imagination plays in interpretation.—Carl Henry argues that the claim that the Bible is literally true in no way requires that only the prose sections serve as the vehicle of this truth: "Some literary techniques more than others sharpen the communication of truth by rousing the imagination, stirring the emotions, and stimulating the will."[74]

According to Roland Frye, it is surely a part of God's wisdom that He raised up people who recorded and preserved the story of our glorious religion in a way "sufficiently dramatic to attract a crowd." More is involved in our Bible than a set of archives and a scholarly report of the events. Technical reports would have attracted little attention beyond a restricted circle of specialists. If, as Christians believe, certain historical events and certain historical understandings are relevant and necessary for all, then these must be conveyed in a manner which can reach and affect all sorts and conditions of humans. Our Bible, therefore, like any great literary work must accomplish a twofold objective. First, it must be basically faithful to the events treated and secondly, it must be dramatic so it can reach a wide audience and convey an indelible impression.[75]

The biblical writers obviously employed certain standard literary devices in order that the history of God's redemptive purpose should be made lastingly and meaningfully relevant to audiences removed in space and time and cultural identity from the original happenings.

Thus we find operative in the Bible the same methods which we have observed in the dramatic histories and other literary forms. It could scarcely be otherwise. As Donald Baillie has written, a photographic portrait of Jesus would not provide us with the most true or the most real acquaintance with Him, and we will generally recognize that the accounts of Jesus' life were all written under the light of the resurrection and Pentecost, as indeed they should have been. The interaction between event and interpretation, between fact and meaning, indicates the affinity between the Gospel narratives and the techniques of dramatic history and literature. Without it, history cannot for long be preserved in a literary form which is at once faithful, vital, and meaningful to generations of men and women.[76]

In a similar manner, much of the Old Testament record was written not only to convey information, but to affect its readers in certain ways. Paraphrase is weakest in its attempts to preserve the noncognitive aspects of a text's meaning. We might perhaps generalize and say that what is lost in conceptual paraphrase is the power and beauty of the in-formed content.[77]

According to Ramm, if a literary genre "plays a positive role in the communication of revelation . . . we should not shy away from it."[78] Barton claims that fundamentalists are seldom students of the humanities, mainly read nonfiction, and consequently do not know how to read the Bible.[79] In contrast, C. S. Lewis, the well-known Christian literary figure, affirms the importance of recognizing literary genre. He sees that the main problem with propositional paraphrase is that it yields a "tasteless" knowing, a knowing bereft of the power and beauty perceived and apprehended by the imagination.[80]

Genre recognition is thus seen as part and parcel of the grammatical-historical method of exegesis. Grant R. Osborne acknowledges this connection when he calls genre or literary form an "epistemological tool" for discovering the literal sense, or intended meaning, of Scripture.[81]

The "later" Wittgenstein points out that many concepts have a given meaning only in particular language-games. Knowing which game is being played is essential. Both philosophical and theological concepts are affected in their meaning by the language-game being played.[82]

That Scripture has many literary forms is no impediment to the truth. In fact, such diversity enhances truth's expression. Furthermore, the diversity of literary forms does not imply that Scripture contains competing kinds of truth; it shows rather that Scripture is about various kinds of fact (i.e., historical, metaphysical, moral, etc.).[83]

It is quite unfortunate that the doctrine of accommodation has lost the prominent place it once held in Christian thought, especially in the writings of Calvin. Dowey gives this brief definition of the term: "Accommodation refers to the process by which God reduces or adjusts to human capacities what He wills to reveal of the infinite mysteries of His Being, which by their very nature are beyond the powers of the mind of man to grasp."[84]

We can call this a symbolic conception of religious knowledge, however, only with the greatest caution. Calvin's viewpoint is different from what we ordinarily think of as symbolic religious knowledge because humans do not choose the symbols for the great unknown as is sometimes implied when the word *symbol* is used. Rather knowledge begins and ends with the self-revelation of God. Before God in pious agnosticism we confess our inadequacy to comprehend the infinite except in so far as God actively approaches and makes Himself known. Calvin would object to a merely symbolic view. In his commentary on Isaiah 6:1, Calvin affirms that the robe, throne, and bodily appearance of God are forms of revelation accommodated to human incapacities. However, lest we should suppose that the prophet Isaiah contrived the manner in which he would paint God we ought to know that he faithfully describes the very form in which God was represented and exhibited to him. The doctrine of accommodation, therefore, clearly posits the reality behind the symbols. Although the symbols in some measure distort that reality, they do so only in order to bring it within the reach of man.

Calvin affirmed that there is no need for reality to agree at all points with a symbol if only the symbol suits sufficiently for the purpose at hand.[85] For example, for John Milton, as for the Christian tradition generally, the use of the upward and downward separation of God and man served as an unpassable metaphoric bulwark against any monist or mystical identification of man with God.[86]

Conclusion

We have noted the challenges, weaknesses, and strengths of recent approaches in literary criticism as they relate to the Bible. We have pointed out that we must resist the suggestion found in much contemporary literary theory that we deny or downplay the historical reference of the biblical text in the face of its literary artifice.

The Bible as literature *or* history is a false dichotomy. It is both and much more.[87]

God chose, however, to reveal Himself to writers who used literary forms. As we have emphasized, the Bible is more like literature than nonliterature. For the most part, we encounter stories and poems in the Bible, not systematic theology, pure historical report, or journalism.[88]

Tremper Longman asks "Why is the Bible not given to us in the form of a *Cambridge Ancient History* or a systematic theology?" The ultimate answer to such questions rests in God's wisdom. However, as we have indicated, there are positive contributions flowing from the Bible's literary forms. For example, to cast truth in the form of a story does lead the hearer or reader to pay closer attention to it and oftentimes to be shocked to reconsider what otherwise might easily become a truism. A proverb is a good, focused example.[89]

Literary approaches to the Gospels complement conventional approaches. For example, a literary approach may enable readers to rediscover value and meaning in the Gospels which have become problematic with approaches that distance texts for purposes of critical examination. The assumptions and strategies of literary criticism allow readers to interact with texts in both critical and creative modes and fashions.

It should also be noted that literature appeals to the whole person. By its very nature, literature appeals not only to the intellect but also to one's will and emotions to a greater extent than, say, the Westminster Confession of Faith or Charles Hodge's *Systematic Theology*.

There is a tendency among some scholars to reduce the Bible to literature and to deny history. Other scholars, particularly those of us whose doctrine of Scripture is conservative, should resist the temptation to ignore the literary aspect of divine revelation by reducing the Scripture to chronicled history and theology.[90]

It should be the goal of all Christians to seek the balance which the Bible itself calls for by its inspired nature and form. In this way we can move "beyond the impasse" concerning the nature of the Bible and its interpretation.

Notes

1. Mark A. Noll, *Between Faith & Criticism: Evangelicals, Scholarship, and the Bible in America* (San Francisco: Harper & Row, 1986), 159-60.
2. Mark Ellingsen, *The Evangelical Movement: Growth, Impact, Controversy, and Dialog* (Minneapolis: Augsburg, 1988), 365-82.
3. Tremper Longman III, *Literary Approaches to Biblical Interpretation* (Grand Rapids: Zondervan, 1987), 7; cf. also David Robertson, *The Old Testament and the Literary Critic* (Philadelphia: Fortress, 1977), viii; and Stephen D. Moore, *Literary Criticism and the Gospels: The Theoretical Challenge* (New Haven: Yale University Press, 1989), xv, xvi.
4. Kevin J. Vanhoozer, "A Lamp in the Labyrinth: The Hermeneutics of 'Aesthetic' Theology," *Trinity Journal* 8 (1987): 28.
5. J. I. Packer, "Infallible Scripture and the Role of Hermeneutics," *Scripture and Truth*, ed. D. A. Carson and John D. Woodbridge (Grand Rapids: Zondervan, 1983), 350.
6. Longman, *Literary Approaches*, 65.
7. Vanhoozer, "Lamp in the Labyrinth," 32.
8. Ibid., 33; cf. Friedrich von Schiller, *On the Aesthetic Education of Man* (New York: Frederick Ungar, 1965), 137, 15th letter, para. 9.
9. Frank Lentricchia, *After the New Criticism* (London: Methuen, 1983), 20, 25.
10. Vanhoozer, "Lamp in the Labyrinth," 33; cf. M. H. Abrahms, *The Mirror and the Lamp: Romantic Theory and Critical Tradition* (London/New York: Oxford, 1979).
11. Paul Ricoeur, *Interpretation Theory: Discourse and the Surplus of Meaning* (Fort Worth: Texas Christian University, 1976), 60.
12. Vanhoozer, "Lamp in the Labyrinth," 38-39; cf. Jacques Derrida, *Writing and Difference* (Chicago: University of Chicago, 1978), 292.
13. Jacques Derrida, "Structure, Sign, and Play in the discourse of the Human Sciences," *The Languages of Criticism and Sciences of Man*, ed. Richard Mackey and Eugenio Donato (Baltimore: Johns Hopkins University, 1966), 249.
14. Robert Detweiler, Introduction to *Semeia* 23 (1982): 2.
15. Vanhoozer, "Lamp in the Labyrinth," 41-43; cf. Robert H. Canary and Henry Kozicki, eds., *The Writing of History: Literary Form and Historical Understanding* (Madison: University of Wisconsin, 1978), 48.
16. Longman, *Literary Approaches*, 25-27.
17. Cleanth Brooks, *The Well Wrought Urn* (New York: Harcourt, Brace, and World, 1947).

18. M. Weiss, *The Bible from Within: The Method of Total Interpretation* (Jerusalem: Magnes, 1984).

19. Terence J. Keegan, *Interpreting the Bible* (New York: Paulist, 1985), 24, 30*f*.

20. Vanhoozer, "Lamp in the Labyrinth," 44; cf. Jonathan Culler, *Structuralist Poetics* (London: Routledge & Kegan Paul, 1975).

21. Keegan, 43, 49-50; cf. Daniel Patte, *What Is Structural Exegesis?* (Philadelphia: Fortress, 1975).

22. Vanhoozer, "Lamp in the Labyrinth," 44*f*.

23. John Barton, *Reading the Old Testament: Method in Biblical Study* (London: Darton Longman and Todd, 1984), 134.

24. Keegan, *Interpreting the Bible*, 79-80; cf. W. Iser, *The Act of Reading* (Baltimore: John Hopkins University Press, 1978).

25. Keegan, 82.

26. Ibid., 83-85.

27. Anthony C. Thiselton, *The Two Horizons: New Testament Hermeneutics and Philosophical Description* (Grand Rapids: Eerdmans, 1980), 293-326.

28. Hans-George Gadamer, *Truth and Method* (New York: Continuum, 1975), 239-45.

29. Roger Lundin, Anthony C. Thiselton, and Clarence Walhout, *The Responsibility of Hermeneutics* (Grand Rapids: Eerdmans, 1985), 25.

30. Longman, *Literary Approaches*, 39; cf. N. Gottwald, *The Tribes of Yahweh* (Maryknoll: Orbis, 1979).

31. Longman, *Literary Approaches*, 39f.; cf. Gabriel Fackre, *The Christian Story: A Pastoral Systematics*, vol. 2: *Authority: Scripture in the Church for the World* (Grand Rapids: Eerdmans, 1987); cf. Katherine Doob Sakenfeld, "Feminist Use of Biblical Materials," in *The Feminist Interpretation of the Bible*, ed. Letty M. Russell (Philadelphia: Westminster, 1985), 56*ff*.

32. Fackre, *Christian Story*, 2:107.

33. Edgar V. McKnight, "Literary Criticism," (unpublished article), 5.

34. R. Alan Culpepper, *Anatomy of the Fourth Gospel: A Study in Literary Design* (Philadelphia: Fortress, 1983), 5.

35. Keegan, *Interpreting the Bible*, 110.

36. Ibid., 106-7.

37. Longman, *Literary Approaches*, 85-86.

38. D. Rhoads and D. Michie, *Mark as Story: The Introduction to the Narrative as Gospel* (Philadelphia: Fortress, 1982), 36.

39. Keegan, *Interpreting the Bible*, 107-8

40. Longman, *Literary Approaches*, 86-87.

41. Ibid., 94-95.

42. J. Culler, *On Deconstruction: Theory and Criticism After Structuralism* (London: Routledge & Kegan Paul, 1982).

43. Lentricchia, *After the New Criticism*, 68.

44. J. D. Crossan, *Cliffs of Falls* (New York: Seabury, 1980), 9-10.

45. P. D. Miscall, *The Workings of Old Testament Narrative* (Philadelphia: Fortress, 1983), 1.

46. Vanhoozer, "Lamp in the Labyrinth," 47*f*.

47. Ibid., 48; cf. Paul Ricoeur, "Biblical Hermeneutics," *Semeia* 4 (1975): 100.

48. E. D. Hirsch, Jr., *Validity in Interpretation* (New Haven: Yale University Press, 1967), and *The Aims of Interpretation* (Chicago: University Press, 1976).

49. Hirsch, *The Aims of Interpretation*, 1-13.

50. Longman, *Literary Approaches*, 48*f*; cf. Barton, *Reading the Old Testament*, 5.

51. Robert K. Johnston, "How We Interpret the Bible: Biblical Interpretation and Literary Criticism," *Proceedings of the Conference on Biblical Interpretation 1988* (Nashville: Broadman, 1988), 51-63.

52. Longman, *Literary Approaches*, 55*f*.

53. A. Berlin, *Poetics and Interpretation of Biblical Narrative* (Sheffield: Almond, 1983), 13; Rhoads and Michie, *Mark as Story*, 3-4.

54. Longman, *Literary Approaches*, 56; R. Alter, *The Art of Biblical Narrative* (New York: Basic Books, 1981).

55. Hans Frei, *The Eclipse of Biblical Narrative* (New Haven: Yale University Press, 1974).

56. Barton, *Reading the Old Testament*, 163.

57. Longman, *Literary Approaches*, 56-57.

58. Ibid.

59. Vanhoozer, "Semantics of Biblical Literature," 67; cf. Anthony Kenny, *Wittgenstein* (London: Penguin, 1973), ch. 2, "The Legacy of Frege and Russell."

60. Vanhoozer, "Semantics of Biblical Literature," 67.

61. "The Chicago Statement on Biblical Hermeneutics," *Journal of the Evangelical Theological Society* 25 (December 1982): 397-401.

62. *Journal of the Evangelical Theological Society* 21 (December 1978): 295.

63. James Orr, *Revelation and Inspiration* (New York: Scribners, 1910), 170*f*.

64. E. J. Young, *An Introduction to the Old Testament* (Grand Rapids: Eerdmans, 1949), 340.

65. Orr, *Revelation and Inspiration*, 65.

66. Bernard Ramm, *Special Revelation and the Word of God* (Grand Rapids: Eerdmans, 1961), 65*f*.

67. Longman, *Literary Approaches*, 60.

68. Ellingsen, *The Evangelical Movement*, 374.

69. Ibid., 376.

70. Longman, *Literary Approaches*, 84.

71. Ibid., 61; cf. L. Ryken, *Windows to the World* (Grand Rapids: Zondervan, 1985).

72. Anthony C. Thiselton, "Speaking and Hearing," in *Christian Faith and Practice in the Modern World*, ed. Noll and Wells (Grand Rapids: Eerdmans, 1988), 139-40.

73. Paul Ricoeur, *Freud and Philosophy* (New Haven: Yale University Press, 1970), 20-56; cf. also *The Conflict of Interpretation: Essays on Hermeneutics* (Evanston, Ill.: Northwestern University Press, 1974), 99-210.

74. Carl F. H. Henry, *God, Revelation and Authority*, 6 vols. (Waco: Word, 1976-83), 4:109.

75. Roland M. Frye, *Perspective on Man* (Philadelphia: Westminster Press, 1961), 15, 34-35.

76. Ibid., 32-35.

77. Vanhoozer, "Semantics of Biblical Literature," 74.

78. Bernard Ramm, *Protestant Biblical Interpretation: A Textbook of Hermeneutics*, 3d rev. ed. (Grand Rapids: Baker, 1973), 144.

79. Barton, *Reading the Old Testament*, 140.

80. C. S. Lewis, "Myth Became Fact," in *Undeceptions*, ed. Walter Hooper (London: Geoffrey Bles, 1970), 42.

81. Grant Osborne, "Genre Criticism—Sensus Literalis," *Trinity Journal* 4 (1983): 1-27.

82. Vanhoozer, "Semantics of Biblical Literature," 83; cf. Thisleton, *The Two Horizons*, 415-22.

83. Vanhoozer, "Semantics of Biblical Literature," 85.

84. Edward A. Dowey, Jr., *The Knowledge of God in Calvin's Theology* (New York: Columbia University Press, 1952), 4.

85. John Calvin, *Calvin: Theological Treateses*, trans. J. K. S. Reid (Philadelphia: Westminster Press, 1954), 112.

86. Edwyn Bevan, *Symbolism and Belief* (London: George Allen and Unmin, Ltd., 1938), 28-31.

87. Longman, *Literary Approaches*, 151.

88. Ibid.

89. Ibid., 151-52.

90. Ibid., 152; cf. Scot McKnight, ed., *Introducing New Testament Interpretation* (Grand Rapids: Baker, 1989), 15-19.

4

Has Theology a Future in the Southern Baptist Convention? Toward a Renewed Theological Framework
R. Albert Mohler, Jr.*

Though the Southern Baptist Convention is no stranger to controversy and crisis, the denomination now faces an impasse of imposing proportions. *Webster's* definition of an impasse as "a predicament offering no obvious way of escape" offers some sense of the challenge facing the Southern Baptist Convention. The denomination is now divided into opposing parties, with a massive and seemingly insurmountable "conflict of visions" creating the impasse.[1]

Indeed, this conflict of visions has produced not one, but several impasses which loom on the SBC horizon. These impasses are theological, political, organizational, and financial. Though each impasse is a critical challenge, the integrity and vitality of the Southern Baptist Convention is most urgently threatened by a theological impasse "offering no obvious way of escape." The purpose of this chapter is to propose a means of overcoming the impasse by reclaiming and restating a shared theological framework adequate to the task. The Southern Baptist Convention has no hope of reclaiming its denominational equilibrium unless it meets the challenge of this impasse.

The theological impasse is both a precipitating factor and a

---

*R. Albert Mohler, Jr., (Ph.D., Southern Baptist Theological Seminary) is Editor of *The Christian Index*, the weekly newsjournal published by Georgia Southern Baptists and one of America's oldest religious periodicals. He has written articles for leading journals in this country and in Europe. Mohler serves as associate Editor for *Preaching Magazine*, a leading journal on homiletics. He has contributed chapters to *Baptist Theologians, Southern Baptists and American Evangelicals*, and other symposiums. His forthcoming works include *A Handbook of Contemporary Theology, The Changing of the Evangelical Mind*, and *Evangelical Theology and Karl Barth*. He is a member of the Atkinson Road Baptist Church in Lawrenceville, Georgia.

product of the twelve-year controversy within the SBC. In the broadest sense, however, it is the inevitable consequence of decades of doctrinal neglect by the denomination at large. The massive expansion of denominational programs and institutions since World War II—an unprecedented period of growth and extension—was made possible by the presence of a powerful reservoir of doctrinal commitment among Southern Baptist churches.[2] Southern Baptists were united by deeply held doctrinal beliefs, a fervent sense of mission, and a methodological commitment to cooperation. In the era of the "Solid South," Southern Baptists, though diverse in style and social convention, shared a common theological framework which stressed a commonly understood set of doctrinal essentials.[3]

But the "turn to program" in the age of expansion was, in retrospect, also to bring a progressive neglect of that common theological framework.[4] The effects of this decline in doctrinal attention were seen even in the 1950s, but came to light in the Ralph Elliott and *The Broadman Bible Commentary* controversies over biblical interpretation in the 1960s. By the late 1970s signs of impending denominational conflict were apparent. The denomination which had sown seeds of benign neglect was to reap a bitter decade of controversy and the current impasse.

The primary issues of controversy in the SBC conflict have been related to the nature and authority of the Bible. Biblical inerrancy has been the most contested term of the debate, though the controversy has also dealt with a constellation of issues essentially related to biblical interpretation and exegesis. With this in view, the SBC conflict is seen in the context of the so-called "Battle for the Bible" in American evangelicalism.[5] Reflecting on the sustained controversy within evangelical circles, historian Mark Noll has questioned whether evangelicals possess a theological framework adequate to sustain simultaneously both critical biblical scholarship and classical doctrinal commitments.[6] This is, indeed, a pressing issue. But it cannot be separated from the larger question: Do evangelicals (and Southern Baptists in particular) possess a theological framework adequate to sustain their identity and integrity as Christian churches? Seen in this light, questions of biblical authority and interpretation are inseparable from other basic theological issues.

Society, Academy, and Church:
The Three Publics of Theology

The Southern Baptist Convention finds itself in the 1990s a confessional denomination in an atheological age.[7] Theological concerns are considered the quaint province of sequestered saints and of only passing interest to any outside the theological tribe. Issues of genuine theological substance are sequestered from the mainstream of congregational life, which is characterized by what Timothy George has termed an "ideology of indifference."[8]

Revisionist theologian David Tracy suggests that theology should recognize three distinct publics: society, the academy, and the church.[9] Yet, none of these publics seems eager to assist in reclaiming an adequate theological framework.

Society

The almost universal progress of secularism has inoculated general culture and society against almost all theological concerns. An essentially atheistic culture recognizes all theological claims as limits to self-fulfillment. The contemporary *Zeitgeist* is absolutely opposed to all theological concerns and thus the public square is open to almost all issues of concern except those of biblical theism. Where theological issues do come to light in debates over ethical issues such as abortion and biomedical ethics, they are moved to the margins of the discussion with a subtle warning that such concerns are essentially sectarian and thus dangerous to the body politic.

The American South, where Southern Baptists are concentrated, was the last region of the country to see secularism take its stranglehold on the public consciousness. By the 1980s the metropolitan areas of the South were as inoculated against theological concerns as their northern counterparts. The Solid South is now, in terms of the public square, solidly secularist.

The hegemony of Enlightenment presuppositions and the autonomy of the individual are givens in contemporary culture. Individuals now inhabit what Oxford sociologist Bryan Wilson terms a "social space" in which theological claims are simply unrecognized—even by those who sit in the pews of the church. Put simply, church attendance is no guarantee that persons will connect the issues and concerns of life with their Christian commitment. Their "plausibility structures" (to borrow Peter Berger's suggestive term) are not inherently theological. We should not be surprised that Western culture sits on the brink of a new dark age.

The Church

Though born of a rich and fullsome theological heritage, the church has largely ceased to see that heritage as a living partner. Amidst the cultural shifts outside the church and multiple distractions within, the church has lost sight of its primary responsibility to guard the gospel and pass its doctrinal commitments from generation to generation. Theology, the pursuit of the true, has been pressed to the margins by the pursuit of the practical, the successful, and even the entertaining.

This phenomenon transcends denominational boundaries and is now a reality within a large number of Southern Baptist churches. These churches have lost the sense of theological vocation evidenced by Baptist forebears, and this declining sense of theological stewardship has been passed from the local congregation to all levels of Southern Baptist life.

The teaching of basic Christian doctrine has been all but abdicated in many churches where the agenda is clearly set by currents in popular culture.[10] So long as this decline is unchecked, the future of the denomination is jeopardized. Southern Baptists risk joining the ranks of atheological denominations living on the residue of a previous generation's doctrinal commitment.[11]

There is no shortage of competing agendas, each with an implicit claim on the church's attention and energy. The pervasive influence of consumerism and the self-movement may be seen in the tendency of churches to address the latest "addiction" diagnosed in popular psychology or the current fixation of the self-help movement.[12] Many churches have made so many concessions to modernity and the secularist mind-set that they are no longer able to recognize their own compromises. These concessions have altered not only the *style* of congregational life, but the *substance* of the congregation's faith and doctrine.

The Academy

Once crowned as the "Queen of the Sciences," theology has been thoroughly displaced within the academy. Departments of religion and divinity schools still dot the academic horizon, but theology plays little part in the intellectual life of American research universities and graduate schools.[13] Theological seminaries, almost uniformly confessional in origin, are the primary locus of serious theological discussion, insofar as it is to be found.

And yet, theological seminaries exhibit a sense of ambivalence concerning their own theological vocation. Who is *their* primary public? Is it society, the church, or others in the academy? For many sectors of American Protestantism the answer is decidedly the academy. Southern Baptist seminary theologians, who entered the postwar period somewhat insulated from the broader theological context, have increasingly addressed themselves to the academy. The press for academic prestige, respect from the theological community, and, among some figures, an intentional mission of opening Southern Baptist intellectual life to contemporary currents in theology and biblical studies, all contributed to an increasing focus on the academy.

This is not to suggest that Southern Baptist theologians have been deficient in individual commitment to the local church, or that theologians have ignored pressing issues within church and society. Indeed, SBC professors are most often models of churchly devotion and service. Nevertheless, the decreasing theological appetites of local churches have been met with decline in theologians who see their primary public as the church, rather than the academy. The essential issue here is the matter of whom one wishes to *address*. Southern Baptists have increasingly looked to pastors as the "public theologians" of the denomination, rather than looking to seminary professors of theology.[14]

And what hath the larger academy wrought? Southern Baptists looking for a way beyond the impasse will find little assistance from the world of contemporary theology. The last half of the twentieth century has seen an almost complete collapse of theology as a discipline. In order to maintain integrity, a discipline must possess commonly accepted norms, formulae, and evaluative tools. All three are lacking in the world of contemporary theology.[15]

Descriptions of the confusion in contemporary theology abound, with books titles such as *The End of the Line?* and *The Shattered Spectrum* setting the tone.[16] Radical pluralism, leading to a situation David Tracy has ably identified as a "blessed rage for order," has been wedded to a pervasive relativism which would surely cause Feuerbach to smile.

What Edward Farley described as "the fall of the house of authority" has brought the very notion of academic theology into question.[17] Postmodern theologian George Lindbeck recently characterized the course of modern theology as "a process of unmediated *aggiornamento*"—an intentional program of the theological reformulation.[18] Such a program—reformulation for modernity's sake—redefines the role of authority in theology. In all too many cases, the authority becomes the theologian or the worldview shared by the theologian.

Foundational to this program is the assumption that the classical Christian paradigm (the tradition of orthodoxy) is irrelevant and/or of little more than historical interest. Indeed, as measured by the canons of modernity, it is often characterized as inherently oppressive and inhibiting, if not dangerous. The older authorities (Scripture, tradition, etc.) are supplanted by the canons of modernity and the magisterium of the academy.

The great postliberal systems of the mid-twentieth century were themselves to fall by the 1960s, leaving a host of variant offspring. As Gordon Kauffman noted:

> As each new turn of this sort was made, it became embarrassingly clear that anyone and everyone could dress up his/her new cause in language and ideas drawn from the Christian tradition and proclaim one more "new theology." Theology apparently had no integrity or standards or demands of its own; its symbols could be used as a kind of decoration for and legitimization of almost any partisan position found in the culture. The once proud queen of the sciences, having lost a sense of her own meaning and integrity, had become a common prostitute.[19]

This loss of meaning and integrity calls into question the validity of the theological enterprise as exercised under the auspices of the academy.

Postmodernity, Paradigm Shifts, and the New Pluralism in Theology

The almost unchallenged establishment of Enlightenment values within the academic community and the virtual reign of modernity came within the context of a theological vacuum. The decline of the great post-Reformation systems in the eighteenth and nineteenth centuries was followed by the collapse of modernism in the early-twentieth century. Neoorthodoxy prevailed but for a brief season; its internal conflicts preventing any lasting establishment.[20]

Into this vacuum came a spectrum of ideological borrowings from both the right and the left, though the academy has been almost uniformly open to the left and closed to the right. The tendency of ideology to supplant theology is increased in the context of a vacuum, and the loss of convictional consensus has opened the way for the triumph of ideological temptations in a myriad of forms.

Under the banners of *postmodernity* and *paradigm shift* a host of new variants ranging from deconstructionism to purely aesthetic theologies came forth in the 1980s. Postmodernity, itself a contested term, provides license for rejecting classical authorities in favor of an updated model of modernity.[21]

The assumption of a "paradigm shift" provides further warrant for the program of radical theological reformulation. The existence of such a shift within the intelligentsia is undeniable. A succession of such paradigm shifts can be traced through the past three centuries, with the major shift seen in the Enlightenment's celebrated "turn to the subject," which has resulted in the a priori assumption of the autonomous individual at the center of the universe of knowledge.

What has this produced in the academy? The range of competing theological options is almost unlimited. The academy embraces theologies of hope, radical (posttheistic) theologies, feminist theologies, multiple models of liberation theology, process theology, narrative theology, aesthetic theologies, and a host of revisionist models which may share little more than a rejection of classical theism and related doctrinal commitments.

Thomas Kuhn defines a paradigm as "an entire constellation of beliefs, values, techniques, and so on shared by the members of a given community."[22] The shift in Western consciousness is nowhere more apparent than within the theological community. There the paradigm shift has become the justification for a myriad of retreats from biblical theism.

Such a situation leads to inevitable conflict between the academy and the church. To the extent a confessional seminary appears committed to the worldview of the larger theological community, the church will view the academy as opposed to the church's own purposes.

The current controversy over theological education reveals nothing less than an underlying *Kulturkampf*—a cultural war and clash of worldviews.[23] The rise of a theological "new class" in the postwar period has led to increasing polarization between the academy and the church.[24]

For the present, the theological academy seems quite satisfied to address only itself, increasingly shorn from all ecclesial roots. Theologians now speak to other theologians, and the church looks on as a bystander. Similarly, the church's own devaluation of theology (whether by resistance to all cognitive issues or by distraction) robs the academy of both audience and authority. If denominational seminaries follow the course of the larger academy, a conflict is sure to result.

This impasse has now reached the sequestered shores of the Southern Baptist Convention. The breakdown of the Southern Baptist evangelical consensus is now almost complete, and neither the churches nor their theological institutions seem either mournfully cognizant of the breakdown or poised to address the loss.

Though many factors produced the present Southern Baptist conflict, this loss of theological focus and commitment was, in and of itself, sufficient to fracture the denomination. Though some may continue to deny any theological erosion, the effects are many and apparent.

Imperatives for a Renewed Theological Framework

Has theology a future in the Southern Baptist Convention? Does the Southern Baptist Convention have a future? These related, indeed inseparable questions lie before a denomination in turmoil. The only hope for the Southern Baptist Convention is a renewed theological consensus wedded to a new model of convictional cooperation. The following imperatives for a renewed theological framework are offered as a proposal toward a reclaimed future:

1. *The Southern Baptist Convention must achieve a common recognition of theological crisis and decline.* SBC conservatives, who have justified their political takeover of the denomination on the basis of theological compromise among denominational officials and seminary faculties, must broaden and deepen their concern to

reflect a more comprehensive theological crisis. Moderates, who have largely resisted the very notion of a theological crisis, must come to see the real gravity of the current hour, both in terms of specific issues of concern and, more importantly, the generalized atheological ethos prevalent within the Convention.

2. *Southern Baptists must strive with intentionality and dispatch toward a new theological consensus.* Denominational debate over the past decade has indicated that some Southern Baptists are resistant to any notion of a new theological consensus and are unwilling to join any process of establishing a new doctrinal synthesis. Others, though willing to cooperate in such and endeavor, see little hope for any new consensus in the midst of the current level of conflict.[25]

Nevertheless, the negotiation of such a consensus is absolutely crucial for the renewal of the Southern Baptist Convention. The 1925 and 1963 editions of *The Baptist Faith and Message* were attempts to negotiate a doctrinal consensus in response to specific crises in Southern Baptist life. The course and intensity of the current conflict will necessitate even greater clarity than that afforded by 1925 and 1963 statements and a more comprehensive theological recovery than any written statement can foster.

The faithful negotiation of any new consensus is endangered by resistance to theological limits on the left and by specific issues of fixation on the right. The only route to stability will be by means of an evangelical Baptist vision which avoids both the rigidity and obscurantism of fundamentalism and the accommodationist concessions of the left.

3. *This new theological consensus must be based on a recovery of the classical Christian paradigm.* The pressures of modernity and the vacuum produced by decades of doctrinal neglect will require that any effort toward theological recovery find its roots within the fullness of the classical Christian tradition. Baptist "distinctives" must be interpreted in terms of a larger and more comprehensive continuity with the larger Christian tradition.

A model of dynamic orthodoxy must be reclaimed within the Baptist tradition. That orthodox tradition must be recovered in conversation with Nicaea, Chalcedon, Augustine, Luther, Calvin, and the Protestant confessions—as well as the sturdy confessional tradition of Baptists developed over four centuries. In sum, any new theological consensus must be rooted within the *consensus fidei* of the Christian church.[26] Nothing less will suffice.

4. *The recovery of the classic paradigm must include a restatement of the evangelical Scripture principle and a clear affirmation of biblical authority.* By "evangelical Scripture principle," I mean a commitment to the complete truthfulness of Scripture. The nature of biblical authority has been the central issue in the current debate, and the current impasse is sufficient to indicate that no new consensus will emerge which lacks a firm recommitment to the authority of Scripture.

This restatement of the Scripture principle must include a clear and balanced affirmation of the Bible's truthfulness and trustworthiness, carefully defined in such a way that the integrity of the Bible is uncompromisingly affirmed even as the legitimate role of "believing criticism" is recognized and valued. Though "inerrancy" has functioned primarily as a weapon of theological warfare in the SBC controversy, it must be recovered in the context of its central meaning and function.

Biblical inerrancy must be posited within the context of a holistic recovery of the Scripture principle within the Christian tradition. Those who claim continuity with the tradition and a high view of biblical authority, but who find the term "inerrancy" problematic, must articulate a doctrine of Scripture which addresses the issue of the Bible's complete truthfulness and which fulfills the function inerrancy has been intended to accomplish.

To affirm inerrancy is not to suggest that it is the most important component of an evangelical Baptist doctrine of Scripture. Inspiration and authority supersede inerrancy as issues of central concern, but this does not indicate that inerrancy is a minor issue in light of present challenges to faith.

The word *inerrancy*, problematic as it is in light of current controversy, must be recovered so as to do justice to the Scripture principle of the church (which speaks to the status of Scripture as God's written revelation) and must deal as well with the difficult but not insoluble issue of the divine/human status of the biblical materials, and with the phenomena of Scripture as well as a doctrine of Scripture. Such an approach is reflected in David S. Dockery's suggested definition:

Inerrancy means *when all the facts are known, the Bible (in its autographs) properly interpreted in light of which culture and communication means had been developed by the time of its composition will be shown to be completely true (and therefore not false) in all that it affirms, to the degree of precision intended by the author, in all matters relating to God and his creation.*[27]

Central to this recovery must be an understanding that inerrancy, while not stipulating a precise theory of inspiration or exegetical method, does indicate a hermeneutical attitude or stance toward Scripture. This may best be described as a "hermeneutic of acceptance" or "hermeneutic of receptivity" over against a "hermeneutic of suspicion."[28] The hermeneutics of acceptance presupposes that the text is truthful and trustworthy, and can incorporate the tools of believing criticism in the task of exegesis and interpretation. Critical methodologies may be employed, but not in such a way that the integrity of the text is questioned, nor the normative status of Scripture compromised.[29]

Debates over the Bible, whatever the terminology employed, must deal with the central issue of the Bible's authority. In the final analysis, either the biblical text or the interpreter will function as authoritative in the encounter with Scripture. The Protestant Scripture principle requires that the text—not the interpreter—be recognized as authoritative. As W. T. Conner commented: "If God is not a God of authority, he is no God at all. If God does not reveal himself, religion is impossible. Therefore, if God reveals himself to man, it must be in an authoritative way."[30] The Enlightenment's famous "turn to the subject" cannot be modeled by the evangelical believer. As D. M. Lloyd-Jones reminded: "Let us not be confused by the modern argument about a changed position. We are still left where believers have always been left."[31]

5. *At the core of this new consensus must lie a foundational reaffirmation of biblical theism.* Such an affirmation may seen axiomatic, but objective biblical theism cannot be assumed as normative in the broader theological community. Indeed, biblical theism has been under sustained theological attack for most of the twentieth century. Revisionist theologies, process theology, much feminist theology, and other current offerings reject biblical theism in favor of a Deity (insofar as Deity is claimed at all) more in keeping with the canons of modernity than the canon of Holy Scripture.

A reaffirmation of biblical theism is a recognition of what is at stake in the larger community and what can be at stake among

Southern Baptists if doctrinal decline is not reversed. Objective biblical theism must undergird the entire theological enterprise. Christian theology is faith seeking knowledge and understanding of the God of Abraham, Issac, and Jacob; the God and Father of our Lord Jesus Christ.

6. *This consensus must also include an unapologetic reaffirmation of salvation through Jesus Christ (fully human and fully divine) alone as the central message of the church.* A bold and unapologetic reaffirmation of the evangelical doctrine of the person and work of Christ; of justification through faith; of salvation through Jesus Christ's substitutionary and sacrificial life, death, and bodily resurrection; and of salvation through Jesus Christ alone, must be the central affirmation of a new theological consensus.

In the midst of increasing concessions to universalism in the Christian community, Southern Baptists must be ready to join other evangelical and orthodox Christians in bearing the "scandal of particularity" against temptations to accommodate the biblical message to the spirit of the age.

7. *Southern Baptist churches must recognize and fulfill their responsibility to extend the gospel through mission, to embody the gospel through authentic discipleship, and to guard the gospel through the discipline of theology in the service of the church.* Southern Baptists have been characterized throughout their history as a "people on mission." A vision for world missions based in an urgent concern for millions who have never heard the gospel has fired and shaped Southern Baptists since the formation of the SBC in 1845.

Recent decades have seen Southern Baptists make significant progress in recognizing their responsibility in embodying the gospel in Christian discipleship. A growing ethical and moral vision has shaped and energized the denomination in the twentieth century. That vision and commitment must grow and meet the challenges of the present and the future.

Those present and future challenges will require that Southern Baptists recognize and claim a responsibility woefully fulfilled to date—contending for the gospel. Mission and evangelism must be linked to the biblical imperative to "contend for the faith that was once for all entrusted to the saints" (Jude 3, NIV). Southern Baptist theologians must be engaged with the wider theological community and modern culture, not merely for academic interest, though that is not to be disparaged, but for a kerygmatic purpose and for the scholarly defense of the faith.

8. *Churches must renew a sense of theological vocation and assist their members to translate theological commitments to daily life.* Churches which fail to educate their members in Christian doctrine will produce a rootless and fruitless generation of spiritually emaciated disciples. Churches must train their members to "convert the question," that is, to see the theological dimensions of issues, events, and choices of everyday life. Unless that translation is made, Christians are doomed to live compartmentalized lives in which their Christian faith is relevant only to churchly activities and concerns.

Churches must be, in effect, little seminaries for growing believers. Without this sense of intentionality in doctrinal education, churches will fail in their responsibility to train disciples. This responsibility cannot be delegated to others. Local churches must recognize and assume their responsibility to educate believers in the gospel, to address the challenges of secular society, and to contend for the faith against the multitude of competing ideologies within and without the church.

Many churches have made their own compromises with modernity and have built large congregations, not on the foundation of the gospel, but at its expense. Whether that "other gospel" be a prosperity theology, the gospel of self-esteem, or some other variant, that church has become a scandal to the cross. Furthermore, churches which have made their own set of concessions to modernity should not be surprised when their students come home from the academy with yet another set of concessions. The church must recognize that it bears the primary and inescapable responsibility for doctrinal education and articulation.

9. *From the churches must come an appreciation for the function of biblical, theological, historical, and professional studies in the service of the church, and they must acknowledge and support confessional scholarship.* Southern Baptist churches must understand, appreciate, and eagerly support the professional and academic training of their ministers and must see the denomination's seminaries as extensions of the church's mission. Churches and seminaries must be linked by common respect and mutual trust.

Seminary faculty members should be encouraged to be fully engaged with the world of professional scholarship in the academy, but the primary convictional commitment of churchly professors must be to the church and not to the academy at large. Churches must sustain and support biblical, theological, historical, and professional studies for their ministers and should be satisfied with nothing less than seminaries which match recognized academic excellence with unquestioned evangelical commitment. The tension between these two standards is the story of theological education in the last two centuries and the most explosive factor in the current SBC controversy.

10. *The academy (theological seminaries) must renew a commitment to the churches as the primary public of confessional theology.* Extending the argument above, the denomination's theological seminaries must make clear their foundational commitment to the churches as the primary public of concern. Seminaries are supported financially by the churches, charged by the churches to train their ministers, and expected to fulfill a ministry to the churches that is both prophetic and priestly.

That is to say, the seminaries should be expected to challenge the churches toward greater faithfulness to the gospel (the prophetic role) and to nurture the churches through churchly theology, biblical studies, and professional disciplines (the priestly role).

Such a partnership assumes that the denomination will not be satisfied with the lowest common denominator of common concern which can be located among the churches and the seminaries, but, rather, that a partnership of vision will be required to establish a level of mutual trust and respect. This requisite level of trust will be possible only if the seminaries make clear their primary public of concern and commitment—and that public must be the churches. This primary commitment must not exclude attention to the other publics as the focus of vital and pressing concern to the academic enterprise. But the seminaries must make clear the distinction between engagement with the broader academy and accommodation to the academy's ethos and worldview.[32]

11. *The Southern Baptist Convention, with the church and academy in partnership, must develop and articulate a set of dual doctrinal parameters.* That is, parameters against obscurantist fundamentalism on the right and revisionist compromise on the left. Both have been very real dangers as the denomination has charted its course. The obscurantism and separatism of fundamentalism (and Landmarkism, its precursor) were rejected by the Convention

at various turns and the Convention responded to threats from the left with *The Baptist Faith and Message* statements of 1925 and 1963.

Bill Leonard is undoubtedly correct in his assessment that *The Baptist Faith and Message* statements, though precipitated by controversy, "also indicate the effort of Southern Baptists to define doctrine in terms general enough to incorporate diverse segments of the convention."[33] The statements functioned as consensus documents which alleviated fears on the right without causing disruption within the agencies and institutions. The 1925 statement effectively ended the controversy which prompted its adoption.[34] The 1963 statement was intended to serve the same purpose, but its effectiveness in suppressing controversy lasted for less than twenty years. Conservatives were not satisfied that their concerns had been adequately addressed.

Southern Baptists have operated for almost 150 years in a tension between *what can be assumed* and *what must be articulated*. In 1845 the founding fathers of the Southern Baptist Convention let it be known that they would establish "no new creed" as the basis for the young denomination. This posture was made possible for the new convention by the undeniable existence of a powerful reservoir of doctrinal conviction among Baptists in the South. Though considerable diversity of opinion existed concerning matters agreed to be secondary, compromise on the cardinal doctrines of biblical Christianity was virtually nonexistent.

The establishment of The Southern Baptist Theological Seminary in 1859 occasioned the first substantial doctrinal statement uniquely formulated for a Southern Baptist constituency. The "Abstract of Principles" established the theological identity of the young seminary and served to provide doctrinal parameters for instruction. Professors were (and remain) required to teach "in accordance with, and not contrary to" the rather comprehensive statement which has remained unchanged since 1859. In an article written in 1874 James P. Boyce, the founder and first president of the seminary, stated that, though some resistance to the notion of a confessional document was present, the Educational Convention which established the seminary agreed that the Abstract should be "a complete exhibition of the fundamental doctrines of grace, so that in no essential particular should they speak dubiously. . . ."[35] Nevertheless, the document was not to take a position on any point "upon which the denomination is divided.''[36] A review of the *Abstract* reveals a document rich in theological content, with explicit articles covering all the central doctrines of the Christian faith. The *Abstract*, seen in light of Boyce's explanation, thus reveals an extensive doctrinal consensus on issues of primary theological concern.

The Baptist Faith and Message statements of 1925 and 1963 also reveal a remarkable degree of doctrinal consensus, though the precipitating factors behind the two statements indicate a growing shift from *what can be assumed* to *what must be articulated*. The pressures and challenges of modernity have inevitably pushed Southern Baptists further along this continuum. The present controversy, and the failure of both *The Baptist Faith and Message* statement of 1963 and the 1987 report of the SBC Peace Committee to establish consensus, indicates that even less can be assumed, and more must be articulated.

Some SBC fundamentalist-conservatives undoubtedly seek doctrinal uniformity on all issues—an accomplishment even more dubious in 1990 than in 1874. Some SBC moderate-conservatives, on the other hand, cite Baptist aversion to creedalism as a basis for denying virtually any level of authority to confessional statements. Both extremes do violence to the Baptist heritage and to prospects for a new denominational consensus.

The Southern Baptist Convention has reflected considerable diversity throughout its almost century and a half of existence.[37] Several distinct Baptist traditions came together in the early Convention, and continue to influence discernable traditions within the contemporary SBC. Nevertheless, a distinction must be drawn between *diversity* and *pluralism*. Diversity reflects the existence of various traditions and points of view within the community. Pluralism, on the other hand, celebrates diversity and undertakes a programmatic encouragement of diversity in conviction and practice.[38]

As Lesslie Newbigin suggests, the "fact of plurality" must be distinguished from "an ideology of pluralism."[39] The Southern Baptist Convention is marked by both plurality and diversity, but it has also reflected a demonstrable evangelical consensus on issues of major theological concern.[40] Advocates of an "ideology of pluralism" within the SBC resist the notion of doctrinal parameters as well as calls for any new theological consensus.

The denomination must resist the ideological temptation of the pluralist agenda even as it seeks to treat the Convention's diverse traditions with respect. The Convention must not be distracted from the process of seeking a new theological consensus lest it concede the battle and dissipate by means of theological chaos.[41]

The process of developing a new theological consensus must be accompanied by the drawing of articulated theological parameters which are commonly understood and affirmed by the seminaries, agencies, and institutions. Such a dual process must give attention to the center of theological concern and to the boundary issues which limit convictional cooperation.

Logicians and phenomenologists describe sets in terms of "fuzzy sets," "centered sets," and "bounded sets." Bounded sets give primary attention to the boundary lines which separate the defining characteristics of membership from the larger community. Centered sets give primary attention to a common core of belief and practice. Fuzzy sets are fluid and have little discernable boundary with the larger community.[42]

The notion of the church of Jesus Christ as a "fuzzy set" is incongruous with the gospel. Christian communions have generally defined themselves as either bounded or centered sets, depending on the dynamics of their organization and their doctrinal commitments. Bounded church sets define themselves over against other belief systems and give a great deal of attention to theological parameters. Centered church sets, on the other hand, tend to give greater attention to the central consensus common to the churches.

The challenges of modernity will not allow Southern Baptists to choose between these two ordering models.[43] Some Southern Baptists have given primary attention to boundaries while others call for them to shift attention from parameters to common affirmations. Such an either/or posture will not meet the challenge now facing the denomination. The Convention must undertake a dual process of defining the center and drawing parameters with unity, not uniformity, as the goal.

To undertake this process is not to suggest that parameters have not existed, nor that seminary faculties operate without regard to the confessional commitments required by their institution. It is to suggest that Southern Baptists need renewed *and clearly articulated* parameters as well as a reaffirmation of the doctrinal center.

Any renewed theological consensus must give attention to the "irreducible minimum" of Christian theology as a basis for beginning the task. Based in the apostolic preaching of the early church, this "irreducible minimum" of doctrinal content served as both center and boundary for the early Christian community.[44] Southern Baptists ranging from theologian William L. Hendricks to Sunday School Board president James T. Draper have called for a consensus based on such primary affirmations, with room left for diversity of opinion on issues such as eschatology, ecclesiology, and worship practices.[45] As Draper commented:

> We must do something to maintain the strength and aggressive ministry that has historically characterized this convention. We cannot allow the cry of "diversity" to intimidate us. Proper balance, within stated parameters, must be demonstrated and nurtured if our historical stance as Southern Baptists is to be preserved.[46]

12. *A process of "theological triage" must be established in order to distinguish first-order issues on which agreement is necessary from second-order and third-order issues on which disagreement is possible.* Triage is the process whereby medical patients are graded in terms of emergency priority. Critical cases receive emergency priority over superficial injuries and chronic ailments. A similar process must be undertaken at the denominational level regarding theological concerns.

Partisans in theological battle see the issues of their conflict as the highest priority of concern. They may or may not be correct. The denomination must foster a deliberate process of prioritization intended to determine those issues of critical priority (on which consensus is necessary) and issues of lesser priority (on which diversity does not threaten cooperation). Such a process is absolutely mandatory in the current situation.

Fissures in Southern Baptist life, ranging from church splits to the "disfellowshipping" of churches at the associational level, tend to be precipitated by disagreements over something less than first-order theological issues. These occurances rarely are prompted by disagreements over the Deity of Christ, the authority of Scripture, Trinitarian affirmations, or substitutionary atonement. Such schisms have tended to follow disagreements over the ordination of women, the exercise of charismatic gifts, the ordination of divorced persons, and issues related to closed communion and alien immersion.[47] This is not to suggest that such issues should not be of concern to the churches. Nevertheless, when debate is focused on these secondary or tertiary issues, the denomination's theological center of gravity is in question.

Southern Baptists must consider which issues require common consent and which should allow for diversity of opinion and practice. Our denominational commitment to cooperation is not for the sake of cooperation in and of itself, but for convictional cooperation based upon a common vision of ministry and purpose, undergirded by and originating in a theological consensus. This process of "theological triage" must be conducted in light of the heritage of the Christian church and with great humility.

13. *Southern Baptists must engage in a genuine process of theological dialogue.* To some in the Convention this call will be seen as axiomatic, to others it will appear naive. Prospects for genuine theological dialogue appear bleak as an institutionalized two-party system is now firmly fixed within the denomination. Neither party seems ready to engage in substantive dialogue or willing to address the "conflict of visions" which has brought the denomination to this current impasse. Yet, no realistic hope for the future of the Southern Baptist Convention exists apart from such a process of dialogue.

14. *The Southern Baptist Convention, long an ecclesiological cul-de-sac, must look beyond itself for allies, models, partners, and resources in this struggle.* The cultural, social, intellectual, and theological isolation of the convention was, perhaps in part, the secret of its success and solidarity in former days. This isolation is also a factor in the current denominational crisis. Southern Baptists must learn from the experience of other denominations and must look to the four corners of the world for allies and partners in faith and mission.

The SBC must enter into dialogue with the larger evangelical community and seek models and partners in theological affirmation, education, and mission.[48] Denominational isolation is no longer possible, but an end to isolation is no guarantee of dialogue with profitable partners. Southern Baptists must judge carefully and honestly the models they wish to follow.

Will Southern Baptists move beyond the impasse? Some have already decided that the challenges are insurmountable and now resist any effort to strive for denominational renewal.[49] It may be that theological recovery and a new Southern Baptist denominationalism do not emerge. If so, the denomination is lost. The Southern Baptist Convention may continue in some truncated and curtailed programmatic form, but its role as a communion of confessing churches united by the gospel will be forfeited.

Yet, hope is not lost. A deep and abiding commitment to the gospel and to cooperative mission continues among the vast majority of Southern Baptists. If the trauma and pain of denominational warfare do not eventually break the ties which have bound these faithful churches together, a hopeful future may yet emerge. If Southern Baptists are willing to dream their denomination anew and probe the depths of their commitments, renewal may come.

In the final analysis, any renewal of the Southern Baptist Convention must come as the work and will of the sovereign Spirit of God. No human striving can produce genuine revival, but we are not freed from our responsibility to act redemptively even as we pray for renewal.

The gospel was entrusted to Southern Baptists, but never to us alone. Should Southern Baptists fail this critical test of faithfulness, the mantle of God's blessing will pass to others who will hold the gospel in trust, for those who have ears to hear.

Notes

1. The concept of a "conflict of visions" has been most effectively articulated by Thomas Sowell in *A Conflict of Visions: Ideological Origins of Political Struggles* (New York: William Morrow, 1987). Sowell's basic thesis is that every political struggle (which would certainly include the SBC conflict) is marked by a foundational conflict at the level of vision—the philosophical presuppositions, worldview, and ideological commitments of individuals on either side of the conflict. One must look beyond the particular issues of debate to the foundational commitments which shape positions on individual issues. As Sowell notes: "One of the curious things about political opinions is how often the same people line up on opposite sides of different issues. . . . A closer look at the arguments on both sides often shows that they are reasoning from fundamentally different premises. These different premises—often implicit—are what provide the consistency behind the repeated opposition of individuals and groups on numerous, unrelated issues. They have different visions of how the world works" (13). This has obvious relevance for the SBC conflict. See R. Albert Mohler, Jr., "The Conflict of Visions," *The Christian Index*, June 15, 1989, 2.

2. Roy L. Honeycutt, Jr., president of The Southern Baptist Theologi-

cal Seminary, has suggested a "programmatic synthesis" which held Southern Baptists together in the postwar period. Roy L. Honeycutt, "Will 'Success' Destroy Southern Baptists?: A Denominationalist's View," in *Evangelicalism: Surviving Its Success*, ed. David A. Fraser (Princeton: Princeton University Press, 1987), 29-44.

3. Such a theological framework is suggested by historian Bill J. Leonard's identification of the "Grand Compromise" which served Southern Baptists throughout their first 125 years. See Bill J. Leonard, *God's Last and Only Hope: The Fragmentation of the Southern Baptist Convention* (Grand Rapids: Eerdmans, 1990). Leonard suggests that this "Grand Compromise" was based on a general consensus regarding core doctrines, with room for diverse positions on salvation (with both Calvinists and revivalists included), understandings of the church (with both Landmarkists and non-Landmarkists included), and other issues the Convention was able to accommodate.

4. Such a neglect may be seen in the diminished attention given to explicitly doctrinal issues in denominational literature after 1950.

5. The term was suggested by Harold Lindsell in his *The Battle for the Bible* (Grand Rapids: Zondervan, 1976). Though the term "inerrancy" had been used by some Southern Baptists for decades, Lindsell should be credited with bringing the word to widespread usage in the 1970s. For an example of an earlier use of the term by a leading Southern Baptist, see J. M. Frost, "Introduction," *Baptist Why and Why Not* (Nashville: Sunday School Board, 1900), 12: "We accept the Scriptures as an all-sufficient and infallible rule of faith and practice, and insist upon the absolute inerrancy and sole authority of the Word of God."

6. Mark A. Noll, *Beyond Faith and Criticism: Evangelicals, Scholarship, and the Bible in America*, Society of Biblical Literature Confessional Perspectives Series (San Francisco: Harper and Row, 1986).

7. The term "atheological" is used here, not in the sense employed by deconstructionists, but as a means of indicating the almost complete absence of genuinely theological concern. Interestingly, this more general absence has been noted by a revisionist theologian as "a form of thinking that bears no manifest sign of the presence of theology." See the foreword to Mark C. Taylor, *Deconstructing Theology*, American Academy of Religion Studies in Religion 28 (New York: Crossroad, 1982), xi.

8. Timothy George, "The Renewal of Baptist Theology," in *Baptist Theologians*, ed. Timothy George and David S. Dockery (Nashville: Broadman, 1990).

9. David Tracy, *The Analogical Imagination* (New York: Crossroad, 1981). See also his *Blessed Rage for Order: The New Pluralism in Theology* (New York: Seabury Press, 1978).

10. Such a shift was noted by Kenneth Chafin, then pastor of South

Main Baptist Church in Houston, Texas, who stated: "The local church desperately needs a healthy interest in doctrine. It is foundational to her understanding and to her action. The claim 'It's not what you believe but what you do that counts' is wrong. The foundation for all that a church does is found in what she believes." Kenneth Chafin, "Communicating Baptist Doctrine in the Local Church," *Baptist History and Heritage* 13 (October 1978): 8-15. Chafin noted that Baptists "have gone through a long period of disinterest in doctrine and are beginning to pay for it" (8-9). Delivered in an address just one year prior to the full eruption of the current SBC conflict, his words were prophetic.

11. See R. Albert Mohler, Jr., "The Decline of Doctrine," *The Christian Index*, February 22, 1990, 2.

12. For a cogent analysis of the self-movement and its influence in contemporary society see Paul Vitz, *Psychology as Religion* (Grand Rapids: Eerdmans, 1980). This is not to suggest that psychology has nothing to say to the church, nor that churches should not direct their ministries toward legitimate human needs. Nevertheless, churches should apply a biblical/theological test to all such "borrowings" from popular culture. Many rest on presuppositions diametrically opposed to Christianity.

13. See Van Harvey, "On the Intellectual Marginality of American Theology," in *Religion and Twentieth-Century American Intellectual Life*, ed. Michael J. Lacey, (Cambridge: Cambridge University Press, 1989), 172-92. Harvey notes: "There are few Protestant Christian theologians in the United States who would not concede that the intellectual enterprise called theology has fallen on evil days in their own country. It is not merely that the basic themes, categories, and types of argumentation of theology are regarded as irrelevant by most intellectuals, but that theological argumentation has virtually become a forgotten and lost mode of discourse" (172).

14. See Walter B. Shurden, "The Pastor as Denominational Theologian in Southern Baptist History," *Baptist History and Heritage*, 15 (July 1980): 15-22. This shift is best seen in the role Herschel H. Hobbs has served as theologian statesman for the SBC. Pastor of First Baptist Church, Oklahoma City, Oklahoma, for many years, Hobbs served as president of the SBC 1962-63, chairman of the 1963 committee on *The Baptist Faith and Message*, preacher for "The Baptist Hour," and author of numerous books. Hobbs has served as the most significant interpreter of Baptist doctrine from the 1960s to the present. W. A. Criswell, longtime pastor of First Baptist Church in Dallas, Texas, has exerted a similar influence in other circles through sermons, books, the annual "School of the Prophets," and Criswell College.

15. Note here the work of Stephen Toulmin of the University of Chicago. In an interesting paper presented to an Association of Theological

Schools seminar, Toulmin suggested: "If theology returns to a tradition of *practice* rather then *theory*, we can take better heart." See Stephen Toulmin, "Theology in the Context of the University," *Theological Education* 26 (1990): 51-65.

16. John H. S. Kent, *The End of the Line? The Development of Christian Theology in the Last Two Centuries* (Philadelphia: Fortress Press, 1978); Lonnie D. Kliever, *The Shattered Spectrum: A Survey of Contemporary Theology* (Atlanta: John Knox, 1981).

17. Edward Farley, *Ecclesial Reflection: An Anatomy of Theological Method* (Philadelphia: Fortress Press, 1982). Farley celebrates this "fall" and suggests that Christian faith must "look for another house in which to live" (168).

18. George Lindbeck, "How My Mind Has Changed," *The Christian Century*, May 9, 1990, 494. He commented: "Now, however, interest has shifted more and more to unmediated *aggiornamento*, the updating of faith and practice by direct translation into presumably more intelligible and relevant modern idioms and actions. This is a revival of the liberal strategy, familiar since the Enlightenment, of letting the world set the church's agenda" (494). The term *aggioramento* was used in the Vatican II deliberations to indicate a process of intentional change.

19. Gordon Kauffman, "Whatever Happened to Theology?" *Christianity and Crisis* 35 (May 1975): 111.

20. The term "neoorthodoxy" is itself problemmatic, but refers here to the spectrum of early-twentieth-century systems including Karl Barth, Emil Brunner, and Rudolph Bultmann in Europe and Reinhold Niebuhr in the United States. In one sense, any term broad enough to include Barth and Bultmann is awkward, but neoorthodoxy has been so established in the current theological vocabulary. See R. Albert Mohler, Jr., "Evangelical Theology and Karl Barth: Representative Models of Response" (Grand Rapids: Eerdmans, forthcoming).

21. The term has also been assumed by more conservative theologians, who indicate by its use the fall of the older modernism and a return to more classical roots. Representative figures would include Thomas Oden, Clark Pinnock, and, to a lesser extent, theologians such as George Lindbeck and Hans Frei at Yale Divinity School. The term is used by some to indicate a posture which assumes the basic assumptions of liberal thought and modernism and seeks to move forward, and is used by others to suggest a mode of thought which rejects some cardinal tenets of modernism, but seeks no return to precritical orthodoxy.

22. See his chapter in *Paradigm Change in Theology*, ed. Hans Küng and David Tracy (New York: Crossroad, 1989), 175. Kuhn has been the primary theorist of "paradigm shifts." See his *The Structure of Scientific Revolutions*, 2d ed., (Chicago: University of Chicago Press, 1970 [1962]).

23. The concept of a *Kulturkampf* (which originally arose in German church/state debates during Bismarck's chancellorship) offers helpful clues to the Southern Baptist Convention controversy. In reality, the conflict has been a cultural war fought on primarily theological terms. But the reality of the progressive/conservative divide in the SBC extends throughout the universe of worldview issues. For a helpful analysis of how such a culture war has shaped another religious body, see George Weigel, *Catholicism and the Renewal of American Democracy* (New York: Paulist Press, 1989).

24. Space does not allow elaboration in this chapter, but the concept of a "new class" opposed to conservative (traditional) values and commitments has been accepted by leading figures on the right (such as Irving Kristol, Richard John Neuhaus, and Peter Berger) and the left (including Alvin Gouldner, et al.). This "new class" is committed to information and ideas as means of changing society, having set itself against the values of the more traditionalist classes in society. Sociologists point to the dominance of new class figures in academia, the service sector, and governmental bureaucracy. The new class worldview now dominates the professional leadership of mainline Protestantism.

25. A glimpse of this dynamic can be seen in "Consensus Challenges '90s, Scholars Say," *Baptist Press*, February 16, 1990, 1-2.

26. Donald Bloesch offers a model of "catholic evangelicalism" which embodies this sense of continuity. See his *Essentials of Evangelical Theology*, 2 vols., (San Francisco: Harper and Row, 1978-79). Another model particularly rooted in the Patristic era is offered by Thomas Oden in his *Systematic Theology*, 3 vols., (San Francisco: Harper and Row, 1986-). A significant Baptist model of engagement with the Christian tradition is seen in James Leo Garrett, *Systematic Theology: Biblical, Historical, and Evangelical*, 2 vols. (Grand Rapids: Eerdmans, 1990-). Garrett's *Systematic Theology* may be the most comprehensive dogmatic effort ever undertaken by a major Southern Baptist theologian. Carl F. H. Henry's six-volume *God, Revelation and Authority* (Waco, Tex.: Word, 1978-85), though not a systematic theology, is a massive engagement with current issues and the classical Christian tradition.

27. David S. Dockery, "Biblical Inerrancy: Pro or Con?," *The Theological Educator* 37 (1988): 25, (emphasis his). See also his chapter in this volume.

28. The "hermeneutics of suspicion" is often associated with Nietzsche, Freud, and Marx but is properly generalized in the course of western thought to refer to all who would take a primary stance of suspicion in regard to the received tradition, whether the tradition is theological, philosophical, or political.

29. See James Leo Garrett's helpful discussion of options when dealing with apparent difficulties within the phenomena of Scripture in his *Systematic Theology*, 1: 165-67.

30. Walter Thomas Conner, *Revelation and God: An Introduction to Christian Doctrine* (Nashville: Broadman Press, 1936), 97-98. D. M. Lloyd-Jones expressed the challenge well in lectures delivered in 1957: "The choice for us today is really as simple as it was for those first Christians in the early days. We either accept this authority [the Bible] or else we accept the authority of 'modern knowledge,' modern science, human understanding, human ability. It is one or the other." See D. M. Lloyd-Jones, *Authority* (London: Inter-Varsity Press, 1958), 60.

31. Lloyd-Jones, *Authority*, 60.

32. An interesting perspective on this tension within mainline Protestantism is seen in the recent work of Tex Sample, professor of church and society at St. Paul School of Theology in Kansas City, Missouri (United Methodist). Sample writes: "Seminary training in the United States basically makes people unfit to serve congregations on the cultural right, and the more a theological school sees itself as committed to the graduate study of religion, the more likely this is to be true. The reasons for this are numerous, but the basic fact is that university and seminary training is socially located in a very different place from the cultural right and operates on the basis of an approach to learning that is as opaque to the local folk as the lifeways of the latter are uninteresting to the former." See Tex Sample, *U.S. Lifestyles and Mainline Churches* (Louisville: Westminster/John Knox, 1990), 83.

33. Leonard, *God's Last and Only Hope*, 69.

34. Though the Convention was to deal with the evolution controversy the next year, it soon ceased to be a major issue of concern at annual Conventions.

35. In James P. Boyce, "The Doctrinal Position of the Seminary," *Western Recorder*, June 20, 1874. Reprinted in *Review and Expositor*, 41 (1944): 18-24.

36. Ibid., 19.

37. See Walter Shurden, "The Southern Baptist Synthesis: Is It Cracking?," the 1980-81 Carver-Barnes Lectures, published by Southeastern Baptist Theological Seminary, Wake Forest. North Carolina, 1981, and in *Baptist History and Heritage* 16 (1981): 2-11.

38. As Edward Farley comments: "The experience of different and competing forms of religion, and even of Christianity, has been in the Christian movement since the days of the Apostle Paul. But the issue of pluralism is not the same as the issue of diversity. A pluralist posture grants legitimacy to the other forms of faith and even celebrates its difference." Edward Farley, "The Modernist Element in Protestantism," *Theology Today* 47 (1990): 139.

39. Lesslie Newbigin, *The Gospel in a Pluralist Society* (Grand Rapids: Eerdmans, 1989), 14.

40. A possible exception to this would be the tension between the Calvinistic and revivalistic traditions regarding the nature of election and the order of salvation (*ordo salutis*). Nevertheless, both traditions within the SBC share a common affirmation of the universal need for salvation, of substitutionary atonement, and of salvation through the atoning work of Jesus Christ alone. The unresolved tension between the Convention's Calvinistic (Reformed) roots and the current reign of revivalism within many, if not most churches, is an underlying factor in the current controversy and has rarely been an issue of public concern.

41. Several mainline denominations are firmly committed to an ideology of pluralism, but the pluralist agenda has come under severe criticism even in some mainline churches. United Methodists officially committed themselves to pluralism as a defining mark of that denomination in 1972 when they adopted a revised theological statement. The 1988 United Methodist General Conference reversed this official commitment by means of a new theological statement. Bishop Jack M. Tuell stated in his episcopal address, "The time has come to say the last rites over the notion that the defining characteristic of United Methodist theology is pluralism." See "United Methodists Bury Theological Pluralism," *Christianity Today*, August 15, 1988, 60-61. Pluralism remains entrenched nevertheless in much United Methodism. The American Baptist Churches, USA, is also dealing with the issue. See "Factions Jostle for Position Among American Baptists," *Eternity*, August 1988, 20-22.

42. A discussion of the technical background to this discussion may be found in Paul G. Hiebert, "The Category 'Christian' in the Mission Task," *International Review of Mission*, July 1983, 421-25.

43. See Mohler, "Evangelical Theology," 299-313.

44. See C. H. Dodd, *The Apostolic Faith and Its Development* (Grand Rapids: Baker [reprint], 1935).

45. I am indebted to Professor William L. Hendricks for his attention to and articulation of the "irreducible minimum." As he comments: "Legalism is an abiding danger to biblical faith. . . . An equal danger to biblical faith is uncertainty or lack of belief. It is impossible to have saving faith in the fullest sense without certain minimal beliefs and awareness of those definitive acts which brought Christianity into being. Faith implies confidence in the object of faith." William L. Hendricks, *A Theology for Children* (Nashville: Broadman Press, 1980), 245.

46. James T. Draper, Jr., *Authority: The Critical Issue for Southern Baptists* (Old Tappan, N.J.: Revell, 1984), 109. Draper's plea was also the theme of his 1983 SBC presidential address in Pittsburgh and was repeated in his address to the 1988 Conference on Biblical Interpretation. He credited William Hendricks with the concept of an "irreducible minimum." See "Southern Baptist Theology Today: An Interview With Dr. James T. Draper, Jr.," *The Theological Educator* 28 (1984): 14-26.

47. These last two issues are linked to Landmarkism and function more regionally than the other issues listed. Arguments over closed/open communion and alien immersion produced the vast majority of associational-level schisms in the convention's first century.

48. A promising example of this process is seen in the Foreign Mission Board's initiatives toward "Great Commission Christians." Another promising dialogue has been sponsored by Southern Seminary in partnership with the Pew Charitable Trusts. That three-year program of evangelical/Southern Baptist dialogue is a positive development which should spawn a larger process of dialogue. See R. Albert Mohler, Jr., "A Call for Baptist Evangelicals and Evangelical Baptists," in *Southern Baptists and American Evangelicals*, ed. David S. Dockery (Nashville: Broadman Press, forthcoming). See also Timothy F. George, "Partly Fearing, Partly Hoping: Southern Baptists and Evangelicals," a review essay in *Perspectives in Religious Studies* (1990).

49. R. Albert Mohler, Jr., "The Synthesis is Cracked: Is the Heart Breaking?" *The Christian Index*, August 30, 1990, 2.

5
Beyond Old Habits and on to a New Land
*Robison B. James**

As I see it, Southern Baptists are at an impasse in the sense of a "deadlock, as in negotiations," or a "stalemate."[1] That may be part of what R. Albert Mohler has in mind when he says in the previous chapter, "an institutionalized two-party system is now firmly fixed within the denomination" (p. 109).

Is there any way beyond this deadlock? One obvious way would be for one party or the other to leave—to opt out of things Southern Baptists are doing, selectively or completely, either at the national level, or within this or that state Baptist convention.

I shall not deal with that possibility. Even if we had a maximum of that kind of opting out, there would still be enough fire in our conflict to keep it burning for decades, flaring up, smoldering on, and eating away at our collective vitality.

Apart from someone's opting out, two things could happen. One side might abandon its principles and surrender. Or there might be a convergent movement from two sides, if not from several sides.

For reasons I will state in a moment, I strongly urge moderate-conservatives not to abandon the principles for which they have struggled. And those on the other side will feel the same way.

The alternative, a "convergent movement," could take at least three forms. There might be a deliberate compromise, or there

*Robison B. James (Ph.D., Duke University) is Professor of Religion at the University of Richmond, the oldest school related to the Baptist General Association of Virginia. He has been on its faculty since 1962. Author of over 40 articles, he is editor and principal author of *The Unfettered Word: Southern Baptists Confront the Authority-Inerrancy Question* and of *The Takeover in the SBC: A Brief History,* which has gone through six printings. James, who served four terms as a member of the Virginia legislature, has been a regular contributor to *SBC Today* (now *Baptists Today*), the main journal of moderate Southern Baptists. He is a member of the River Road Baptist Church in Richmond, Virginia.

might be a more or less unconscious "backing off." Neither of these options strikes me as both promising and likely to happen, or certainly not if it were pursued entirely apart from the third possibility.

And the third possibility? It would have to be a work of God—and I emphasize that fact—but it is at least conceivable that there could be a convergent movement from two or more sides *onto new ground*. That new ground would allow the parties to remain true to their principles and yet affirm one another, learn from one another, and share fully in the leadership of the denomination.

What This Chapter Tries to Do

In trying to persuade Southern Baptists to occupy this new and promising land, I pursue three purposes in this chapter. The first is to describe and recommend seven features of the new land that beckons us. Because I have room to deal only with the biblical issues, the new ground I will be pointing us toward is new biblical ground. I shall refer to it as "the new land."

We cannot leap to that promised land in a single bound, however. We are "in the wilderness"—at an impasse—and some deeply ingrained habits hold us there. Thus, as a second purpose, I diagnose and raise warnings about several "old habits." Each is the opposite or the absence of one of the seven things I recommend.

My third purpose is to respond to as many of the things said in chapters 1-4 as I have room for.

Mohler and Dialogue Among Baptists

I begin by applauding Mohler's proposal for a dialogue between the parties. Or I applaud that idea on the assumptions, with which I believe Mohler agrees, (a) that the dialogue would make use of researched, written exchanges over periods of time, and (b) that some of the people involved would be well versed in the relevant subjects, biblical, historical, and theological.

On the other hand, I am uneasy with the way Mohler presents some of his "imperatives." For example, he defines at considerable length the structural type of doctrinal parameters we must have and then says we should dialogue. Though I do not think he intended it that way, this procedure could create the impression that the results of the dialogue are being laid down before it starts.

I have reservations at another point also. Though Mohler sets forth fourteen imperatives, none of them is distinctly Baptist, or even recommends anything distinctly Baptist. That implies (again inadvertently, I feel sure) that our being Baptists is our problem, or part of our problem, anyway; and that the solution is for us to quit being Baptists, or to quit being so serious about it.

And that leads me back to the "weighty reasons" why I believe moderate-conservatives should not surrender their principles. Whether these people want it or not, and whether they are worthy of it or not, recent history has saddled them, in the providence of God, with a solemn task. If I understand it correctly, this task is not only to uphold the highest ideals of uncompromisingly honest, unfettered, believing inquiry, but also to uphold at least the following nonnegotiable features of Baptist identity:

> the equal priesthood of believers;
>
> the democracy within the church that such equality entails;
>
> freedom not just as a civil liberty, but as a freedom in Christ (Gal. 5);
>
> separation of church and state;
>
> free cooperation rather than forced conformity in carrying out the mission of Christ together;
>
> the right of individual interpretation under the Spirit, and the duty to engage in it, even for denominational employees; and finally,
>
> the plenary authority of the Bible as contrasted with this or that denominational pronouncement about the Bible, a principle that rings out clearly in the preamble that introduces and controls *The Baptist Faith and Message*.[2]

Just Living Our Theology Is Not Enough

Nancy Ammerman's penetrating analysis of the Southern Baptist struggle makes it clear why moderate-conservatives lost (or why they lost at the national level, which is the subject of her book). They lost, not because they lacked sufficient numbers or resources, but because they lacked something the other side had, namely, a cohesive agenda and a coherent message.[3]

I would recast Ammerman's point by saying that moderate-conservatives lost at the national level because they were not able to articulate the theology they were in fact living—or not in a sufficiently biblical and robust way. I hope this chapter will be of help in that regard and that it will prompt others to help. In any case, moderate-conservatives must articulate "the faith that is in them" in a more compelling way than they have thus far done.[4] This does not mean that the new land that beckons us is moderate-conservative turf. It is biblical ground for all Baptists. But it is new. Both sides, and not just one side, will have to pull up stakes and move their tents to settle there.

What Does the Bible Make Central—Ongoing Relation or Doctrine?

The first feature of this new land is the fact that those who live there agree with the Bible that our *ongoing relation to God in Christ* has priority over right doctrine or "orthodoxy."

I believe this first point holds the key to whatever chance we have of moving beyond the impasse. In addition, as I will make clear, the other six features of the new land confirm this one. The seven features comprise an interlocking network in which they reinforce and clarify each other.

As to this first point, I must be clear. I am not talking about relation to God in Christ *without* sound doctrine. The question is one of priority. Both doctrine and ongoing relation are important. We certainly must affirm both.

But which must conform to which?

Do we require our doctrines to conform to our living, ongoing relation to God in Christ, as I believe the Bible mandates? Or do we require our ongoing relation to Christ to conform to doctrines— that is, to doctrines which (in that case) must be based, partly if not entirely, on some foundation *other* than Christ and our living relation to Him (1 Cor. 3:11)?

Let me state another caveat. I am not playing "relation to Christ" against "biblical teaching." Quite to the contrary I am asking, "What does the Bible teach?" Or, in case the Bible does not want its way of dealing with us to be viewed purely as "teaching us things," I am asking, "What does the Bible most centrally *press upon* us, or *get across* to us, or what is it like when the Bible really *has its way* with us?"

The answer is that when the Bible really has its way with us, though we will find ourselves believing biblical doctrines, we will not be *primarily* believing biblical doctrines. Primarily we will be believing in Christ. The Bible never says, "Believe in the doctrine of the incarnation and you will be saved." It says "Believe in the Lord Jesus Christ and you will be saved" (Acts 16:31, NIV).

To put this provocatively: We do not believe in doctrines. We believe *through* them, and *in terms* of them, *in* Jesus Christ.

The Heart of the Bible

This point may be clearest in the Gospel of John. The great New Testament scholar C. H. Dodd points out that John came up with a characteristic emphasis upon one way of talking when he spoke about believing in Christ.[5] John found that he had a problem with the usual Greek phrase for "believing." The usual Greek expression, Dodd explains, almost "inevitably connoted simple credence, in the sense of an intellectual judgment." For example, it connoted that we believe (or judge) that this or that doctrine is true.

John came up with his characteristic emphasis because he wanted to bring out "the moral element of personal trust or reliance" (Dodd's phrase), as distinguished from intellectual belief. John wanted to continue the emphasis on personal trust that was clear in Hebrew and Aramaic, an emphasis that was also "integral to the primitive Christian conception of faith in Christ."[6]

This sense of personal trust is always present when John speaks of believing in Christ. For example, it is present and prominent when Jesus says, "Trust in God; trust also in me" (14:1, NIV). But though it is present, it is not always uppermost. John often uses his characteristic expression in such a way, Dodd says, that it makes this fact clear: Our believing in Christ also means we recognize and accept "the claim of Jesus to be the revelation of God."[7]

But note. Even in that case—even when we are believing the doctrine *that* Jesus is God's revelation—we are still face to face with our Lord. We are still in a personal relationship with him. The reason is that we are responding in faith to a claim that *Jesus Himself* is making.[8] Our situation is basically the same as Thomas's when he encounters the resurrected and ascended Jesus and exclaims, "My Lord and my God!" (John 20:28, NIV; see v. 17).

Thus the Gospel of John, even when it teaches us a doctrine, keeps us in a face-to-face, personal relationship with Christ. John will not let us "turn to one side" away from our Lord, so that we could merely believe this or that doctrine *about* Him as though He were not there confronting us all the time. For He is there. Always. That is precisely the point of the rich teaching that we are in Him, and He in us (John 14—17).

Though some parts of the New Testament are not as clear on this point as John, Paul agrees with John.[9] And in the other Gospels, people respond directly to Jesus and follow Him in personal trust and obedience. And that pertains to later times, too, when Jesus was no longer on earth, for these Gospels have the uncanny power to confront us directly with Jesus now, years later. In fact, Matthew is explicit and emphatic on precisely that point. "I am with you always," says the risen Lord; and earlier Jesus says, "For where two or three come together in my name, there am I with them" (Matt. 28:20, RSV; 18:20, NIV). The underlying issue here is why the New Testament was written. John's answer is not wrong for any of the books. They were written that we might enter into believing, ongoing relation with Christ, and in that way have life in Jesus' name (John 20:31).

These thoughts bring us about as close to the heart of the Bible as we can get. And the implication is clear. Doctrine is to conform to our ongoing relation to God in Christ, not the other way around, because the whole purpose of biblical doctrine is to bring about that living relationship.

I say again, however, that there is important doctrinal content in biblical revelation. When we state it, we may go hurtfully astray, or we may be nourishingly adequate. But that does not change the fact that the test of right doctrine, or "orthodoxy," is the question, Does it render our ongoing relation to Christ in such a way that this relationship flourishes in us and reproduces itself in others?

I conclude that God's revelation in the Bible is not basically a matter of doctrinal truths so that, in the first instance, we are to believe them. Rather, God in the first place reveals *Himself* to us in

Christ, encountering us and offering us the chance in Christ to participate in His life and relate to Him now and eternally.[10] If we reverse that priority, or even put doctrine and relation on a par, we are not letting the Bible have its way with us. Rather, we are resisting the Bible's authority in a way that has profound, far-reaching consequences, as we shall see.

Are Baptists Pietists or Scholastics?

This first feature of our new biblical land is a very Baptist feature and, with qualifications, it is a very pietist feature as well. Clark Pinnock, who knows us well, says it well: "It seems to me that 98% of Southern Baptists are simple biblicists, *pietists rather than doctrinalists* in their orientation, what Mark Noll calls the Baptist way of inerrancy."[11]

The Bible gives strong support to the things Pietism emphasizes, that is, our close personal involvement with Jesus in Bible reading, prayer, Christian fellowship, and so on. Further, I believe we should continue to emphasize and luxuriate in that kind of religion.

More needs to be said, however. In the Pietist emphasis, the stress falls upon the way Christ enters into our personal life story. But the Bible is clear that God wants us to enter into His story, too—into the huge story of His dealing with the world.[12] We are to be caught up in the awesome, overarching drama of God's love affair with His world (John 3:16-17; 2 Cor. 5:19; Hos. 2:11).

I have tried to take account of this in the language I have used. I have not said the central thing in biblical revelation is our "inner experience with Christ." That might be Pietism and nothing more. Instead, I have said the central thing is our "ongoing relation to God in Christ." That affirms the Pietist elements, but it is also intended to play up the way we are involved in the overarching drama of God's dealings with the world.

In chapter 1, Dockery speaks of what I have just called the overarching drama of God's larger story. Dockery says,

Central to Scripture is the unifying history of God's redeeming words and acts, of which the life and work of Jesus Christ serve as the ultimate focus.... (p. 21)

Jesus Christ binds and unites together everything in Scripture—

beginning and end, creation and redemption, humanity, the fall, history, and the future. If this overriding unity is neglected, Scripture can become denatured. . . . (pp. 21-22)

That breathtaking vista takes us beyond Pietism while, at the same time, it is able to affirm everything Pietism affirms.

David Kelsey gives a succinct account of the way Pietism arose. First came the massive doctrinal systems of Protestant scholasticism in the generations after Luther and Calvin. Then, in the late 1600s, Pietism appeared as a reaction against this "high intellectualism." The reason for the reaction, Kelsey explains, is that, for scholasticism, "*personal trust* is understood to depend on faith . . . [in the sense of] *intellectual assent* to the truth of certain theoretical doctrines revealed by Scripture." Priests turned that around.[13]

Much of today's evangelicalism is the intellectual heir of Protestant scholasticism. What should we say, then, of the way some Southern Baptists have taken a strong interest in evangelicalism, including non-Baptist evangelicalism? I believe we should learn to talk about *two kinds* of evangelicals. We should prefer "non-scholastic evangelicals" without disparaging anything we may be able to learn from the often well-educated "scholastic evangelicals."

J. Gresham Machen as an Intellectual Father of Fundamentalism

One person who could be called a scholastic evangelical is the great Presbyterian scholar of old Princeton Seminary, J. Gresham Machen (1881-1937). In this section, I discuss Machen's small book of 1923, *Christianity and Liberalism*.[14] My purpose is to make it clear that when I speak later of "fundamentalism," I am not dealing in cheap stereotypes, and I am not using the word as a term of abuse.

I must also be fair to Machen. He is more than an intellectual father of fundamentalism. But he *is* a "fundamentalist father." And that is the respect in which I deal with him here. In particular, I deal with him as the author of his 1923 classic.

Fundamentalists recognize Machen's book as the "Fundamentalist Manifesto." They say it "represents the best scholarship of the day against Modernism,'' and that it is ''the classic treatise on conservative Christianity and its antithesis, Liberalism.''[15]

Machen is especially pertinent to our current impasse because there is a clear divide between his outlook and the outlook of E. Y. Mullins of The Southern Baptist Theological Seminary and W. T. Conner of Southwestern Baptist Theological Seminary, the leading and most representative Southern Baptist theologians of the 1900-to-1950 period.[16] Mullins's 1924 book, *Christianity at the Cross Roads,* is a counterfundamentalist book[17] that contrasts sharply with Machen's book, though the two men respected each other's Christianity.[18]

One of the most apt ways to state what has happened in the SBC since 1979 is to say that our ascendant fundamental-conservatives are going back to the 1920s and 1930s and siding with Machen (and sometimes with J. Frank Norris) rather than siding with Mullins and Conner.

That is an extremely important switch. A generally Mullins-Conner kind of theology has undergirded SBC institutions right up into the 1980s, cooperation-based and relatively inclusive as these institutions have been. In 1962, for example, near the height of the Ralph Elliott controversy, Herschel Hobbs made an appeal for unity and diversity in his SBC presidential address. The logic of that address turns upon ideas and distinctions that Hobbs derived from Mullins's book, *Christianity at the Cross Roads.*[19]

In his chapter on doctrine, Machen argues as follows. If we had been in Jesus' vicinity during His earthly ministry, we could have had a personal relation to Him. We could have trusted Him. ''But alas,'' Machen writes, ''we are not with him, and the way is far. How shall we come into His presence?''[20]

Machen continues, ''Trust involves a personal relation between the one who trusts and him in whom the trust is reposed.'' And how can this be brought about? ''[I]n this case,'' Machen continues, ''the personal relation is set up by the blessed theology of the Cross.''[21] The latter statement accurately epitomizes Machen's line of argument through this entire context.[22]

We note carefully. Because our Lord is now far away (!), *doctrine* must overcome the gap. Doctrine is certainly important, as I have urged. But as our biblical study has made clear, it is not doctrines that are ''there'' for us to put our weight on. We rest our weight on Christ. Astonishingly, that is missing in Machen's classic 1923 discussion.[23]

Contrast a Baptist, E. Y. Mullins. In his antifundamentalist (and antiliberal) book of 1924, Mullins says religion is "a personal relation of fellowship between God and man."[24] Elsewhere Mullins says the Bible should be regarded "as a living thing, like an organism, full of life and power, instinct with the life of the God of human experience."[25]

Why didn't Machen talk like that? True, he was neither a Baptist nor a typical Pietist. But there is something else. In a sense that I will explain later, Machen was deaf to the "symphonic pluralism" of the New Testament. He tended to read the New Testament as all of one piece *as a system of doctrine*. Thus he failed to hear the distinctive voices of Acts, John, and Paul.

It is in Acts, we may recall, that we read of Christ's bodily ascension into heaven. That is a clue. In Acts, the distance between heaven above and earth beneath has *separating* significance. That distance separates us on earth from Christ in heaven.

In John and Paul, however (neither of whom recounts Jesus' bodily ascension), that is not the way Christ's exaltation to His Father is understood. John and Paul do not suggest that, in His ascension, Christ *left* us. They routinely speak of Christ as here, among us, with us. He is in us, and we are in Him.

Furthermore, in John the Spirit wells up within us like a refreshing spring of water (John 7:37-39; 4:13-14), whereas in Acts the Spirit is poured out and falls upon us from above (Acts 2:2-3, 33; 10:44). Apparently it falls "from a distance," because, in Acts, Christ is in heaven, at the right hand of God, until He comes again (Acts 1:3, 7, 11; 3:21).

The New Testament broadcasts in stereo, if not in quadriphonic. Acts is on one channel, Paul and John on another, and so on. Any effort to squeeze all that into a doctrinal system that our minds can master will flatten everything into monaural transmission. And, as Machen demonstrates, it also tunes out the near and living Christ.

Is Doctrine Master or Servant?

This leads me to the first of the "old habits" I want to discuss. It is the habit of making doctrines equal or superior to our ongoing, "quadriphonic" relation to God in Christ.[26] I sincerely believe that if we could break this habit, that would do more than any other single thing to get us beyond our impasse.

Let me explain. Your doctrines and my doctrines may differ at some significant point, perhaps in our doctrine of Scripture. Even so, we can share leadership in missions, evangelism, and theological education *if* the crucial question (other than ready competence) is whether you and I are mutually related to Jesus Christ as Savior and Lord, living faithfully in Him and for Him.

In fact, we not only can share leadership; if the Bible tells us to keep our relation to Christ primary over doctrines, then the Bible *obligates* us to share leadership.

Or it probably obligates us in that way. My doctrines may be confused enough that, as a practical matter, they do not orient me effectively for the task at hand. Or your doctrines and mine may be so diverse that we cannot work together, practically speaking.

But notice where that puts the question. It is the practical question of putting into effect our relation to Christ, and our relation to each other in Christ. If you and I are both Baptists, mutually sharing in Christ, then we are obligated to see whether, at the practical level, we can share leadership. It would be scripturally disobedient to turn that upside down, put doctrine on top and say, "I see doctrinal differences here. That ends it. There can be no practical venture toward shared leadership."

As this makes clear, getting doctrines right is not an end in itself. Though I think Mohler would agree with that statement, I wonder whether he weighs it heavily enough. If he did, I doubt that he would have been quite so gloomy about the state of doctrinal teaching in the SBC. Granted, we should have done better. But when Mohler and others have leisure to *document* the supposed decline in teaching doctrines, they should ask this question: Did the SBC produce fewer doctrinal studies since 1945 because the SBC produced and promoted more biblical studies?

If that turned out to be the case, it would be consistent with the kind of people we are. For us, and for the Bible, too (as I believe I have shown), our formulated doctrines are servants, not masters. It is their job to serve our Lord and us by helping us do more important things, such as to live more fully in Christ and for Him, or to introduce someone to Him, or to understand the Bible better, or to preach well, or to be an effective missionary.

Doctrine is not superior to those things. It is not even on a par. Thus it should not be the master.

Fundamentalism and Our Impasse

Both Dockery and Mohler say something about the post-Second World War history that lies behind our present impasse. Though I agree that, during those years, Southern Baptists were not adequately schooled in their convictions, I see the main problem at a point they do not mention. I see the most serious omission in the decades after 1945 in this way: SBC churches were taking in people willy-nilly without instructing, training, and forming them *in the distinctive features of Baptist faith,* including the Baptist principles I listed; and without exposing them to informed biblical study.[27]

So a void was left. And what filled that void as thousands failed to learn their Baptist ABC's? The largest and most dynamic thing appears to have been fundamentalist religion. Thus the ground was prepared for our recent controversy and our current impasse.

As I see it, our impasse is more or less equivalent to the fact that a fundamentalist spirit is ascendant in the denomination. People who try to do church work with fundamentalists find they are at a perpetual impasse so long as they do not subscribe fully to some prescribed creed, *and* so long as they do not agree that the creed shall be used as a litmus test to exclude people from leadership.

Fundamentalism and Fear

I am using the term "fundamentalism" in the narrower sense that has been common since the 1950s, a sense in which it refers to a recent movement, one that took its distinctive shape at the end of World War I.[28] Fundamentalists are North American Protestants who are very conservative theologically and socially, but are distinguished *from other conservatives* by a certain spirit. It is a spirit that is militant or fighting, intolerant, often separatist, and sometimes cantankerous if not mean as well.[29]

Underlying these traits there appears to be a deep-seated fear, a fear that shows itself in something we might call a "trauma-reaction syndrome." The "trauma" combines a sense of being threatened by modern trends (except for modern technology) with a feeling that key convictions of Christianity are being attacked.

In response to these perceived threats, there is a self-protective recoil. That is the "reaction." Of course, it is natural and wholesome for religious groups to preserve and protect their convictions. The question is how they do it. I shall describe the typically fundamentalist reaction in a moment.

Before I do that, I should say that I have derived the idea of a trauma-reaction syndrome in considerable measure from George Marsden, the premier historian of American fundamentalism.[30] He does not state it, and might not like the term, but in my judgment he talks about it in several places. For example, after noting certain developments early in this century, Marsden continues:

> *In reaction,* the new fundamentalist coalition emerged. . . . In the face of the modernist *threat* to undermine the fundamentals of evangelical faith, a threat magnified by the accompanying cultural revolution, much of surviving evangelicalism took on *a fundamentalist tone.* The perennially upbeat mood of the nineteenth-century movement was now tempered by accents of *fear and negativism.*[31]

Fundamentalist Doctrines: Is There a Non-fundamentalist Inerrancy?

I now want to deal with the "reaction" part of the trauma-reaction syndrome. In that reaction, certain convictions are specified as essentials; they are defined in a heightened, combative way; and these doctrines, which may or may not have been central before, now preempt much of the center of ongoing fundamentalist religion.

When convictions that were not central are made central, a religion is changed. Thus fundamentalism is new.[32] And when convictions are defined in a heightened, combative way, they are changed.

The most basic example is probably the "heightened supernaturalism" of fundamentalism.[33] Partly because this extreme kind of supernaturalism draws disproportionately from the apocalyptic parts of the Bible, it departs from the poised, balanced supernaturalism of the Bible's overall testimony to God's mighty acts.[34]

And the effects ramify. For example, the historic Christian doctrine of incarnation affirms something—a union of divine and human—that extreme supernaturalism can hardly conceive, much less believe. The subbiblical supernaturalism of fundamentalists almost inevitably pushes them into Apollinarianism, Nestorianism, Monophysitism, or Docetism. They want to be orthodox. But their fundamentalism makes it almost impossible.

Is biblical inerrancy another example? Is it a heightened, combative redefinition of the historic Christian confidence in the trustworthy truthfulness of the Bible? Without question, inerrancy originated in that way, that is, as part of the trauma-reaction syndrome I have described. The negative character of the word, which is only some 150 years old,[35] tells us as much.

But is a "nonfundamentalist inerrancy" possible? If inerrancy is put forth *with sufficient humility,* with the word qualified so that it is recognized as the commanding symbol it is (somewhat as Dockery and the 1978 Chicago statement qualify the term), and if the proviso is included that acknowledging the complex concept is enough, and using the word to identify oneself is not required—then I might on those conditions acknowledge it, if that would enable us fully and mutually to accept one another's leadership.

The "Symphonic Pluralism" of Scripture

I move now to a second feature of the new ground that beckons us. It is the fact that people who occupy that new land can hear the full chorus of voices in the Bible without trying to make them all sing the same part.

An example is Herman Ridderbos, the Dutch evangelical from whom Dockery takes some of his ideas in chapter 1. Ridderbos deals sensitively with what he calls the "pluriformity of interpretation of salvation in Scripture," which should not disappoint us, he indicates, but astonish us "with the manifold grace of God."[36]

In this connection I like to speak of the "symphonic pluralism" of the biblical witness. Of course I am not using "pluralism" to refer to the kinds of things Mohler rightly warns us about (pp. 106-7). Furthermore, I am talking about "symphonic" pluralism, a way of speaking that draws attention to the concert of the Bible as a whole, and to the harmony of its parts.

Even with the adjective "symphonic" attached, however, there may be some shock value when this noun is applied to the Bible. If so, this way of speaking is intended to be like the sudden loud chords in Haydn's *Surprise Symphony*. The purpose is to jar us and wake us up, repeatedly, in order that we will not miss what is in front of us, namely, the fact that the Bible has a rich and many-voiced diversity as well as a powerful, undergirding unity.

What kind of diversity am I talking about? To speak only of the New Testament, we have already seen the difference in the way Christ's exaltation to the Father and the coming of the Spirit are understood. In addition, there are things in the New Testament that seem to lead to high Calvinism and things that do not seem to lead in that direction. There are charismatic gifts there. There are apparent reasons for women in ministry, and there are apparent reasons against women in ministry. There are intimations of diverse eschatological views. There are robust differences between Paul and James concerning justification by faith. And with respect to Christology, or the doctrine of Christ, there are healthy differences between Luke and Acts on the one hand, and Paul and John on the other hand.[37]

This taste of the Bible's symphonic pluralism makes it clear how this second feature of the new biblical land reinforces the first. The magnificent variety of Scripture tells us almost in so many words that we must let relation be primary over doctrine. It tells us we are bound to be frustrated if we try to locate the unity of Scripture at the level of a doctrinal system.

That does not mean the Bible lacks unity, of course. It only means we should look for it where the Bible puts it, namely, in the fact that God seeks, through a history of saving acts that centers in Jesus Christ, to relate us to Himself, now and eternally.

The Bible will forever frighten us if we try to tame its manifoldness in an ironclad system. But if we yield to it, if we trust ourselves to the living relation it offers us in Christ, then the angels sing, and we hear the harmony of the whole.

More Narrow Than the Bible: The Irony of Fundamentalist Exclusivism

This leads directly to the second "old habit" we must outgrow if we are to escape our wilderness impasse and advance to the land of promise. I refer to our fundamentalist habit of excluding people because, supposedly, they are not true to the Bible.

This habit is heavy with irony. If we knew the Bible, if we were aware of its majestic symphony, we would see that many of the people we exclude have a basis in the Bible for the way they confess Christ and for the way they view the Bible. And we would also see that *we* are the ones who are disobedient to Scripture, because we will not embrace the diversity God put in the Bible.

What has gone wrong? Somewhere along the way, we or our teachers have cut the Bible down in size so that it fits some neat bundle of teachings we have put together. Next we assume, and this is the fatal step, that the New Testament affirms nothing broader than our set of ideas. Then we use our cut-down Bible to cut people down. The mighty sword of the Spirit has become a dagger of division.

But it is our fundamentalism that has cut the Bible down to dagger size. If we followed the real Bible instead of the cut-down Bible, we would realize that we have fellowship in Christ with a lot of people we thought were unworthy to share leadership with us.

Using "Word of God" in Its Primary Biblical Sense

A third characteristic of the new biblical land I am trying to describe is the fact that the people who live there speak as often of the "Word of God" in the Bible's primary sense (which is the word being delivered "live") as they speak of the "Word of God" in the Bible's secondary sense (which is the Bible).

The New Testament uses the following (and cognate) expressions fairly frequently: "the word of God," "the word of the Lord," "God's word" and "the word."

Traditional Bible believers assume that these expressions routinely refer to the Bible. They are mistaken. Usually the New Testament is referring to something distinct from itself. Most often it is talking about God's word being delivered "live" to this or that person or group, on this or that occasion.

John Reumann summarizes the New Testament evidence as follows:

'the word (of God, or of the Lord)' refers, in order of frequency of reference, to (1) a message, generally of good news, from God and about him, at work in his people Israel, in Jesus Christ, and in his church; (2) Jesus Christ himself; and (3) scripture (the Hebrew writings, the emerging Christian books of the canon).[38]

In July 1990, Paige Patterson agreed that the first meaning is the New Testament's usual one.[39] That is to be welcomed.

Because Reumann's first sense is used most often in the New Testament (and because of some things I say later about the Bible's inspiration), I believe we must recognize this as the primary biblical sense of "Word of God" for Christians.

The Book of Acts is a key example. It is not talking about the Bible but about the witness to Jesus, or the preaching about Jesus, when it says "the word of God increased," or "the word of God grew and multiplied," or "the word of the Lord grew and prevailed mightily" (6:7, 12:24, 19:20, RSV; cf. 1:8; 4:31, 33; 6:2).

Similarly, 1 Peter says, "You have been born anew, . . . through the living and abiding word of God." The author explains: "That word is the good news which was preached to you" (1:23, 25, RSV).

And in Hebrews, chapter 4, we read the following:

The word of God is living and active, sharper than any two-edged sword, piercing to the division of soul and spirit, of joints and marrow, and discerning the thoughts and intentions of the heart. And before him no creature is hidden, but all are open and laid bare to the eyes of him with whom we have to do (Heb. 4:12-13, RSV).

What is impressive here is that the idea of "the word of God" involves "God speaking," that is, "God actually present" in such a personal way that He peers into human hearts.

Clearly "word of God" in this primary sense is not thought of as something split off and separate from God, such as a book we could hold in our hands or place upon a table. Instead, God is *there,* speaking live with people through words that are sounding in the voice of a spontaneous human agent, such as an apostle.

This fact—the "thereness" of the God who now speaks—gives an enormous boost to the idea that, in Scripture, God's *relating* to us is primary over the doctrines involved in what is going on.

Making the Word of God of No Effect
Through Our Tradition

By contrast with the New Testament usage, Baptists and others have an almost ironclad tradition. It is the third "bad habit" on my list. When we say "Word of God," we mean the Bible, period. We sometimes drill this into people so continuously that they are made virtually deaf to what the New Testament usually means by that expression.[40] Jesus could well say to us, as He did to the Pharisees, "Thus you nullify the word of God by your tradition" (Mark 7:13, NIV).

The text I have just quoted is interesting, however. It is one of the few places where the New Testament speaks of *Scripture* as the "word of God." Which is to say: There is biblical warrant for us to say the Bible is the Word of God.

I am not trying to undo that way of speaking, however. I speak that way myself; I do so with conviction; and I think we should keep it up. My point is that we are using the *secondary* sense of "Word of God" when we talk like that. My plea is that we give the primary sense equal time so we don't suffocate it.

It is not a very good commendation for any group that claims to have a correct view of the Bible when its way of using the Bible routinely obscures something important. That, however, is what some of our conservative evangelical tradition does. In place after place, where we see or hear the expression "Word of God" in the New Testament, this tradition stifles the main reference the text has in mind.[41]

By sharp contrast with our bookish religion, New Testament religion takes place overwhelmingly within the sphere of dynamic interpersonal relationships (including God's relation to us), a sphere in which the written word rarely has a direct role to play.

We have become aware in recent years that the New Testament is a "putting to writing" of testimony, exhortation, and instruction that has its home in *oral-aural transactions*. New Testament faith is an oral faith. The books were written not for readers but for hearers. In most instances, they were written to be read by a reader to a community who were to receive it by ear. Even the solitary reader got it by ear as he read to himself or herself, never silently.[42]

Is this whole thing not a scholar's quibble, however? Do we not have, written down, the *things the apostles and others said* as they delivered God's Word—live—in New Testament times?

Yes, we do. We have what was said. But by what right do we decide that "what was said" is all we care about, and "God's now saying it" doesn't matter? We cannot get that idea from the New Testament.

I think I know where we got the idea, however. Our antibiblical tradition makes perfect sense if we have determined ahead of time, no matter what the Bible says, that *doctrine* is the center of everything. In that case, all we need is "what was said." That gives us the doctrine.

But if God's *relating to us in Christ* is the center of biblical revelation, then we need something else. We need God really there, saying it, relating to us while He speaks. That is precisely what the New Testament gives us. Or that is what the New Testament *will* give us, if we do not muffle it with a less-than-biblical tradition.

Inspiration in the New Testament Sense, Or Bookish Religion?

I turn to a fourth characteristic of the new land. In that land people embrace both halves of the New Testament idea of inspiration, both the "here-and-now" part and the "there-and-then" part. They believe that the same Spirit who, long ago, "inspired" the Bible to be written, also "breathes into" or "in-spires" the Scripture now. The Spirit is present in it and speaks through it.

Consider the main biblical statement on inspiration, 2 Timothy 3:16. The *King James Version* reads, "All scripture is given by inspiration of God." The *New International Version* translates better: "All Scripture is God-breathed."

The exegesis of this statement that I offer was suggested to me by Clark Pinnock,[43] but Pinnock may have gotten it from Karl Barth. In addition, as Barth notes, the main insights are in Luther and Calvin, though they were lost in the next century.[44]

We first note that the 2 Timothy context is drenched with expression about how Scripture is powerful unto salvation and the like. We must read the statement that all Scripture is inspired or God-breathed in keeping with that insistent context.

If we do, it becomes clear that the central point is not that in the past the Spirit caused the Bible to be written. That point is made, true; but the central point is that the mark of Scripture is that it is full of the Spirit *here and now.* The reason the Bible has the power to change our lives in the profound ways we hear about in this context is that God's breath or Spirit is in it.

We should feel confident in reading 2 Timothy in this non-bookish, spiritual way because of what Paul says in 2 Corinthians 3.[45] Paul makes at least five points in that short chapter: (i) The Bible as words written in a book kills us and condemns us. (ii) The Spirit, not the letter, gives life. (iii) The Spirit and the Lord Jesus Christ are one and the same. (iv) "Where the Spirit of the Lord is, there is freedom" (v. 17, NIV). And (v) when we turn to the Lord, the veil over Scripture is removed and we are related to the Lord— not to a book but to our living Lord.[46]

Paul is warning us in these points against the fourth bad habit in my list, "bookish religion," or the habit of fixing on the Bible as a written text and making the book decisive as a book rather than meeting the living God *in* the text. Paul is telling us not to do that, but to be open to the Spirit who speaks in Scripture, and to *turn to the Lord* who meets us there.

Strikingly similar is Jesus' warning to certain hostile Jews in John: "You search the scriptures, because you think that in them you have eternal life; and it is they that bear witness to me; yet you refuse to come to me that you may have life" (John 5:39-40, RSV).

To conclude this section: The New Testament's persistent emphasis upon the fact that Scripture is where we meet and hear the Spirit is one more confirmation of my first point, namely, that the central thing in biblical religion is not doctrine but God relating to us—in this case God the Spirit and Christ the Spirit.

Let me append two clarifying points. First, my stress on Spirit religion does not mean I want to woo the believer away from the canonical books. Quite to the contrary, my point is that those books are "God-breathed." They are where we *meet* the Spirit. I believe God uniquely binds Himself, in the ongoing work of His Spirit, to these sixty-six books.

And second, there is an important sense in which I am urging that we be very bookish indeed. I am urging that we "go by the book," the Bible. But I am pointing out that if we do that, the book itself makes us alive to the Spirit. The book itself keeps us away from bookish religion—which is our fourth "bad habit."

Authority Needs Criticism

The fifth feature of our new land is that people who live there see this fact clearly: Without the uncompromising use of critical scholarship, the Bible cannot be fully authoritative for any Christian group today. Thus biblical authority does not merely permit, but requires the use of biblical criticism. Plenary authority demands uncompromising, undiluted criticism.

The logic of this point is so simple I was able in 1985 to explain it to an angry young man who was waiting to speak at a microphone during the Dallas SBC meeting. He wanted to ask a seminary president why SBC seminaries teach biblical criticism.

I asked the young man, "What would you say about a scholar's effort to learn all he can about how God gave us the Bible through its human authors? Should we hear about that in our seminaries?"

"Yes," the young man answered.

"Well," I followed up, "that is what biblical criticism is. It is the effort to find out as best we can how God gave us the Bible in the first place, through the various human authors God used."

It is true that, in this conversation, I was explaining how someone who believes *God brought the Bible into being* will employ historical criticism. I was speaking of the "believing criticism" that influential evangelicals such as Mark Noll recommend.[47]

But the fact that we believe does not require us to restrict the work of the critic, or to tell the scholar what conclusions to reach. Exactly the opposite! If we really believe God has given us this book, we must leave the scholar who investigates it free to help us understand it, and how it came into being, humanly speaking. If we tell the researcher ahead of time what conclusions to reach, we are prescribing how God must have done it rather than being open to how God did it. We don't set standards for God!

As a footnote, I express a reservation about one thing in Walter Harrelson's immensely valuable, moving chapter. His Aunt Zora did employ historical criticism. It told her that God's command to commit genocide and kill babies is not part of the Old Testament's historically controlling, central understanding of His character. But

Aunt Zora moved to a theological judgment, not a historical conclusion, when she said God could not have said that (pp. 40-41).

Imprisoning the Bible in a Cocoon

One reason critical approaches are so important for biblical authority is that every religious group builds a cocoon around the Bible. The cocoon is what the people in that group have made of the Bible in their religious life. Their cocoon is their preconceptions about the Bible, their interpretations of it, and their favorite selections from it.

Of course, a certain amount of that sort of thing is inevitable. But in many cases it is not the full truth when people in this or that Christian group say the Bible is their authority. Their authority is not the Bible. Their authority is what they have made out of the Bible. Their authority is their cocoon. Making this cocoon our authority is the fifth bad habit that would hold us in the wilderness.

If the Bible is to break free from that—and it must break free, again and again, if biblical authority is not to be a farce—critical scholarship will do much of the liberating work. Biblical criticism is our best tool for cutting through the cocoon and getting back to what the Bible is, and what the Bible means, as God gave it to us. (I am not leaving the Spirit out. The Holy Spirit is not a tool.)

This does not mean that every ordinary Christian must directly use biblical criticism, though many should. I am speaking corporately of what any Christian group must do. The scholars do their work, and the results must be packaged and disseminated to the people.

An important qualification is necessary at this point. Critical study is necessary, but it is not sufficient. Such things as theological interpretation are necessary *along with* criticism—historical, literary, and other kinds of criticism. And, more important by far, critical study can never take the place of being open to the Spirit and listening to what the Spirit has to say in the text.

But we must not forget that denominations are like silkworms. They are busy cocoon-makers. If solid biblical study is not being regularly disseminated throughout a denomination, its leaders and followers will settle into exotic or unloving notions of the Bible. And it then becomes a very bad joke indeed when they claim that the Bible is their authority.

Southern Baptists Flirting with Idolatry

The situation I have just described is to be found in the Southern Baptist Convention. Only it is worse. We do not merely have a bad joke. We also have something bordering on idolatry. I refer in particular, though not exclusively, to the way certain parts of the 1987 Peace Committee Report are now being used.

In that report, four interpretations of the Bible are identified, interpretations that are widespread among Southern Baptists. That is Southern Baptists' cocoon, of course. Or it is part of our cocoon, anyway. It is part of what we make of the Bible.

But now this cocoon, rather than simply the Bible, is to be our authority. Those who do not agree with it are not to exercise any leadership in the denomination, though their money is welcome.

Why does this border on idolatry? The Bible is the Word of God. But my interpretation of the Bible is not the Word of God, and neither is yours. If I call you to task and tell you that you must subject yourself to what I have made of the Bible as though it were the Word of God itself, that is a clear violation of the Second Commandment. It means I am telling you that you must bow down and subject yourself to *something I have made* as though it were absolute, as though it were the very Word of God.

In an exchange of papers at the University of Richmond in July 1990, Paige Patterson responded to this point by stating that it is not idolatry when a denominational group insists upon certain doctrines. He is right. It may or may not be creedalism, but it is not idolatry.

But that is not what I was talking about. At least in some key instances, we are not just being told we have to accept one more doctrine in a list of doctrines. We are being told what the Word of God itself *is*. The voice of God Himself is being constructed for us, after a certain image, and we are being told that we must bow down and give consent to that as the very Word of God.

In order to understand this, we have to reflect on what it means to accept the authority of the Bible in the only way we should accept it as mature Christians, namely, as God's Word—as God's Word in the Bible's senses of that term.[48]

Accepting biblical authority in that way is not a question of whether I accept this or that doctrine about Scripture. It is a question whether I believe God is addressing me there. It is a question whether I am ready to hear in these texts the speech of the Holy One who holds the destiny of all things in His hand. It is a question whether I agree that God is confronting me here, in Scripture, with that with which I must deal, in life and in death.

If Southern Baptists are simply being told that we must accept one more doctrine among others, whether that doctrine squares with the Bible or not, that is creedalism, not idolatry.

But if those who intend to enforce the Peace Committee Report understand what it means to accept "the Bible as God's Word" as authority, they are promoting idolatry as surely as Jezebel was.

Perhaps the most charitable conclusion is that most or all of the enforcers of the report are not promoting idolatry. They just do not know what it means to accept the Bible both as God's word and as our authority. They only know how to promulgate and enforce certain doctrines or theories *about* the Bible.

Conforming to the Humility of Scripture

People who are rigidly certain and dogmatic about religious truth may claim to be "very biblical." But they cannot be biblical, because that kind of self-certainty is not characteristic of the biblical witnesses overall. Appropriate humility is the sixth feature of the new biblical land we can see from afar.

Granted, some parts of the Bible are rather self-assured. But shall we make only them our canon? That is what fundamentalism does. It barricades itself within its *canon within the canon*.

By contrast, if we let the Bible as a whole have its way with us, we will come to terms with the fact that the various parts of the Bible *differ in their degrees of self-assuredness*.

Consider first the Old Testament. I think of Jeremiah's probing, self-correcting meditations (Jer. 11:18-23; 12:1-6; 15:10-21; 17:14-18; 18:18-23; 20:7-12, 14:18). I think also of Jeremiah's saying, according to Harrelson, that we can be sure God has spoken to a prophet if the prophet speaks faithfully, that is, if the prophet's word is *discussable* and stands up;[49] I think of the Book of Proverbs, which is at numerous points so very open to being instructed from ordinary mundane experience, and I think of the groping, questioning, uncertain spirit in which virtually all of the Book of Ecclesiastes proceeds.

Turning to the New Testament, I think of the way Paul corrects himself and indicates that he made a mistake when he said how many people he had baptized in Corinth (1 Cor. 1:14-16), and I think of the tentativeness with which Paul expresses some of his judgments in chapter 7 of 1 Corinthians.

And I think, finally, of the prologue to the Gospel of Luke (1:1-4). Luke tells his readers he had followed the standard procedures for research and the existing conventions for writing historical narrative as they prevailed in pagan antiquity.

The cumulative weight of this and other evidence is overwhelming. We spurn the Bible's authority and refuse to let it have its way with us if we insist on being more dogmatic and self-assured than it is.

John Newport's chapter, extremely valuable throughout, exploded into special life for me when he came to the contributions of recent literary approaches to the Bible. Especially pertinent here is the idea that God "accommodates" to our capacities in communicating His truth to us in the Bible, as Calvin believed (p. 85). That insight could help some of us come closer to the humility of the Bible.

Is "Uptightness" Characteristic of the God of the Bible?

In order to present a last, seventh characteristic of our new biblical land, I should like to adopt the word *uptight* as a term of art and say that the God to whom we relate in the Bible is not uptight. By that I mean He does not have a legalistic mind-set and a meticulous, hyperscrupulous nature.

If the Bible is to be believed, God is far less uptight about some things than we are. If readers detect some irreverence in what I am saying, they are probably correct. But I hasten to explain that I got it from Jesus and Paul.

There was a nonconformity about Jesus that was breathtaking. He resolutely refused to be uptight about a lot of things the legalists of His day wanted Him to worry about.

In the parable of the prodigal son, the father abandons all dignity and *runs*—unheard of for a man of his age in that day—to embrace the despicably delinquent younger brother. And the older brother, the uptight fellow who punctiliously kept all the rules turns out to be the butt of the story (though the father loves him too, of course).

And consider the string of stories in Mark 2:1 to 3:6, especially Jesus' important saying, "The sabbath was made for humankind, and not humankind for the sabbath" (Mark 2:27, NRSV).

Allow me to paraphrase that. Jesus says, in paraphrase, "God gave the rule about the Sabbath in order to meet real human needs. Human beings were not created in order to jump through the hoop of a rule that has no relation to their needs or interests."

If we do not recognize that as humanism, we are not paying attention. Jesus was not a secular humanist, of course; but He was a humanist. And He thought His Father was a humanist, too.

So far as Paul is concerned, we have already seen the shocking things he says in 2 Corinthians 3. There Paul confronts the Scripture, the very Instruction or Law of God, and says it will kill us and condemn us if we do not turn from the letter of Scripture to the living Lord, the Spirit, who meets us there.

The fact that God is not uptight does not mean He is a picture of laid-back indifference, however. Far from it! God cares passionately. It is His will, stronger than death, to encounter us and to establish a *relation* with us, if we will have it so. "God *so* loved the world that he gave his only Son, that whoever believes in him . . . [might] have eternal life" (John 3:16, RSV).

People become like the God they worship. That suggests that there may be something wrong with fundamentalist religion, because fundamentalists tend to be uptight, and God is not. Something about their view of the Bible makes it hard for God—the real God who is not uptight—to get through to them.

Conclusion

Early on I said our impasse is more or less equivalent to the fundamentalist spirit that has taken control of the denomination. That may sound as though I have argued for freedom. In some ways I have; but I have mainly argued for authority—for the authority of the Bible, for letting it have its way with us.

My point is that the fundamentalism that creates our impasse not only divides us, it is resistant to Scripture in several ways. Let us review.

This kind of fundamentalism tends to muffle the New Testament so that the main meaning of "God's Word" is not noticed. It ignores the Spirit's inspiration of the Bible in the full New Testament sense. It promotes a bookish faith that is alien to New Testament religion. It hamstrings the critical scholarship that might force it to confront the Bible as God gave it. It flirts with idolatry as it holds up a cocoon and says that must be the Word of God for us. And it spins its doctrines in a soundproof room, where the symphonic grandeur of the Word of God cannot be heard.

Further, this kind of fundamentalism is at odds with the Pietist quality of Baptist life; it reverses a biblical priority by making our relation to Christ (which unites us) conform to formalized doctrines (which may divide us). Much narrower than the Bible itself, it denies leadership if not fellowship to people whose faith is also grounded in Scripture. By its teachings and its attitudes, it tells people that God is uptight, and thus derails the Bible in the very thing the Bible is after, namely, relating us to God, the real God.

And finally, because of a self-certainty that contradicts the humility of the Bible, the fundamentalism that generates our impasse usually refuses on principle to listen to such things as I say here.

Will that continue? Or will we break some of these old habits? There is a good land. It is not so far away. Maybe some of us will go over and occupy it together.

Notes

1. *Webster's Third New International Dictionary of the English Language* (Springfield, Mass.: G. & C. Merriam, 1961), 1132. *American Heritage Dictionary,* Second College Edition (Boston: Houghton Mifflin, 1982), 644.

2. See Robison B. James, ed., *The Unfettered Word* (Waco: Word, 1987), 139-41, 142-43.

3. Nancy T. Ammerman, *Baptist Battles: Social Change and Religious Conflict in the Southern Baptist Convention* (New Brunswick, N.J.: Rutgers University Press, 1990), 178-81.

4. Ammerman aptly says that the agenda tacitly followed by many denominational leaders from the 1960s into the early 1980s was "progressive," that it involved opening the denomination to new trends regarding race, biblical scholarship, women's ordination, etc., and that these leaders were "reluctant to hit the trail in open support" of that agenda when they were attacked. (Ammerman, 179). This might create the impression (though Ammerman indicates otherwise elsewhere) that the denomina-

tional policies followed were theologically vacuous accommodations to contemporary culture. To the contrary, some impressive theology was implicit and sometimes stated. I deal only with elements of it in this chapter.

5. *Pisteuein* followed by *eis* with the accusative rather than the dative.

6. C. H. Dodd, *The Interpretation of the Fourth Gospel* (Cambridge: Cambridge University Press, 1958), 183.

7. Ibid.

8. Here I move beyond Dodd, who fails to take account of the fact that in John it is Jesus who characteristically speaks the claims we are to believe (cf. Dodd, 183-84). By contrast, Bultmann sees this point clearly. (In fact, he overstates it.) He says, "In John believing Jesus or his words is believing in him, for proclaimer and proclaimed are the same[,] as the proclaimed himself meets us and speaks with us." R. Bultmann, *"pistis,"* in Gerhard Kittel and Gerhard Friedrich, eds., *Theological Dictionary of the New Testament,* translated and abridged in one volume by Geoffrey W. Bromiley (Grand Rapids: Eerdmans, 1985), 856.

9. Especially illuminating to me are Romans 4:5 and 2 Corinthians 5:17-19. For the whole question see Bultmann in *TDNT,* 853-57.

10. See Charles Talbert, "The Bible's Truth Is Relational," in James, ed., *The Unfettered Word,* 39-46.

11. Clark Pinnock, "What Is Biblical Inerrancy?" in Michael A. Smith, ed., *The Proceedings of the Conference on Biblical Inerrancy 1987* (Nashville: Broadman Press, 1987), 75, emphasis added.

12. The New Testament uses the term for "regeneration," *palingenesia,* twice. Titus 3:5 says God "saved us through the washing of rebirth [*palingenesias*] and renewal by the Holy Spirit" (NIV); and in Matt. 19:28 Jesus says, ". . . at the renewal of all things [*en te palingenesia*], when the Son of Man sits on his glorious throne, you who have followed me will also sit on twelve thrones" (NIV). The Titus passage tells how God becomes part of our personal story in our rebirth. But the Matthew passage makes it clear that this is the case because we are thereby enfolded within God's story, the story of His rebirthing His creation (cf. Rom. 8:22-23).

13. David H. Kelsey, "Protestant Attitudes Regarding Methods of Biblical Interpretation," in *Scripture in the Jewish and Christian Traditions,* ed. Frederick E. Greenspahn (Nashville: Abingdon, 1982), 153, Kelsey's emphasis altered.

14. J. Gresham Machen, *Christianity and Liberalism* (New York: Macmillan, 1923).

15. Jerry Falwell, ed., *The Fundamentalist Phenomenon,* with Ed Dobson and Ed Hinson (Garden City, N.Y.: Doubleday, 1981), 226, n. 14; 242, n. 32.

16. James Leo Garrett, "The Teaching of Recent Southern Baptist

Theologians on the Bible," in Michael A. Smith, ed., *Proceedings Of the Conference on Biblical Inerrancy, 1987*, 289, cf. 289-98.

17. William E. Ellis's study, *A Man of Books and a Man of the People* (Macon, Ga.: Mercer, 1985), shows Mullins as antifundamentalist and as a prototype of later moderate-conservative SBC leaders.

18. E. Y. Mullins, *Christianity at the Cross Roads* (Nashville: Sunday School Board of the SBC, 1924). See George Marsden, *Fundamentalism and American Culture* (New York: Oxford University Press, 1980), 216. My copy of Mullins's book is from the library of my late father, W. K. E. James, who studied under Mullins at Southern Seminary.

19. With Mullins, 26-38, compare Herschel H. Hobbs, "Presidential Address," *Annual of the Southern Baptist Convention 1962*, 82-83. Hobbs confirmed his indebtedness to Mullins in a letter to me of April 7, 1970.

20. Machen, *Christianity and Liberalism*, 43.

21. Ibid., 44.

22. Ibid., 40-44, 71-72.

23. Elsewhere Machen acknowledges the role of the Spirit, but in this fundamentalist classic, neither the Spirit nor the real Christ plays a role at this point. Machen, *Christianity and Liberalism*, 40-44, 71-72.

24. Mullins, *Christianity at the Cross Roads*, 51.

25. Mullins, *Freedom and Authority in Religion* (Philadelphia: Griffith and Rowland, 1913), 382.

26. A sophisticated version of this bad habit is the scholastic "high intellectualism" that we met earlier.

27. Historian Walter Shurden has called attention to this in numerous speeches, for me notably in a series of addresses at River Road Baptist Church, Richmond, Virginia, in the spring of 1985. Shurden believes this SBC failure is especially attributable to the decline of the Sunday evening Discipleship Training program.

28. Fundamentalists both in the current narrow sense and in a broader sense came into being around this time. But around 1950, the term was narrowed so that it usually refers now only to the narrower group.

29. Marsden, *Fundamentalism and American Culture*, 4, 141-95, 231; H. Leon McBeth, *The Baptist Heritage* (Nashville: Broadman Press, 1987), 568-78, 755-76. Compare George W. Dollar, *A History of Fundamentalism in America* (Greenville, S.C.: Bob Jones University Press, 1973), xv: "Historic Fundamentalism is the literal exposition of all the affirmations and attitudes of the Bible and the militant exposure of all non-Biblical affirmations and attitudes."

Marsden rightly states that fundamentalism was "created" after the First World War, *Fundamentalism and American Culture*, 149. On that point, Bill J. Leonard's excellent *God's Last and Only Hope* (Grand Rapids: Eerdmans, 1990) could mislead. His pages 4-9 can be read to suggest that fundamentalism originated with the publication of a *prefundamentalist* series of pamphlets (cf. Marsden, 119), namely, *The Fundamentals* of 1910-15. But that would imply, for example, that E. Y. Mullins, the articulate antifundamentalist president of Southern Seminary, was a fundamentalist, since he wrote an article for *The Fundamentals*.

30. This "trauma-reaction syndrome" also parallels Ammerman's view. She writes, ". . . as various forces presented challenges to their faith, they. . . intentionally organized against a real threat to what they believed—the threat and the organization are what distinguish fundamentalists from ordinary believers or traditionalists" (*Baptist Battles,* 16).

31. G. M. Marsden, ed., *Evangelicalism and Modern America* (Grand Rapids: Eerdmans, 1984), xii-xiii, emphasis added.

32. Fundamentalism is modern because it defines itself in terms of modern threats and cannot be what it is apart from those threats. As Ammerman says, "Fundamentalism only exists where there is conscious opposition to the forces of change, and conscious opposition can only exist where there *are* forces of change." Ammerman, *Baptist Battles,* 155.

33. Marsden sees this as characteristic of dispensationalism (Marsden, *Fundamentalism and American Culture,* 62). I see this heightened supernaturalism as characteristic of fundamentalism overall. That is not much of an expansion, because most fundamentalists are dispensationalists.

34. In discussing J. G. Machen above, I pointed out that, in Acts, the heaven-to-earth distance has separating significance. The apocalyptic literature provides an Old Testament parallel. For example, Daniel 9:21-23 shows that Gabriel, dispatched when Daniel begins his lengthy prayer, comes "in swift light" (v. 21, RSV) and reaches Daniel at the end of the prayer. That assumes a considerable distance. Israel's classic prophets, on the other hand, provide a rough analogy to John and Paul, for whom the heaven-to-earth distance does not separate. The Assyrian army is the rod of God's anger, and God takes Cyrus by the hand when he sets the exiles free (Isa. 10:5-19; 45:1-7). The balanced, "stereophonic" supernaturalism of the Bible unites both these ways of thinking.

35. Paul D. Feinberg, "The Meaning of Inerrancy," in *Inerrancy,* ed. Norman L. Geisler (Grand Rapids: Zondervan, 1980), 291-92.

36. Herman Ridderbos, *Studies in Scripture and Its Authority* (Grand Rapids: Eerdmans, 1978), 5, *et passim.*

37. For a far fuller analysis, see James D. G. Dunn, *Unity and Diversity in the New Testament,* 2d ed. (Philadelphia: Trinity, 1990).

38. John Reumann, "The New Testament Concept of the Word," *Consensus: A Canadian Lutheran Journal of Theology,* 5 (1979): 15; cf. 4 (1978): 15-14, and 5 (1979): 15-22.

39. Paige Patterson, "Response" to Robison B. James, "Beyond the Impasse: Study That Enables Us to Heed," University of Richmond Pastors' School, Richmond, Virginia, July 12, 1990.

40. On rare, self-conscious occasions we speak of Christ as God's Word, but that has no real impact on our routine practice.

41. At the May 1987 Conference on Biblical Inerrancy at Ridgecrest, North Carolina, former SBC president Adrian Rogers quoted some fifteen New Testament passages which refer to "the Word of God" and said they were speaking of the Bible. M. A. Smith, *Proceedings,* 125-27. The next day at a news conference, inerrantists Clark Pinnock and Kenneth Kantzer pointed out that in all but one of Rogers's cases (Pinnock), or in all but a few (Kantzer), "the Word of God" means the gospel message, not the Bible. R. B. James, *The Unfettered Word,* 85n.-86n.

42. Paul J. Achtemeier, "*Omne Verbum Sonat:* The New Testament and the Oral Environment of Late Western Antiquity" (Society of Biblical Literature Presidential Address, 1989), *Journal of Biblical Literature* 109 (1990): 3-27. Cf. Lou H. Silberman, ed., "Orality, Aurality and Biblical Narrative," *Semeia 39* (Decatur, Ga.: Society of Biblical Literature, 1987).

43. Clark Pinnock, *The Scripture Principle* (San Francisco: Harper & Row, 1984), 63-64, cf. 39-40, 55.

44. Karl Barth, *Church Dogmatics,* vol. 1, part 2 (Edinburgh: T. and T. Clark, 1956), 514-26.

45. Christopher D. Stanley, drawing upon Dietrich-Alex Koch's *Die Schrift als Zeuge des Evangeliums* (Tübingen: Mohr, 1986), says Paul received "a totally new view of Scripture" as a Christian. The *locus classicus* is 2 Corinthians 3:12-18. "Paul sees the text," Stanley says, "as a 'witness to the gospel' whose true meaning is opened up only to the believer, through the testimony of the Spirit." Stanley, "Paul and Homer," *Novum Testamentum* 32 (1990): 49.

46. Dockery warns against thinking that in 2 Corinthians 3 Paul is pitting the Scripture which the Spirit inspired against the Spirit. I agree that Paul is not doing that. But we must not squelch the fiery apostle. Paul is pitting Scripture by itself, which is death-dealing, against Scripture filled with the Spirit, which is life-giving.

47. Mark A. Noll, *Between Faith and Criticism* (San Francisco: Harper & Row, 1986), 163-66.

48. When we consciously join a religious community, we ipso facto accept its sacred writings as authoritative. For Baptists, however (if not for others), I believe we should go beyond that. The Bible should also become authoritative directly and personally.

49. The textual basis is Jeremiah 23, cf. verse 28. Walter Harrelson, "Passing on the Biblical Tradition Intact" (audiotape), address delivered, Pastors' School, Southern Baptist Seminary, Louisville, Kentucky, August 9, 1990. Professor Harrelson expanded and confirmed this insight in a telephone conversation on October 12, 1990.

6

Beyond the Impasse—Fidelity to the God Who Speaks
*Paige Patterson**

Even after twenty-five years, one of my most poignant memories from seminary days is as vivid as though the event had only just occurred. My closest friend in college, Happy Miller[1] and I resigned college pastorates and made the 750-mile trek southeastward to New Orleans. The excitement of the challenge of street preaching, the joy of seeing lives categorically altered by a meeting with the Lord Jesus, and the blessing of having lived through the torrential rains of a hurricane the second week of classes finally gave way to the necessity of parsing, conjugating, and memorizing, while imbibing coffee strong enough to disintegrate any spoon left in the brew too long. Happy was never a decisive leader, but he was a powerful preacher, more persuasive than he ever knew. Everyone liked him. He was just as much at home with a farmer from Mississippi as he was with Ben Hurr,[2] a former railroad executive from Baltimore.

Then I began to watch the joy fade from Happy's face. He did not wish to share his faith anymore. He no longer craved opportunities to preach. His church attendance began to falter, a pattern I had noted among some of our professors who chose to stay at home on the Lord's Day. One day I confronted Happy. "Why is this happening?" Happy, as well as I, had already heard in a Baptist college

---

*Paige Patterson (Th.D. New Orleans Baptist Theological Seminary) is president of The Criswell College and Associate Pastor of the First Baptist Church, Dallas, Texas. He has also served churches in Texas, Arkansas, and Louisiana. Patterson is a contributor to *The Holman Bible Dictionary, The Criswell Study Bible,* and *The Believer's Study Bible,* for which he served as managing editor. He is a consulting editor for *The New American Commentary* and has written commentaries on the *Song of Solomon, Titus, 1 Peter,* and *1 Corinthians.* Patterson is in constant demand as a preacher and Bible Conference leader. He is one of the best known leaders of the movement that gained ascendancy in the Southern Baptist Convention in the 1980s.

classroom we shared that there was never an Adam, a Noah, or a Jonah. But we had comforted ourselves by noting that it all balanced out since we were also told that there were three Isaiahs. But now in seminary, the attacks on the reliability of the Bible began anew.

Happy confessed that he had accepted his New Testament professor's claim of the superiority of historical-critical studies. This professor maintained that whatever Jesus did at the last supper was almost certainly embellished by Paul, who in his recording of this event made it something which Jesus never anticipated. Happy wondered how he personally had been so gullible all those years; he further questioned the integrity and understanding of the West Texas preachers who had never told him about this "superior" scholarship and "selective" enlightenment.

The seeds of doubt could not be jarred loose. Taking hold strongly, the roots ran deep into Happy's heart. Sorrowfully, I watched as he gradually lost confidence in his call to preach, became decreasingly interested in theological and biblical studies, and finally left the ministry altogether. My deepest regret is that he is not the only young man plucked from calling and service.

Noel Wesley Hollyfield's master's thesis, completed at Southern Seminary in 1976,[3] is a startling reminder that something has gone wrong in Baptist higher education. His thesis demonstrates that the longer students remain at Southern Seminary, the less orthodox they are likely to be. Some even begin to question the existence of God. One may fault the statistical sample; another may decry the formulation of the survey questions; others may debunk the entire project. Still, the information is alarming.[4]

Clayton Sullivan's sad but colorful account of his own experience at Southern Seminary confirms the Hollifield study and goes so far as to provide at least some of the answers for such a loss of commitment to orthodoxy.

> As a seminarian, still in my mid-twenties, I found myself baffled. I was more certain of what I *didn't* believe than I was of what I *did* believe. Southern Seminary had destroyed my biblical fundamentalism but it had not given me anything viable to take its place. That's the weakness of the historical-critical method: its power to destroy exceeds its power to construct. The historical-critical method can give you facts and hypotheses but it cannot give you a vision.[5]

Thus armed, Clayton Sullivan embarked upon his pastoral career. But here, too, he found disappointment. What he had imbibed in historical-critical studies provided little point of contact with the people he served.

> As a neophyte minister in Tylertown, I experienced reality shock. My seminary training, for which I am still appreciative, hadn't prepared me for life's rawness and pain. Indeed, I began to think that much of what I'd learned in Louisville was not relevant to the pastorate. I had moved back to Mississippi able—at the drop of a hat—to discuss "the Persian background of Deutero-Isaiah." I knew fourteen reasons why the last chapter of Romans was a misplaced letter of Paul to the church in Ephesus. But when you're talking to a woman whose husband has been killed in a head-on collision with a logging truck, issues like the authorship of Deutero-Isaiah are beside the point.[6]

Clayton Sullivan is no fundamentalist. He has, in fact, indicated his fervent hope that the conservative resurgence in the Southern Baptist Convention would fail utterly. But he does not obscure the path down which his studies at Southern Seminary led him. He says,

> The more I read, talked, and listened, the more I found it impossible to ignore reservoirs of sincerity and piety in non-Christian religions. Increasingly I found it difficult to deny alternative religious experiences. To this day I recall the impact made upon me when for the first time I studied in detail the life of Edgar Cayce, the famous psychic. Cayce's life was the springboard that caused me to consider seriously reincarnation, a belief held by thinkers as diverse as Plato, Emerson, and Goethe. Subsequently I have looked at reincarnation through the spectacles of writers like Ian Stevenson and Geddes MacGregory and against my will, resisting every step of the way, I have come to see reincarnation's plausibility.[7]

And again,

> The Muslims, Sikhs, Jews, and Buddhists I encountered took their religion as seriously as Christians take their religion. As I came to know these "non-Christian" religionists I had no desire—nor did I see any need—to "convert" them to the Christian faith. To have broached such a possibility would have been insulting or embarrassing. Rather I wanted to listen and to learn from them for I intuited in them God's presence. In other words, on the campus of

both Temple and USM I had a head-on collision with *religous pluralism,* perceiving that I live in a world in which numerous religions—with millions of devotees—exist side by side. Southern Baptists are not the only ones. Christians are not the only ones. There are numerous religious alternatives open to mankind.[8]

One can scarcely be amazed at these kinds of conclusions when a professor now teaching at Southern Seminary has written concerning the need of Christians to open themselves to the wider implications of world religions.

The conclusion leaves me with mixed feelings about the applicability of my findings to the church today. Negative sentiments arise out of the way in which early Christianity narrowly defined the boundaries for God's people. Its expansion was related to an exclusivism and intolerance to which I could not subscribe. Early Christianity grew for the same basic reasons that conservative American churches are now growing. If my thesis is correct, the major eccelesiastical and theological forms had much to do with inculcating and conserving this spirit, helping continually to motivate the Empire-wide effort. Indeed, they figured prominently in inciting the effort to enlist not only non-Christians but others who claimed to be Christians—schismatics, heretics, and others. Did the covenant have to be so narrowly defined and applied through Christianity's institutional life?

Today, it would appear, the covenant and thus the mission of the church could be defined with a greater measure of tolerance. This would not necessitate an abandonment of monotheism nor of the conviction that some sort of special revelation occurred through Israel and Christ and the church. It might necessitate, however, the acknowledgment that the one God has disclosed himself in particular ways through other cultures and religions besides these.[9]

As much as anyone, I am aware that these failures and a host of others like them do not admit to a simple cause-effect evaluation. No facile explanation could possibly suffice. All the blame cannot be headed upon the historical-critical method or upon the professors with whom these people studied. A significant portion of the failure, if it be thus construed, must rest upon Happy Miller and Clayton Sullivan. One might counter the approach above by asserting that it is ''anecdotal'' and by citing cases in which ''fundamentalists'' were ill-affected by ''fundamentalist'' mind-sets.

Nevertheless, when the exercise of a particular approach to the interpretation and understanding of the Bible leaves strewn in its path not only individuals whose faith has been shattered but also institutions that have strayed from the vision of their founders and sometimes even the denomination which gave them life, one can conclude little else than that the method is fatally flawed either in its essence or its application or in both. Furthermore, when churches influenced by pastors whose training was largely devoted to the historical-critical approach show alarming tendencies to loss in attendance and especially to decreasing evangelistic impact, one cannot resist the suspicion that there may be a substantive connection.[10] This leads to important questions: What exactly is the historical-critical method? Are there ways in which it may and should be useful to reverent readers of the biblical witness?

Defining the Historical-Critical Method

According to Charles Talbert, the role of biblical criticism is simply to determine "the meaning of the writing, not to disparage it."[11] The five questions which the biblical critic must ask relate to the isolation of the best manuscript tradition; the identity of the types of literature being studied; the identification of the authors of biblical materials, together with the circumstances and purposes surrounding the writing; the discovery of the organization of the material; and the location and evaluation of significant parallel materials in extrabiblical literature.[12]

George Ladd's definition of the historical-critical method is this:

> Criticism means making intelligent judgments about historical, literary, textual, and philosophical questions which one must face in dealing with the Bible, in light of all the available evidence, when one recognizes that the Word of God has come to men through the words of men in given historical situations.[13]

As I have responded elsewhere to such a definition,

> Defined in this way it is difficult to see what possible objections could be sustained. Furthermore, note should be made that such "critical" efforts hardly constitute a novelty in the modern world. Early "critics" such as Papias and Jerome and Reformation "crit-

ics'' such as Luther and Erasmus sought the same sort of answers as do modern "critics" even though they did not develop the technical jargon characteristic of more recent critical inquiry. Why then would anyone object to the use of historical-critical methodology in the interpretation of Biblical materials?[14]

The problem is that the definitions provided by Ladd and Talbert remind me of a very tall man with a very short blanket. What is covered is clearly covered, but much is not touched. In fact, practitioners of historical-critical methodologies frequently make bold assumptions and draw unwarranted conclusions which have a way of becoming codified as "truth" if the theories appear with relative frequency in a sufficient number of journals and monographs. Almost all my college and seminary professors argued passionately, if not convincingly, that the Pentateuch was the product of multiple sources and extensive redactions, that "Q" was no doubt a lost but essential tradition lying behind major aspects of the "gospel traditions," and that Mark was certainly the first gospel. Students were seldom, if ever, made aware of arguments to the contrary presented by able conservative scholarship. Other "liberal" scholars who venture to question the "assured results of scholarly research" are sometimes dismissed with little hearing. Such is the case with Kikawada and Quinn, who present an intriguing case for the unity of the Pentateuch,[15] and William Farmer, who has provided serious arguments for Matthean priority and doubts that "Q" exists or ever existed at all.[16] As Kikawada and Quinn put the matter,

> However imposing the consensus, the documentary hypothesis remains as hypothesis. Its formulation may well have represented the dawn of a new day for biblical scholarship, but the days have their dawns and their dusks.[17]

Not only are "the assured results" of historical-critical scholarship frequently shown in time to be in error, but also some of those who were formerly practitioners of the historical-critical methodology have not only abandoned it entirely but also have written perceptive critiques of the approach and urged evangelical Christians not to succumb to its siren appeal. Eta Linnemann in her cogently argued *Wissenschaft oder Meinung* has announced her "retirement" from critical scrutiny of the New Testament, though certainly not from careful research into the meaning and exposition of the text. This new departure for Linnemann, after her writing of several highly acclaimed historical-critical studies, signals her conviction that, upon reflection, there is a distinction to be made between reverent scholarship which grapples with all-important issues impinging upon the meaning of the text, on the one hand, and the historical-critical methodology, which she now believes to be seriously flawed, on the other. She is so adamant about this that she says,

> That is why I say "No!" to historical-critical theology. I regard everything that I taught and wrote before I entrusted my life to Jesus as refuse. I wish to use this opportunity to mention that I have pitched my two books *Gleichnisse Jesu . . .* and *Studien zur Passionsgeschichte,* along with my contributions to journals, anthologies, and *Festschriften.* Whatever of these writings I had in my possession I threw into the trash with my own hands in 1978. I ask you sincerely to do the same thing with any of them you may have on your own bookshelf.[18]

Actually, Walter Harrelson's delightful anecdote about his Aunt Zora (in chapter 2 above) illustrates precisely the nature of what is for so many the objectionable feature in the common utilization of historical-critical methodology. Aunt Zora, like nephew Walter, dismisses the text for no better reason than that she found the text offensive to her aesthetic sensibilities. No textual problems or widely disparate variant readings cast doubt on the authenticity of the text. Nothing in the text itself suggests that its author doubted that the Canaanites and Midianites were to be destroyed as an act of God's judgment upon those nations. The God made in Aunt Zora's image, simply would not do anything like that. Harrelson says that such an act "is untrue to the character of the God of the Bible," when he should have said that "such an act is untrue to the character of the God of the Bible as I have conceived him to be."

Again Harrelson says that "critical-historical scholarship still operates on the principle that prophets do not customarily prophesy in advance about named kings who have not yet been born."[19] Yet, Harrelson admits that the historical-critical consensus of yesterday is often radically altered by contemporary formulations.[20] So why jettison the biblical text, which is still to be disproven, in favor of current historical-critical conclusions, which may be abandoned by the more enlightened research of the twenty-first century?

Walter Harrelson's intent is to preserve Christian truth for future generations. This sincere desire is misguided for two reasons. First, one cannot call into question the validity of some aspects of the historicity of the text without raising substantive questions about the theology of the text. Karl Barth candidly admitted this to be the case saying,

> We have to face up to them and to be clear that in the Bible it may be a matter of simply believing in the Word of God, even though it meets us, not in the form of what we call history, but in the form of what we think must be called saga or legend. But the vulnerability of the Bible, i.e., its capacity for error, also extends to its religious or theological content.[21]

Or again,

> The men whom we hear as witnesses speak as fallible, erring men like ourselves. What they say, and what we read as their word, can of itself lay claim to be the Word of God, but never sustain that claim. We can read and try to assess their word as a purely human word. It can be subjected to all kinds of immanent criticism, not only in respect of its philosophical, historical and ethical content, but even of its religious and theological. We can establish lacunae, inconsistencies and over-emphases.[22]

Eta Linnemann recognizes the sincerity of historical-critical scholars but finds the approach flawed at several points.

> In its own eyes, historical-critical theology wants to lend assistance to the proclamation of the gospel through an interpretation of the Bible that is scientifically reliable and objective. There is, however, a monstrous contradiction between what it says it wants to do, on the one hand, and what it actually does, on the other. In light of all I have already said, it should be patently obvious that the manner in which historical-critical theology handles the Bible does not further the proclamation of the gospel, but rather hinders it—in fact, it even prevents it. But worse yet, it is by no means clear that we are dealing here with an approach that yields objective and scientifically reliable interpretation of the Scripture as it claims. It is simply not true that historical-critical theology has replaced subjective impressions with a well-grounded discovery of the truth through careful weighing of arguments.[23]

Second, Harrelson's optimistic portrayal of the functioning of historical-critical methodology scarcely does justice to the overwhelmingly predominant posture of its practitioners. R. P. C. Hanson and A. T. Hanson are refreshingly plainspoken about the conclusions of at least the majority of historical-critical scholars.

> There are certain conclusions that stand out, certain basic assumptions which must considerably modify how we use the Bible. Here are a few taken very much at random. Many more could be added.
> (a) Everything narrated in the Old Testament about the history of Israel up till the entry into Canaan is either myth or legend. Solid history only begins after the entry, and even then there is a considerable element of legend.
> (b) Mark is the earliest of the four gospels and was used by both "Matthew" and Luke in the composition of their gospels.
> (c) The Fourth Gospel does not give us a picture of Jesus as he actually appeared in history.
> (d) Paul did not write the Pastoral Epistles (I and II Timothy and Titus). They probably belong to the early years of the second century. It can safely be claimed that the best scholars in all Christian traditions would accept these conclusions.[24]

The Hansons continue by assuring the reader that the Bible cannot be taken as a handbook for theology,[25] Christian worship, an accurate account of the origin of the world, or of mankind, or even of Israel.[26] Under no circumstances, the Hansons allege, does the Bible contain any significant "revealed" information about the future.[27] Indeed, the Bible is no more reliable than other similar documents of its age.[28] In fact, the Hansons conclude, "Historical criticism of the Bible has challenged two widely held beliefs about it; that it is inerrant and that it is inspired."[29]

If the Hansons's conclusions must be rejected, commendation is nonetheless in order for their forthrightness. The veneer of innocence which adorns historical-critical studies in the thought of Harrelson, Talbert, and Ladd frequently proves to be a thin disguise for the devastating doubt and skepticism often engendered by such studies. In this regard Clayton Sullivan, Karl Barth, R. P. C. and A. T. Hanson, Eta Linnemann, and Gerhard Maier are more reliable as guides to the nature and consequences of historical-critical studies than Harrelson, Talbert, or Ladd.

Studies prepared by Southern Baptists will provide us with the most appropriate samples from which to determine whether Talbert and Ladd have given us the whole truth about the nature of the historical-critical method or if Linnemann and other former practitioners are correct in their distrust of the idea that the historical-critical method does not result in the disparaging of the Bible.

A popular and widely used introduction to the Old Testament written by three Southern Baptists is *People of the Covenant* by Henry Jackson Flanders, Robert Wilson Crapps, and David Anthony Smith. Here is a sampling of their persuasions. Concerning the general nature of Old Testament history, we are informed as follows:

> The historical narratives in the Old Testament, for the most part, are not firsthand contemporary records comparable to those found in the inscriptions and records of other ancient peoples. Instead they are religious works which have gone through a long history of compiling, editing, and copying. These include traditions of Israel's origins, a history of Israel in the land of Caanan, and a priestly overview of all Israelite history.[30]

In other words, the firsthand records of ancient peoples are more likely to reveal actual history (i.e., what really happened, than is the Old Testament, replete as it is with "traditions" of Israel's origins and a "priestly overview of history"). No proof for this startling avowal is offered. In fact, no evidence, impressive or unimpressive, is marshaled. One is just left to believe that this must be so.

Later we are informed of the origins of some of the patriarchal stories.

> Inevitably various units of tradition must have been written down and copies of them treasured as religious possessions of tribal and local communities. So, for example, certain tribes treasured the traditions about Abraham while others preserved the Jacob stories.

> Units of tradition were woven into cycles of stories stamped with peculiar emphases and experiences of Israel's various tribes. These tribal traditions, recited at annual religious ceremonies, were gradually welded into great Israelite "sagas." Among them were "sagas" on the patriarchs, the deliverance from Egypt, the wandering in the wilderness, the giving of the law of Sinai, and the conquest of Canaan. Such traditions became shaped by liturgical usage and reached a fairly uniform oral form prior to the rise of the monarchy under Saul and David.[31]

Beyond the Impasse: Fidelity to the God Who Speaks

We are nowhere informed that this "reconstruction" is a hypothesis. The reader is left to assume that this is in fact what transpired. No footnotes alert the reader to other evangelical perspectives, and if the express declaration is absent, the hint is certainly present that the "sagas" of patriarchal oral deliverance were only partially accurate by the time they were inscribed during the monarchial period or later.

Of course, one is not to worry about this. The essential religious message of the patriarchal sagas is there, and, in any case, what exactly happened is not that crucial. Never mind if Abraham never really set out to sacrifice Isaac, as G. Henton Davies argued in the original Genesis volume of *The Broadman Bible Commentary*.[32] Or if you prefer another version, perhaps there was some sort of effort made in a momentary "polytheistic lapse" of Abraham, which was later reconstructed by the priestly community to show the value of faith. Either way, the incident allegedly did not happen as stated in Genesis 22 and confirmed in Hebrews 11.

But if the sacrifice of Isaac did not take place, who is to say that Abraham and Isaac were ever really there at all? What of the actual origin of God's chosen people? In whom shall we vest the authority to make these decisions?

Someone may wish to point out that this is a discussion about Old Testament materials reporting facts alleged to have happened four thousand years ago, noting that the New Testament era is closer and admonishing us of the need to focus more on Jesus. Here, however, according to Glenn Hinson, the situation is only relatively improved. While there is no justification for a skeptical attitude about the historical event of Jesus of Nazareth, this is not to say that the Gospels offer us reliable history.

> All sources, however objective they claim to be, have biases. They reflect the slanted viewpoints of their authors. At the same time most possess, in varying degrees, some element of fact. The fact that none of these is absolutely factual, however, does not take away all of their value. What it takes away is the dogmatic certainty with which historians in the past sometimes operated. With dogmatic certainty out of the question the historian speaks in terms of relative certainty. He approaches all sources critically and seeks to evaluate their accuracy from as many sides as possible. In the case of the Gospels one can safely conclude that a kernel of historical fact underlies the early Church's handling of the material.[33]

In fact, one cannot even be sure about Jesus' birth in Bethlehem, though one may breathe easier knowing that the Gospels are probably right in ascribing to Jesus humble origins.[34] And what of John the Baptist? We cannot be sure of the picture of John in the Gospels since "modern scholarship" has shown that the authors of these materials were engaged in a polemic against a John the Baptist sect.[35] "Embellishment undoubtedly occurred" in the Gospel stories about the healing narratives, and besides, they would have been reported very differently in our scientifically enlightened age and modern world view.[36] Clearly, Jesus, who expected the return of the Son of Man and the consummation of all things within His own lifetime, was in "error."[37] It is possible to go on and on. It is not possible to show that such affirmations do not disparage the biblical materials. Furthermore, one cannot dismiss Hinson as an uncharacteristic practitioner of the historical-critical method.

Other examples of the use of historical-critical methodologies that result in the disparaging the Scriptures include those of Trent Butler of the Sunday School Board and Roy Lee Honeycutt of Southern Seminary. When I speak of "the disparaging of the Scriptures," I do not speak of intent but of consequence. I have reason to believe that neither man set out to disparage the Scriptures.[38]

Nevertheless, Butler's 1983 commentary on Joshua declared that historical-critical scholarship produced multiple instances of embellishment in Joshua. Butler indicated that some passages are anachronistic. Redactors bungled narratives and borrowed popular "folklore" from their cultures, which they then presented as actual events. The Deuteronomist fashioned words to put in the mouth of Rahab the harlot of Jericho. Based on his historical-critical investigations, Butler reconstructed for us what took place at Jericho.

> Israel has taken up a popular story centering around the ability of a prostitute to trick a king and gain freedom for two men. Israel has transformed this into a story preparing for the conquest of Jericho. The two men are spies sent out by Israel to conquer the land, that is the city-state ruled by the king of Jericho. The story has then been placed at the front of the conquest narratives as a whole to introduce the theology of conquest. The Deuteronomist has then made the story the basis for this theological creed. The growth of the story thus represents a manifold theological interpretation. Each generation of Israelites has learned something new about itself and its God through telling and retelling the story of Jericho's favorite prostitute.[39]

According to Butler, the story of Israel's "favorite prostitute" has religious significance, perhaps even a lesson to be learned, but he maintains that the events did not happen as the book of Joshua records. Under such circumstances, his conclusion is unavoidable: The Bible not only errs but, worse still, deliberately errs. No wonder Eta Linnemann and Clayton Sullivan became disillusioned, even if their ultimate trajectories sent them scrambling in opposite directions. Both, being thoughtful individuals, could see the logical conclusions to which the historical-critical methods relentlessly drove them.

Roy Honeycutt, in a 1964 article in the *Review and Expositor,* "assumes," on the basis of historical-critical study, that Deuteronomy was a growing body of "oral tradition" finally finished in the sixth or seventh century B.C. He is not sure how much of Deuteronomy can be legitimately ascribed to Moses.[40] An actual angel probably did not speak to Elijah since people today do not conceive of the migration of "physical beings" from heaven to earth.[41] Calling down fire from heaven on five hundred could not have been according to God's plan since such is clearly immoral.[42] Gray is probably correct that the axe head was retrieved with dexterity and a long pole rather than floating to the top as 2 Kings reports.[43] Moses probably did not see an unconsumed burning bush,[44] and the children of Israel did not have the tabernacle while they were in the wilderness.[45]

This last conclusion is especially disturbing since any number of critical historical events relate directly to the existence of such a tent in the wilderness. How did Honeycutt determine that witnesses from both the Old Testament and New Testament eras made such a mistake? What "discovery" of the "assured results of modern scholarship" eliminated the tabernacle in the wilderness? Whatever Honeycutt's intentions may have been, his earlier published works questioned the accuracy of Scripture and enthroned human judgment above divine revelation. This he has done without providing a single compelling reason of any sort for accepting the assumptions he has made about the reliability of his historical-critical conclusions.

From this sampling, one cannot conclude that all use of the historical-critical method is wrong or that use of this method has contributed to the fall of Happy Miller and Clayton Sullivan. But it certainly is possible to demonstrate from the above sampling that there are potentially catastrophic dangers lurking in the uncritical employment of historical-critical methodology. From surveys, such as those of Hollyfield and Ammerman, and from the impact of such methodologies on the evangelistic and missionary effectiveness of churches and even denominations, one can certainly conclude that the deleterious results of the uncritical use of the assumptions of the historical-critical approach ought to inspire profound caution.

Using the Historical-Critical Method

If the historical-critical approach to the Bible has some merit but is sufficiently hazardous as to demand great caution, then how ought we to proceed? Millard Erickson provides a general answer when he says,

> Biblical criticism, then, if carefully used and based upon assumptions that are consistent with the full authority of the Bible, can be helpful means of shedding further light on the meaning of the Scripture. And although the Bible need not satisfy biblical criticism's criteria for authenticity to be accepted as dependable, when it does satisfy those standards, we have additional confirmation of its reliability.[46]

To extrapolate further, we can perhaps lay down the following guidelines, not as a final position but as a place to begin.

Truth must be followed wherever it leads.—Confidence in the inerrancy of the Bible in no way precludes rigorous historical, scientific, philosophical, or theological investigation. Those who seek to interpret the Bible correctly must remain open to truth as it emerges from any discipline.

Scholars, like other scientists, should be free to examine all the evidence, bark up all the trees, and paddle up all the creeks.—The only limitation here is that if heaven is real and hell is authentic and Jesus is the only way to avoid one and reach the other, a certain stewardship of time is incumbent upon a Christian scholar. In other words, some trees are so clearly empty that the scholarly steward probably should not waste much time scouting their barren branches.

The historical-critical approach to the Bible is itself a reality.—As such, seminarians, college students, and even local church saints must be made aware of its claims and conclusions. As an option in the agora of thought, this approach may not be treated as though it did not exist. The presentation of its claims and approaches, void of caricature and misrepresentation, should be candidly and honestly made. Where conclusions of such an approach are demonstrably true, they must be embraced. Where such are merely probable, they may be accorded "viability status" as clearly distinct from "factual status." In those cases where historical-critical conclusions are uncertain, dubious, or clearly wrongheaded, then they must not be advocated. To the contrary, we must attempt to show "why that dog won't hunt," and provide a clear and ringing evangelical alternative which we also endorse and advocate. The fatuous assumption that good education does not indoctrinate not only fails to understand the basic meaning of "indoctrinate" but also is patently and logically absurd. For example, the idea of a medical school which does not indoctrinate is unthinkable.

Historical-critical scholars must be held to the same standards of probability and certitude which govern all legitimate inquiry into history.—Absolute integrity must be demanded in distinguishing fact from hypothesis. Wherever hypotheses and assumptions lead to contradiction or disparagement of the inspiration and accuracy of the Bible, these must be abandoned in favor of faith. Furthermore, Southern Baptists attempting to practice the historical-critical method must be as candid as Karl Barth and the Hansons in admitting that the whole question of revelation and unique inspiration are often very much in question as historical-critical scholars pursue their research.

Because we have experienced the Bible to be true so often, we must not accept any conclusion calling its veracity into question on any point unless that conclusion can be indubitably established. —Because of the form of the text and our distance from it and, most especially, because of the fallenness of our own minds, we may often have to take a page from the phenomenologists and simply bracket some text, admitting that we cannot fully comprehend or reconcile it with other texts. But we must not declare it faulty until we know beyond reasonable doubt that this text in its autographic form was incorrect.

Almost totally absent from historical-critical discussion is the illuminating role of the Holy Spirit in the life of the individual believer-priest or in the confessing community.—Perhaps this is because of the tendency among advocates of this method to create a de facto priesthood of scholars. In any event, the present impasse cannot be overcome without full recognition of the role of the Holy Spirit in both inspiration and illumination.

Other approaches to the Bible which recognize the value of the text in its present form often provide greater promise for the exegete. John Newport's assessment (in chapter 3, above) of the nature of various literary approaches to the Bible, together with the contributions and limitations of these methods, is an excellent general introduction to this rapidly developing phenomenon.

Finally, the notion that a canon somehow exists within the canon must surely be jettisoned.—Gerhard Maier alleges that this idea was prevalent among the early practitioners of the historical-critical method.[47] Robison James had denied this and stated that Maier's work is a piece of ''very bad scholarship.''[48] No proof is offered. No response is made to Maier's citations from the works of Semler, Kummel, Kassemann, and Braun, all of whom make it clear that they are seeking to identify the canon within the canon.

Conclusion

How then does all this lead us "beyond the impasse"? To answer that question, we must not only work out an agreement about the use and misuse of critical procedures in biblical studies, but also we must understand the nature of the mind-set of those involved in the conservative resurgence. Although I resist the pejorative term "fundamentalist," Richard John Neuhaus offered an analysis of the situation in American society which is to some degree analogous to the circumstances prevailing in Southern Baptist life.

> The activist fundamentalists want us to know that they are not going to go back to the wilderness. Many of them, being typical Americans, also want to be loved. They explain, almost apologetically, that they did not really want to bash in the door to the public square, but it was locked, and nobody had answered their knocking. Anyway, the hinges were rusty and it gave way under pressure that was only a little more than polite. And so the country cousins have shown up in force at the family picnic. They want a few rules changed right away. Other than that they promise to behave, provided we do not again try to exclude them from family deliberations.

Surely it is incumbent on the rest of us, especially those who claim to understand our society, to do more in response to this ascendance of fundamentalism—and indeed to religion in general—than to sound an increasingly hysterical and increasingly hollow alarm.[49]

Frank admission by Chauncey Daley[50] and more recently Bill Leonard[51] to the effect that the established Southern Baptist bureaucracy did not open the door to more conservative pleas helps to establish the fact of the rejection and even the ridicule that many conservatives keenly felt. A trail of broken promises to "look into" problems and unfulfilled admonitions to "just trust us to take care of this mistake," has led to mistrust that will not be completely rectified overnight. The avalanche of articles in denominational press and state papers assigning unworthy motives to conservative leaders has done little to convince conservatives than any new openness would prevail on the part of moderates if the current pressures at the point of ballots were to be relaxed. For us to move beyond the impasse, moderates must be able to show that they recognize that the developments of the past twelve years represent the concerns of a large segment of Southern Baptist life and not just those of a new alleged oligarchy of leaders. Further, those concerns must be addressed, as Neuhaus poignantly stated, without "increasingly hysterical and increasingly hollow alarm." The country cousins did come to the Baptist picnic, and they probably will not go away anymore. And, they may not be nearly so uncultured and poorly tutored as some have imagined.

On the other hand, the country cousins must learn that not all of their more cultured cousins are bona fide heretics just because they, for example, make guarded use of historical-critical methodology. Their suspicions may be understandable, and we may not blame them for showing up at the family picnic with boxing gloves on, but if they are to have a reasonable role in a civil picnic, they must "hear their cousins out" and not "punch their cousins out" everytime someone moves.

In regard to the use of the historical-critical method, I have not altered my persuasion provided in a prior paper. I can do no better than to cite it again, since it represents both my mind and my heart.

Given the fact that we must seek and accept truth from all sources, the reverential use of historical-critical method should not be rejected. The usual accompanying presuppositions of error, mistake, anachronism, etc. in the Bible must be relinquished. Every effort should be made to utilize the best sources available to the scholarly community in order to ascertain what precisely it is that God is saying to us through the biblical authors. This is an awesome responsibility and must be pursued with a full sense of accountability before God. Scholars from religiously liberal and neoorthodox perspectives and skeptical scholars from the secular city will provide the world with theories which call into question the truths of Scripture. Until a factual or theological error is actually substantiated beyond every reasonable doubt, it remains for Southern Baptists and other evangelical scholars to use the historical-critical method only insofar as it helps us capture meaning and never to the extent that it risks breeding doubt in a malleable public. Whenever the critics beckon us to embark upon an odyssey to locate a canon within the canon, we must stoutly resist knowing that such a pilgrimage is as futile and as destructive as was the search for the Holy Grail. The words of God through Malachi to the priests of Israel are applicable to theologians, pastors, and teachers today.

"For the lips of a priest ought to preserve knowledge, and from his mouth men should seek instruction—because he is the messenger of the Lord Almighty. But you have turned from the way and by your teaching have caused many to stumble; you have violated the covenant with Levi," says the Lord Almighty (Mal. 2:7-8, NIV).[52]

Notes

1. The name is fictitious because of my love for him. The story is real.
2. This really is his name.
3. Noel Wesley Hollyfield, "A Sociological Analysis of the Degrees of 'Christian Orthodoxy' Among Selected Students in the Southern Baptist Theological Seminary," (Th.M. thesis, Southern Baptist Theological Seminary, 1976).
4. As a matter of fact, no refutation of Hollyfield's study has appeared. Furthermore, in a recent book entitled *Baptist Battles* from Rutgers University Press, Nancy Ammerman's sociological surveys extend those of Hollyfield to a broader base, showing, for example, that lay people who attended Baptist colleges and universities tend to be less conservative than those who attended state schools. Ammerman also provides significant evidence showing that the seminaries, particularly Southern, Southeastern, and Midwestern, with their focus on critical studies,

were the principle agents of change to more liberal perspectives. "It is little wonder that the Convention's colleges and seminaries were the primary target of the discontented right wing. Colleges and seminaries had created both the ideology and the social networks, both the sources of meaning and belonging, out of which the old establishment was constructed. They were largely responsible for the changes in belief fundamentalists sought to oppose. Our statistical testing of responses from survey respondents confirmed what fundamentalists already knew—their foremost enemy was the denomination's educational system." Nancy Tatom Ammerman, *Baptist Battles* (New Brunswick: Rutgers University Press, 1990), 163.

5. Clayton Sullivan, *Called to Preach, Condemned to Survive* (Macon: Mercer, 1985), 79.

6. Ibid., 117.

7. Ibid., 179.

8. Ibid., 179-80.

9. E. Glenn Hinson, *The Evangelization of the Roman Empire* (Macon: Mercer, 1981), 287.

10. Once again, Ammerman's surveys demonstrate far greater commitment to the sharing of their faith on the part of the "fundamentalists" than on the part of the "moderates." Seventy-four percent of conservatives opted to share their faith when possible as opposed to only 18 percent of moderates. (*Baptist Battles*, 111.)

11. Robison, B. James, ed. *The Unfettered Word* (Waco: Word, 1987), 62.

12. Ibid., 62-64.

13. George Eldon Ladd, *The New Testament and Criticism* (Grand Rapids: Eerdmans, 1967), 37.

14. Paige Patterson, "The Historical-Critical Study of the Bible: Dangerous or Helpful?" *Theological Educator* 37 (1988): 47.

15. Isaac M. Kikawada and Arthur Quinn, *Before Abraham Was* (Nashville: Abingdon, 1985).

16. William R. Farmer, *The Synoptic Problem: A Critical Analysis* (Macon: Mercer, 1981).

17. Kikawada and Quinn, *Before Abraham*, 13.

18. Eta Linnemann, *Historical Criticism of the Bible*, trans. Robert W. Yarbrough. (Grand Rapids: Baker, 1990), 20. Although the character of this book is primarily that of a testimony, Linnemann is now preparing a more extensive refutation of the historical-critical approach.

19. See p. 45.

20. See pp. 47, 49-50.

21. Karl Barth, *Church Dogmatics,* (Edinburgh: T&T Clark, 1963), 509.

22. Ibid., 507.

23. Linnemann, *Historical Criticism,* 89.

24. R. P. C. and A. T. Hanson, *The Bible Without Illusions* (Philadelphia: Trinity, 1989), 6-7.

25. Ibid., 12.   26. Ibid., 13.   27. Ibid., 14, 66-89.

28. Ibid., 39.   29. Ibid., 43.

30. Henry Jackson Flanders, Robert Wilson Crapps, and David Anthony Smith, *People of the Covenant* (New York: Ronald, 1963), 8.

31. Ibid., 22-23.

32. G. Henton Davies, "Genesis." *The Broadman Bible Commentary,* vol. 1 (Nashville: Broadman, 1969), 198.

33. E. Glenn Hinson, *Jesus Christ* (Wilmington, N.C.: McGrath, 1977), 56-57.

34. Ibid., 60.   35. Ibid., 61.   36. Ibid., 66.   37. Ibid., 76.

38. What I have reported is an accurate presentation of the writings of these men at the time they wrote their respective works. However, I have been informed that there has been indication on the part of both that they would not offer these interpretations of biblical material if they were to rewrite their commentaries today. While I am encouraged by such developments, it, nevertheless, is the case that these are representative writings which establish the fact of serious theological drift in our Southern Baptist institutions and agencies—a drift that had to be addressed.

39. Trent C. Butler, *Joshua, Word Biblical Commentary* (Waco: Word, 1983), 34.

40. Roy Lee Honeycutt, "Deuteronomy and the Teaching Church," *Review and Expositor* 61 (1964): 288.

41. Roy Lee Honeycutt, "II Kings," *The Broadman Bible Commentary,* vol. 3 (Nashville: Broadman, 1970), 277.

42. Ibid., 229.   43. Ibid., 242.

44. Roy Lee Honeycutt, "Exodus," *The Broadman Bible Commentary,* vol. 1 (Nashville: Broadman, 1973), 312-13.

45. Ibid., 447.

46. Millard J. Erickson, *Christian Theology* (Grand Rapids: Baker, 1983), 104.

47. Gerhard Maier, *The End of the Historical-Critical Method* (St. Louis: Concordia, 1977).

48. Robison B. James, "The Historical-Critical Study of the Bible: Dangerous or Helpful?" *Theological Educator* 37 (1988): 64.

49. Richard John Neuhaus, *What the Fundamentalists Want* (Washington, D. C.: Ethics and Public Policy Center, 1985).

50. Chauncey R. Daley, Audiotape of Lecture by Chauncey R. Daley, presented at The Southern Baptist Theological Seminary, July 1984.

51. Bill Leonard, *God's Last and Only Hope* (Grand Rapids: Eerdmans, 1990).

52. Patterson, "The Historical-Critical Study of the Bible," 57.

7
Setting Our Feet in a Large Room
*Molly Truman Marshall**

Psalm 31:8 offers this assurance of God's covenantal faithfulness: "you have set my feet in a broad place" (NRSV). The psalmist is speaking not only of God's enduring care, but of the spacious freedom the faithful people of God enjoy. Perhaps the image of a "large room" can help us in these days of heightened animosity among competing parties in our denomination, each attempting to lay claim to the true Baptist "room." Moving beyond the impasse may be possible only through a renewed acknowledgment and commitment to the anchor of our faith, the love of God expressed to us through Jesus Christ. This common confession provides our entrance into the broad place which, we might discover, is more expansive than our current climate might suggest.

It matters greatly that we attempt to strengthen our bonds as Christians in the one body of Christ during this time of rapid fragmentation. All of the contributors to this volume believe in mutual education and mutual conversion and, most important, retain a sense of hope about our work together. Theological reflection, in my judgment, is best done in community; the constructive criticism we will afford one another can keep us on track, and the breadth of shared vision can enlarge our particular provinciality.

This chapter is not one of the programmatic chapters, rather it is

---

*Molly Truman Marshall (Ph.D., Southern Baptist Theological Seminary) is Associate Professor of Theology at The Southern Baptist Theological Seminary, where she also has served as Associate Dean of the School of Theology. She has contributed to *Baptist Theologians, Mercer Dictionary of the Bible, Holman Bible Dictionary,* and *Becoming Christian.* She is the author of more than a dozen articles that have appeared in a variety of journals. About half of her publications deal with issues related to women in the church or in ministry. She has served as editor of *Folio* and has delivered lectures at numerous colleges and seminaries. Marshall is a member of the Deer Park Baptist Church in Louisville, Kentucky.

designed to interact with the primary themes of the other authors, especially the significant contributions of John Newport on literary-aesthetic approaches to biblical hermeneutics and of Albert Mohler on his proposal for a renewed theological framework for Southern Baptists. By engaging their chapters, the contours of my own approach to Scripture, theological construction, and ministry will come into view as we look to a possible theological consensus that might lead our denomination beyond the present cultural, ideological, and theological impasse.[1]

My own roots in Southern Baptist life are very deep. My great-grandfather, W. S. Wiley, began working in Indian Territory in 1887. My mother, who grew up in his home, tells of peering over the upstairs banister in an attempt to listen to the conversation of historic Baptist forebears such as E. Y Mullins, J. M. Frost, and I. J. Van Ness, who came to Muskogee to visit him and encourage him in his work of planting churches among the Indian tribes transplanted to that area. My "goodly heritage" continues with his daughter, Clema Wiley, who graduated from the WMU Training School in Louisville in 1920, the oldest living alumna until her death four years ago. While she sat at the back of A. T. Robertson's New Testament classes and dared not say a word, I have, ironically, inherited his old office at Southern Seminary. Thus, I am concerned both about continuity and appropriate development in our shared Baptist life.

A Literary-Theological Approach to Biblical Hermeneutics

Newport has offered a wide-ranging taxonomy of the influence of contemporary literary or aesthetic approaches on biblical hermeneutics. Wisely, he has pointed out the philosophical presuppositions that undergird these analyses, particularly those which put them at odds with the traditional evangelical approach.

Analyzing several representatives of the methods he surveys allows him more than a cursory evaluation of their merits and serious deficiencies. His considerable comprehension of these disparate emphases is commendable, and he has painstakingly assessed a large amount of material before forming his tempered conclusions. Certainly we can find substantial agreement with most of his delineations; however, at a few points we might want to press for more clarity or finer discriminations.

Professor Newport is correct to insist that while Holy Scripture is literature and can be illumined through the canons of literary theory, it is more than an aesthetic object without historical and authorial moorings. Original context and author do offer major clues to proper interpretation, as he insists, yet the text's meaning is not exhausted by those two parameters. Perhaps the work of Brevard Childs and James A. Sanders, loosely defined as canonical criticism, can offer further interpretative insight as their approaches do greater justice to the diversity of the entire Bible, attending to the ways in which earlier communities of faith understood and reshaped the texts as Scripture.[2] Employing these hermeneutical methods does not set the text adrift, a possibility that Newport rightly inveighs against, but will balance authorial intent with the ongoing quest of the community of faith for meaningful interpretation.

Further, these approaches will allow interpreters to go beyond the limited scope of the literal sense of biblical passages to discover the levels of meanings held by the texts,[3] or what earlier scholars have called the *sensus plenior*. By definition this perspective on Scripture refers to "the deeper meaning, intended by God but not clearly intended by the human author, that is seen to exist in the words of Scripture when they are studied in the light of further revelation or of development in the understanding of revelation."[4] While this hermeneutical method cannot be adopted without qualification, its emphasis on the "fuller sense" or "excess of meaning" has continued to influence contemporary scholarship shaped by the new hermeneutic.

E. D. Hirsch's accentuation of an author-centered interpretive method provides a substantial buttress for Newport's concerns about retaining the priority of the author over against the "horizon" of the interpreter. Surprisingly, Newport did not contend that the reason for retaining the biblical authors' intents as primary has to do with an understanding of Spirit-inspired authority. While a certain authority should be granted to the author of a particular literary work, the description of Scripture as "God-breathed" sets it apart from other literary contributions. Although we realize that this is not Hirsch's concern, yet because Newport wants to conscript his view for biblical hermeneutics, it offers an appropriate nuance to Hirsch's perspective.

Newport's weightiest criticism is that literary or aesthetic approaches tend "to deny referential function to the biblical text." While this is not a new issue in biblical hermeneutics (it has been simmering for at least two centuries),[5] in many contemporary methods it has reached a boiling point, as Newport notes. To maintain that a work renders a "world within the text," though, does not necessarily mean that the interpreter is arguing there is no world outside the text.[6] While many biblical interpreters disavow a strict "correspondence" theory of truth, which believes that the assertions of the text correspond absolutely to external reality (i.e., literal historical events), they would not attempt to limit truth to a world created within the literary tradition of the Bible. We should heed Newport's caution, however, because a literary approach to Scripture needs to be complemented by historical-critical methods.

Similar evenhandedness could have mitigated the author's contention that the various literary approaches "tend to lead to one-sided, distorted results." Granting that each of these methods of interpretation has some truth, he implies that they are employed conjointly and are, therefore, contradictory. Moreover, he declares that Marxist and feminist readings "distort the text by insisting that their themes are the primary interpretive grids." In a manner similar to Hirsch, Newport wants to limit the influence of the interpreter's context on the perception of meaning. My own understanding of the "ideological readers" who use these hermeneutical devices is that they are more interested in correcting an imbalance in interpretation than furthering another form of myopic reading. Liberationist and feminist interpreters, in particular, are concerned for the neglected justice themes within the texts, but not a reduction to these only.[7] They desire that Scripture remain for them the dynamic Word of God, and "passing on the biblical tradition intact" (Harrelson's fine phrase) requires that they allow its truth to intersect the specific needs of oppressed people. Yet much critical reserve is in order here, for all of us carry certain ideological concerns that press our interpretations toward distortion.

Newport acknowledges elements of truth in the feminist approach, and he wisely delineates among the varied methodological accents of those who congregate under the "feminist" umbrella. The work of evangelical feminists such as Aida Besancon Spencer, Ben Witherington III, David M. Scholer, and E. Margaret Howe has enabled the church to see new dimensions in Scripture concerning women and encouraged a more inclusive view of ministry.[8] Yet, not all feminist scholars share this high regard for the Bible. With Newport we should resist the diminishment or abandonment of biblical authority that accompanies many of these approaches. Those who move in a post-canonical direction in their theological construction are jeopardizing their claim to be working within the Christian tradition. Most objectionable is the regular distortion of the word *theology* by appending it to writing in which the emphasis on personal experience is tantamount to self-deification.[9] By contrast, Christian theology is properly concerned with the One God whom we confess as Trinity.

My senior colleague in theological education concludes his survey with a judicious assessment of the possible contributions of recent literary approaches. Especially insightful is his appreciation of the diversity of literary forms through which God's truth comes to readers of every epoch. The pluriform character of the Bible requires literary and theological sensitivity and a proper interfacing between a "hermeneutics of suspicion" and a "hermeneutics of reception."[10]

Toward a Renewed Theological Framework

Mohler has not only offered a set of imperatives that he believes can guide our denomination's movement toward theological renewal, but he has sketched a percipient description of the context in which this work must be done. Undergirded by a wide survey of contemporary scholarship, he laments the absence of theological thinking in our epoch and, with some demurring, we can agree with him.[11]

Mohler's description of an "atheological" context refers to a lack of explicit theological conversation employing classic theistic categories; however, we must remember that theological concerns are never absent from the human quest for meaning and hope. In the struggle for belief, persons begin to realize that the facts of the world are not the end of the matter, as Wittgenstein taught us. Yet Mohler's perception that a part of our vocation as theologians is to help interpret the implicitly theological questions of the persons around us that they might desire to know and be known by the living God is certainly correct.

But we may differ in our understanding of the theological vocation. Theology must be more than the "pursuit of the true," as Mohler describes it. Surely it has the intellectual component, *fides quaerens intellectum,* but the practice of theology involves our redemptive action in the world, which the more scholastic approach suggested by his chapter threatens to eclipse. Theology has to do with "truth-telling" in both word and deed. The true test of the adequacy of any theological perspective is not its strict adherence to a particular confessional tradition, but whether or not it spurs our passionate willingness to be salt and light and leaven for our own "perverse generation." We can affirm Mohler's understanding of "authentic discipleship" expressed through mission and evangelism. Putting the gospel into practice—the praxis of the gospel—will allow theological reflection to be aimed at clarifying the relationship between God and the church. A deepened relationship will, in turn, make possible an active witness to this relationship to the world in order that it be persuaded and welcomed to relate to both God and church.

The absence of serious theological reflection today is the result of doctrinal neglect by the churches, according to Mohler. We cannot gainsay this conclusion; albeit, we might add that it is also the result of widespread confusion about the role of "communities of conviction"[12] (and here we should confess *especially* in the churches) in moral and theological formation in the public sphere. Reclaiming the church's prophetic role as an enduring "community of conviction" will compel it to speak to the contemporary moral uncertainty in the dilemmas of human experience. Although we might not want to return to the Puritan experiment in New England, surely the passion of these Christian forebears that the gospel must invade every sector of human life is worthy of our emulation.

Believing that the controversies surrounding Ralph Elliott's study of Genesis and *The Broadman Bible Commentary* were fomented by this doctrinal inattention, Mohler calls Southern Baptist churches to strengthen one of their primary ministries, theological education, which includes the rigorous teaching of basic Christian doctrines as well as the hermeneutical sensitivity needed to "rightly divide the word of truth."

It is worth contemplating whether the "decline in doctrinal attention" has also been abetted by the failure of seminary-educated ministers to pass on the historical-critical method in a clearly articu-

lated and relevant manner. In their attempts to pander to consumerism in religion which has little interest in the "reason [for] the hope
that is within" (1 Pet. 3:15), they have failed to nurture the maturing
discipleship required to move from a "borrowed" to a more personal faith.

Of course, blame might be placed on theological educators for
failing to apply the methodology more clearly to the concerns of
ministry; yet, I fear that seminary graduates have often reverted to a
pre-seminary pattern of proclamation and biblical exposition because they lacked facility or boldness in conveying to the laity the
positive contributions historical-critical studies can make. Indeed,
as Harrelson has argued, historical-critical study has an indispensable role if the biblical heritage is to be passed on faithfully.

In his call for a renewed theological framework, Mohler presupposes a "commonly-understood set of doctrinal essentials" which
have guided us, but he believes these can no longer be assumed. We
might question whether they were *ever* assumed to the degree he
envisions. As Bill Leonard argues in *God's Last and Only Hope:
The Fragmentation of the Southern Baptist Convention,* our denominational forebears articulated Baptist doctrines in ways that could
include the diverse theological traditions which contributed to our
identity as Southern Baptists. Indeed, they resisted "all attempts to
define basic doctrines in ways that excluded one tradition or another, thereby destroying denominational unity and undermining the
missionary imperative."[13] In Mohler's view, however, the present
situation in Baptist life calls for greater clarity than articulated in the
1925 and 1963 statements or, for that matter, in the Abstract of
Principles, the doctrinal guidelines for the faculty of The Southern
Baptist Theological Seminary.

Is the clarity Mohler seeks actually a narrowing of Baptist affirmations? There is a marked inattention to religious liberty and the
priesthood of all believers in his proposal, which appears to be a
narrowing commensurate with the fundamental-conservative political and theological agenda. Most problematic is his call for an
official understanding of the nature of Scripture, something Baptists
have always staunchly resisted. When one party determines how
language can be employed (i.e., the meaning of "inerrancy"), a
consensus of beliefs can hardly emerge.

Mohler suggests that this new theological consensus would be
based on "the" classical Christian paradigm. At this point, his

proposal needs further clarification. Ostensibly, he is calling for a reformed faith, perhaps even a dogmatics deeply rooted in the life of the church. A serious engagement with the "radical" wing of the Reformation, where our roots lie, might lend greater balance—lest Baptist distinctives be buried under the more dominant magisterial Reformers who were more concerned with "national" churches than with "gathered" churches. Moreover, we must acknowledge that the insights of the Protestant confessional tradition are offered in a specific historical context—with all the robust concreteness and limitation which that implies.[14] Surely our Baptist beginnings are in this tradition—and we must strengthen our common heritage with all of Christ's church—but we must not lessen Baptist dependence upon Scripture by assuming a confessional posture that has not been our identity historically.[15]

Suggesting a vocational ambivalence on the part of seminary professors in Baptist life, Mohler maintains that the "decreasing theological appetites of local churches" have been met by scholars who have increasingly addressed the academy rather than their appropriate primary public, the church. Faculties in Baptist seminaries will, most likely, disagree with this assessment. Seminary professors' ministries are anchored in the life of the church: we preach there, we teach and learn the Bible there, we conduct revivals in many different church settings, we help churches grow Sunday Schools, we help in missions emphases, we speak at Baptist Student Union conventions, we train choirs and write hymns for worship, to name only a few of our churchly activities. We do this because it is our vocation; we love the church and seek to offer our gifts within that part of the body of Christ we call Baptist. Because the concerns of the academy are often irrelevant to the ministry of the church, many of us have, in the main, neglected the academy because of the strength of our commitment to the local church. There is no question about where professors understand their primary accountability to lie. We see ourselves as ministers who are called to equip vocational ministers—not persons who just happened to choose religious studies as our major field in graduate school. We have an abiding love for students, the churches that nurtured and sent them, and the congregations they will serve after graduation.

Futher, Mohler suggests that our denominational seminaries are imbibing the intoxicating brew of the theological academy without cognizance of "the breakdown of the Southern Baptist evangelical consensus." His perspective that a loss of theological focus and commitment is regnant in our seminaries which, in turn, might be blamed for the doctrinal neglect in the churches is suspect. In the past decade, the systemic creation of suspicion about "what is being taught in our seminaries" has contributed greatly to our current fragmentation. In my opinion, this has done more to breed mistrust than persons "losing their faith" while in the process of theological education.

While Mohler rightly stresses our common commitment to the authority of Scripture, he does not articulate how one moves from an affirmation of biblical authority to theological formulation. Southern Baptists have always been biblical; however, we have not known how to ground our theological convictions in an informed understanding of the witness of Holy Scripture. Anyone assuming that there is *one* "scriptural view" that can supply the foundation for our theology ignores the richness of the biblical materials in which a retraditioning process is always at work.[16] Theology strives to encompass the whole of the biblical message, but one's historical horizon always leads to the accentuation of certain elements and the neglect of others. Perhaps it will be more fruitful for us to speak of the Scriptures as the "norming norm" (*norma normans*) rather than as a foundation for theology.

Envisioning a reciprocal relationship between the study of Scripture and theology would allow a more adequate interfacing of the two.[17] We cannot attempt the study of the Bible without bringing along our theological assumptions, which are given form by our cultural horizon and personal experience. Neither the "modern view of the world" should determine what carries authority, nor can a correct a priori understanding of the Scripture simply be assumed. The Bible will always raise questions about the penchants of contemporary theology, and theology will undoubtedly continue to pose questions to the Bible. In the reciprocity of theological reflection and scriptural study, the community of faith continues its desire to be addressed by God and to speak of God in the most informed way.

Among his imperatives is the interesting proposal for a process of "theological triage" that could allow a greater "convictional cooperation." Delineating "first-order" theological issues from those less crucial, Mohler elevates the Deity of Christ and His sole sufficiency for salvation, and the utter trustworthiness of Scripture as doctrinal beliefs which have priority.

Placing other issues such as the role of women in ministry in a secondary status is understandable, given these foundational concerns, but it is not an insignificant matter. When Calvin wrote about church order, he classified the question of woman's proper role in the church among "indifferent things," those aspects of Christian freedom neither commanded nor forbidden by God and subject to change.[18] Would Mohler also place qualifications for ministry in general as an "indifferent" or second-order concern?

Evidence of the importance of churchly concern about women in ministry is the measure of attention evangelical scholars and organizations have devoted to its exploration over the past two decades. And, as we know, the debate is far from settled. Closer to home, we are aware of the divisions among Southern Baptists on this issue, but perhaps we can grow toward a more accepting attitude toward those with whom we disagree. Because we affirm the liberty of conscience and the autonomy of the local congregation, there should be room for churches who affirm the role of women in ministry and for those who do not. Accordingly, a church voluntarily cooperates with others and should resist control by any outside body. Hence, many congregations in our denomination believe without reservation that Scripture, our Baptist theology, and our ecclesial polity encourage the calling and giftedness of women for all roles of ministry.[19]

The strong accent on theological vocation, attention to missions, ethical renewal, and ecumenical concern found among Mohler's other imperatives are worthy of responsive consideration on the part of all Baptists. The jeremiad in his chapter, however, is a call for those on both the right and the left to embrace doctrinal parameters as a necessary characteristic of denominational identity. To my knowledge, the moderates of our Convention have never contended that there is no need for such. They simply have protested such a structure being imposed in a creedal way. "Voluntarism" has always been a treasured part of our Baptist heritage.[20] While Mohler notes key theological essentials which obviously must be included within the "doctrinal parameters," I found interesting the absence of affirmations about this Baptist distinctive as well as others relating to the dignity and liberty of each believer.

The call for encompassing theological renewal is timely and

Mohler's analysis and proposal deserves our careful reflection. We must put aside mutual suspicion and distrust to engage in serious theological dialogue which can foster convictional cooperation for the service of Jesus Christ and His world. This will require confession and repentance for our own distinctive genre of spiritual triumphalism which has brought us to the brink of denominational catastrophe.

Entering the "Large Room"

More than a few among us are concerned that Southern Baptists have been captured more by the "theology of glory" than by the "theology of the cross."[21] Our denominational successes have contributed to an imperious attitude toward other Christian traditions, toward Christian brothers and sisters within our denomination and, we confess, toward the scandalous cross on which our faith depends. Because the denominational "product" sold so well for so long, we have had little patience with those for whom faith was a "dimly burning wick" (Isa. 42:3, RSV). Weakness and hiddenness, the garb of the cross and the means of God's disclosure, were expendable parts of the commodious gospel regnant among us.

In this final section, we will return to the image of the "large room" as the place all can enter through the common confession of the crucified, buried, and risen Savior. We will examine, first of all, the cross of Christ which allows us to enter our true "home" through our reconciliation with God; second, how Scripture bears witness to this chief disclosure of God and thereby points the way for us; and, third, the manner in which gospel and Scripture enable us to extend the glad welcome into God's spacious salvation. Undergirding this analysis is the presupposition that incarnation, the Word ever becoming flesh, is God's chief means of revelation, which takes a threefold form. In the descending order of importance, they are: the eternal Word of God enfleshed as the Christ; the Bible as God's Word clad in human words; and our contemporary proclamation of this Word as we bear God's image and witness to our world.

It is not possible or desirable to pretend that the Enlightenment did not occur. While we do not need to place the knowing subject at the epistemological center as Descartes's method enjoined, we cannot gainsay its call for liberation from the shackles of ignorance. Indeed, it is constructive to incorporate some of its insights into an understanding of God's ongoing revelation to humanity.[22] Thus, the following brief overview of the relationship of Scripture, theology, and praxis bears the marks of historical-critical scholarship and contemporary hermeneutical theory.

Going Home by Way of the Cross

John A.T. Robinson described Jesus as one of whom two stories must be told.[23] The story of the Son is contextualized in the very life of God, revealing God's inexorable movement to redeem—which is the story "according to the spirit." And the story of Jesus of Nazareth reveals the true identity and destiny of human beings, who are through their creation by God potentially in the image of God's Son, but are sinners needing God's forgiveness—which is the story "according to the flesh." Let us examine each of these perspectives, in turn.

Although we know that it is not possible to separate the story of Jesus Christ from the witness of Scripture, we have to decide where to begin in our study. Thus, the present order of analysis, in which we attempt to say something about the life and death of Jesus which antedates the biblical text, suggests something about the priority of importance.

Several generations of biblical scholars stand in debt to C. H. Dodd's study of apostolic preaching. In this pivotal book he outlines the *kerygma* of the primitive Christian community as "the proclamation of the facts of the death and resurrection of Christ in an eschatological setting. . . ."[24] This occurs "according to the Scriptures" (meaning the Hebrew Scriptures), yet the historical reality of the death and resurrection of Jesus Christ both precedes the New Testament's witness and conscripts, to a major degree, the Old Testament for this Christological interpretation.

James Barr has insisted that for these early believers, "the Old Testament, though authoritative, was no longer the communicator of salvation . . . ,"[25] which seems to be the sense of John 5:39-40: "You search the scriptures, because you think that in them you have eternal life; and it is they that bear witness to me; yet you refuse to come to me that you may have life" (RSV). Early Christian faith was not controlled by Scripture (the Old Testament), but rather it served as the source for Scripture (the New Testament). Only the preaching of Jesus Christ as crucified and risen communicated salvation in the Christian sense. The *kerygma* functioned, then, as an "essential verbal authority."[26]

The Old Testament provided categories and traditions for interpreting the life of Jesus Christ, hence any Marcionite dismissal of its relevance is unsatisfactory. But it could not serve as the controlling and delimiting authority for the church, as Barr writes, "With Jesus there came something new, something that burst the limits of what the Old Testament knew about; and for the expression of that something new it was both necessary and right that Jesus' teaching should go far beyond what scripture then authorized. . . . "[27]

Jesus' teaching is remembered primarily because persons encountered the very presence of God in Him. With God's vindication of Him in resurrection, His disciples perceived His true identity as one who discloses the very heart of God. In the death of Christ, says Paul, God manifested righteousness and condemned sin in the flesh (Rom. 8:3). This ontological movement in God transcends the Hebrew Scripture's understanding of covenantal righteousness. Much of this older material describes the prohibitions to human closeness to the Holy One (Ex. 33:7-11) or the fearfulness of the people to encounter God. The sinfulness of humanity rendered persons sacrally unworthy to draw near to God; however, in the New Testament we see the nearness of God in the poured-out life of the Son.

A clear example of this new understanding is found in Luke 7:35-50, the story of a meal at the house of Simon the Pharisee; it is remembered because of the extraordinary scene in which the woman washes Jesus' feet with her tears and dries them with her hair. We recall that the host of the dinner party was less than pleased and sought to upbraid Jesus for His lack of discernment about the sort of woman this was. "If this fellow were a real prophet, he would know who this woman is that touches him!" (v. 39, NEB). A real prophet would not be so careless as to allow an unclean woman to taint him, he muttered. Simon is voicing a legitimate Old Testament understanding; one who represents the holy should not come too near the unholy for fear of contamination. In Christ, God has overcome these prohibitions to nearness.

The reconciling movement of God in Christ most clearly reveals that God takes initiative toward the sinner. The familiar words,

"God commendeth his love toward us, in that, while we were yet sinners, Christ died for us" (Rom. 5:8, KJV), provide the heart of our confession. The crucified one reveals the righteousness of God, but it is not a righteousness that demands perfect obedience to the law. It is, though, a righteousness that grants a new standing before God, demonstrating the wideness of God's mercy. The truth about God is that God suffers in our place in the death of the Son in order to change us from "enemies into friends" that we might no longer relate to God with dread, but in grateful love. God suffers the humiliation of the cross for the sake of our reconciliation. God justifies sinners through their faith in the Son, a righteousness determined by God's scandalous standards. We who are reconciled have no cause to bar entry into the hospitable space provided by God, for it is by God's mercy that any return to their true home.

The crucifixion of Jesus reveals to us the lengths to which God will go to redeem, even bearing the sin of the world. While the death of the Son is a new event in the life of God, it is, by no means, the first expression of "the cross in the heart of God," as H. Wheeler Robinson never tired of reminding Old Testament scholarship. Jesus Christ is our window into the very being of God.

The cross of Christ tells the truth about humanity, also. It serves as notice that we are sinful, incapable of meeting God's standard of right living, and incapable of saving ourselves. The cross reveals the moral affront our sin is to God; it is a costly and violent rebellion that scapegoats the one who alone has lived truly for God and others. The crucified God (Luther's phrase) shows the provisionality of the Old Testament sacrificial system through the surpassing efficacy of God's own self-emptying, suffering "even death on the cross."

Our pride finds this description of God and the character of grace an affront. Yet locating truth in the cross is essential, for it is only here that the proud heart is able to hear God's unmistakable address. Because of the depth of God's love, we learn something of the dignity and significance God grants us and all those for whom Christ died. In Christ we see all that humanity was intended to be but never was because of our sin and all that we are not but which we will become through resurrection. As my teacher John Robinson was fond of saying, "Jesus is the only truly normal person who ever lived."

Scripture Points the Way

Holy Scripture serves the church by standing as the *sine qua non* witness to the story of salvation. In our view of Scripture it is important to remember that the "center of gravity" in the Bible must be its faithful narration of God's mighty acts culminating in the cross of Christ, not "the perfection of the text as a document by itself," as Clark Pinnock so aptly puts it.[28] Scripture does not give authority to Christ, but Christ authorizes Scripture as a book of promise through His faithful demonstration of God's power to save. As Paul writes in 2 Corinthians 1:20: "For in him every one of God's promises is a 'Yes' " (NRSV).

Perhaps we can find agreement on what might be called a functional view of Scripture. Augustine's approach can assist us, for he rarely tried to prove the character or inspiration of the Scriptures, but simply "took the inspiration for granted because of the effect the Bible had on people."[29] Building on Augustine's insight, the Reformers trumpeted "the power of the Bible to convey a sense of encounter with the divine and to elicit a religious response from the hearer."[30] Specifically, Luther's hermeneutic, which contends that the distinctive character of Scripture is that it urges or promotes (*treibt*) Christ, continues to shape our Baptist understanding of the function of the Bible for theology and faith.

Luther wrote (without a shred of the self-doubt plaguing many contemporary theologians) in his sturdy preface to the Book of James: "All the sacred books agree in this, that all of them preach and inculcate Christ. And that is the true test by which we judge all books, when we see whether or not they inculcate Christ. Whatever does not teach Christ is not yet apostolic. . . ." Southern Baptists' own 1963 confession, which still offers adequate guidance for our theological consensus, states "The criterion by which the Bible is to be interpreted is Jesus Christ."

This view suggests both a "scripture principle"[31] and a hermeneutical method for relating the Testaments and finding the center of gravity within the biblical literature. Luther's lyrical metaphor: "Scripture is the swaddling clothes containing the Christ" echoes this understanding. Christ stands above Scripture, giving it enduring authority and is, at the same time, rendered to us by Scripture.

David Dockery suggests that it is helpful to regard the human-divine nature of the Bible as analogous to the humanity and divinity of Jesus. Yet, Christ is the Incarnate Word and Scripture the written Word; one expresses and one refers, as John Macquarrie puts it in his *Principles of Christian Theology*.[32] Of Christ we confess: "conceived by the Holy Spirit," but we describe Scripture as "God-breathed"—analogous to our human forebears whom God's own breath awakened. Thus, Scripture bears witness to the life of God, yet does not bear the life of God as did Jesus. Nor should we speak of the biblical writers as possessing the Spirit in the same manner as the one who "baptized with the Holy Spirit." Truly both Christ and Scripture disclose God's initiative, yet Christ retains priority as the expressive Word of God.

As Christians we confess that our knowledge of God is interpreted by our knowledge of Christ. While Scripture should not be viewed as coextensive with the truth of God, just as Christ is thoroughly of God *totus deus,* but does not subsume all of God *totom dei,*[33] it reliably serves as the key source for the story of Christ and must be treasured for its unrivalled historical proximity.

In his valedictory address at Cambridge University during the Michaelmas term of 1980, Professor C. F. D. Moule described the distinctiveness of Scripture with this analogy: knowledge of an ancient meteorite can only be obtained by studying its crater; in the same way, Scripture portrays to us the impact of the Christ-event. Therefore, Scripture's distinctive function is its primary witness to the life of Jesus Christ. Further, what Scripture points to is "a self-authenticating reality. . . which secular history cannot deny."[34] It serves to give the community the kind of stability needed for the people of God to preserve an identity.

George Lindbeck provides us with additional insight as to the interpretive method which might best allow Scripture to function in this manner. He urges the contemporary interpreter to assume that Scripture "creates its own domain of meaning and that the task of interpretation is to extend this over the whole of reality."[35]

His suggestion is reminiscent of the approach of the early Christian interpreters who sought to "incorporate the Hebrew Scriptures into a canon that focused on Christ, and then, by extension, to embrace extrabiblical reality."[36] Typology or figural representation were traditional exegetical devices to accomplish this. For example, Moses or David were, in some respects, typological foreshadowings of Jesus. This method of interpretation allowed believers to "make the story of the Bible their story," Lindbeck recounts. Accordingly, the cross should not be viewed as "a figurative representation of suffering nor the messianic kingdom as a symbol for hope in the future; rather, suffering should be cruciform, and hopes for the future messianic."[37]

This method, however, could not withstand the onslaught of modernity, as Hans Frei's pivotal study has shown. An overly rationalistic bias and a positivist view of history dismembered the biblical narrative, preventing the reader from hearing the Bible's story.[38] Consequently, Frei and others, such as Lindbeck and Hauerwas, who call themselves "postliberal" and Pinnock, who calls himself a "postmodern,"[39] have turned more in the direction of narrative theology in their search for orthodoxy.

What is the benefit of this old-new approach? Lindbeck recommends an "intratextual" approach to the biblical narratives, that is, an approach that reads all passages in light of the Scripture's Christ-centered unity (in conformity to the church's trinitarian rule of faith) and interprets all extrabiblical realities by its measure (canon). Lindbeck believes such an approach not only will allow Scripture to interpret Scripture (that hallowed tenet of the Reformers) in its true theological meaning but will also redescribe "reality within the scriptural framework rather than translating Scripture into extrascriptural categories." Further, he believes the "normative or literal meaning must be consistent with the kind of text it is taken to be by the community for which it is important."[40] The Bible, used in this manner, has a consensus and community-forming potential sorely needed for the people of God who presently lack a *sensus fidelium.* Another significant benefit is a new appreciation for the meaning of the narrative. Therefore, we need not view the biblical materials as a scientific account of creation, an existential analysis of the human condition, or a source of clues for the reconstruction of history; its primary function is, in the words of David Kelsey, "to render a character... offer an identity description of an agent,"[41] namely God. To this Moule adds, "Scripture performs its distinctive function when it brings us to God through Jesus Christ."[42]

My colleague Rob James is fond of suggesting "we need to let the Bible have its way with us." When we allow the Scriptures to function in the manner for which they were intended—as that which conserves and communicates revelation, which is the story of God's redemptive history with humanity—it will ably bear witness to the story of Christ which makes us free. That Scripture is wholly trustworthy is not at question among us; how we will let it transform us, and transform the way we live, is the pressing question.

Extending the Welcome

Human freedom does not require the absence of God, as John Paul Sartre believed. To the contrary, human freedom is only made possible by the liberating action of God. Being set free "from the law of sin and death" allows the human to join with God in the transforming work of salvation. When we are "obedient to the cross of truth" (Merton's phrase), our hearts are opened toward others, even as God's grace has included us.

Our guidance for redemptive actions on behalf of others comes from what Rosemary Radford Ruether calls the norm for biblical faith, the "prophetic-liberating tradition."[43] This recurring theme in Scripture is the creative dynamic that corrects ideological deformations among God's people and once again relates God's redemption to the concrete needs of people pushed to the margins of society. The tradition of liberation is clearly heard in the Old Testament prophets and is brought to its ultimate expression in the preaching of Jesus concerning the *basileia,* the rule of God.

Have we as contemporary Baptists forgotten this focus of Scripture? It seems that we spend more energy finding ways to exclude persons for doctrinal variances than we spend extending God's welcome with our money, our voices, and our embrace. Our early forebears were certainly concerned about liberty—and not simply their own.[44] But sinful humans, even those of us being redeemed, are always tempted to sacrifice the freedom of others in order to ensure our own, which constricts the spaciousness of the "room" in which God's people dwell.

Elizabeth Schussler Fiorenza contends that in some of the later writings of the New Testament we can discover the marginalization of oppressed groups such as women and slaves so as to make the Christian presence less offensive in a situation conducive to persecution. The freedom of the leadership was preserved at the expense of these other sisters and brothers in Christ,[45] which is a gross distortion of Christian freedom. We must listen to the internal prophetic critique within Scripture for it can galvanize new sensitivity in different epochs. Hence, we must not hesitate to use new methods of interpretation (such as the feminist one from which I am drawing) with a "hermeneutical flexibility" (Patterson's term) as we seek to respond to the insistent cries of contemporary persons.

Further, we can trust that the Spirit of God will lead us to new insights on the biblical tradition as we wrestle with the pressing needs of our time. It will remain important that this venture in interpretation be undertaken within the community of faith, not in imperious isolation.[46] The left wing of the Reformation—our Anabaptist forebears who well knew that Spirit, Scripture, and community must remain in dynamic relationship—can provide timely assistance.

What, then, is the spacious freedom which the truth of God makes possible? It is primarily freedom for redeeming relationship with God and with others. Christ beckons us to saving relationship, and we have opened our arms to His embrace. Truth, as we can testify, usually makes itself known in personal form, as Kierkegaard taught us, and we must express God's truth through our living. Salvation provides a gradual healing that allows us not only to know how welcome we are in God's presence, but how expansive God's welcome is.

The cross has overcome our fear of God and removes any basis for considering ourselves enemies of God. It also removes any ground for pretension; we should not presume judgment upon those whom God counts as righteous. Further, those who have not accepted God's righteousness in Christ through faith should be regarded as ones for whom Christ also died—and who need to be told just that. Freed from the preoccupying and self-defeating attempt to save ourselves and please God, we can offer ourselves in service for those still in bondage.

The biblical view of freedom always involves social-ethical responsibility, for liberation was not meant to be possession for the few; rather, it is a dynamic relationship which must not be consigned to the safe area of doctrine. God's redemptive truth must become, in the words of Paul Fiddes, "a powerful motive in transforming the actual situation of people today."[47] Though the assessment of Dockery and Mohler that Southern Baptists are guilty of doctrinal neglect and accentuation of programs is most apt, we should not welcome an epoch of scholasticism that so preoccupies us we neglect pressing evangelistic and justice concerns.

This will require that we strengthen our relationship with God, which can come about through prayer, meditation upon Scripture, and service. We become most like that which we set our hearts upon. It is not possible to be a maturing Christian, prompted to live for God and for others, without discerning our lives within the biblical story. There we will be instructed, corrected, and thoroughly furnished for every good work. A patient listening to the gospel will "form our minds," as Basil Pennington writes.[48] We will be reminded of the freedom we have in Christ to find new ways of ministry in His name. Through the biblical narrative we will hear again, by the amplification of the Spirit of God, the calling to bear witness to God's truth which comes to us in gospel form and which our lives help extend.

Conclusion

In dialogue with the first four chapters, I have called for theological renewal based upon a return to *theologia crucis* rather than *theologia gloria*. As our point of departure for theological construction, the cross tells the truth about God, the Christ, and humanity. This hermeneutical norm can assist greatly, I believe, toward a theological consensus. That God chooses to redeem sinful persons through Jesus in the cross is certainly the heart of our faith and is the fulcrum for whatever else we say in Christian theology.

We must learn to discriminate between those strands in Scripture where Scripture most fully bears witness to its focal truth and those strands in which that focal truth is subordinated to lesser concerns. Historical-critical studies and some of the insights of literary-aesthetic approaches can help us in this task.

Theology functions in the service of understanding and ministering, never seeking knowledge for its own sake, but always concerned about its shepherding role.[49] While the Bible and our present denominational hour urge us to "contend for the faith," theology is misused when it becomes an instrument for wounding other Christians or driving them out of the "broad place."

Getting beyond our present impasse will require humility, repentance, and the will for "convictional cooperation," as Mohler winsomely calls it. Only the providential grace of our God can bring about a new spirit of cooperation; only the wisdom borne of God's Spirit can instruct a way forward together.

Notes

1. In my opinion, the current "impasse" in Baptist life has more to do
with cultural shifts and fundamentalist ascendancy than with one's view of
Holy Scripture. While fundamentalist-conservatives have maintained that
the authority and trustworthiness of Scripture (i.e., inerrancy), is the
central issue, I believe our fragmentation is the result of many complex
sociological, ecclesiological, and theological issues. Robert Wuthnow, *The
Restructuring of American Religion* (Princeton: Princeton University Press,
1988), 198, offers this description of the mid-1970s: "The growing influence of a more conservative element within American evangelicalism . . .
was . . . a function of trends in culture at large. . . ." Cf. Nancy Tatom
Ammerman, *Baptist Battles: Social Change and Religious Conflict in the
Southern Baptist Convention* (New Brunswick: Rutgers University Press,
1990), 128*ff*. The studies of each of these eminent sociologists demonstrate
how the Southern Baptist controversy reflects much larger cultural currents
in American society. Another factor, rarely discussed in the current internecine atmosphere, is the lack of women's voices helping shape the Convention's agenda. The particularly male character of our controversy is
evidenced in the initial election of twenty men to the SBC Peace Committee.
Only after some women complained were two women added.

2. See Childs's *Introduction to the Old Testament as Scripture* (Philadelphia: Fortress, 1979) and *The New Testament as Canon: An Introduction*
(Philadelphia: Fortress, 1985). What matters for Childs is the final canonical
form, which alone can be called Scripture for a community of faith and
practice. He does not use the term "canonical criticism" lest it be misunderstood as no more than one more form of biblical criticism among others. The
canon, rather, is the horizon in which biblical criticism can occur, in his
opinion. James A. Sanders has attempted a very different and perhaps more
helpful approach in *Canon and Community: A Guide to Canonical Criticism*
(Philadelphia: Fortress, 1984). Cf. idem, *From Sacred Story to Sacred Text*
(Philadelphia: Fortress, 1987). Sanders differs from Childs in resisting exclusive
focus on the final form of the texts and attending more to the canonical process which involves both selection of materials and hermeneutical strategies.

3. Paul Ricoeur is most helpful in this regard, especially his *Interpretation Theory: Discourse and the Surplus of Meaning* (Fort Worth: Texas
Christian University Press, 1976). Cf. idem, *Essays on Biblical Interpretation* (Philadelphia: Fortress, 1980), and his earlier work *The Conflict of
Interpretations* (Evanston: Northwestern University Press, 1974).

4. Raymond E. Brown, "More-Than-Literal Senses," in Raymond
Brown, Joseph Fitzmyer, and Roland E. Murphy, eds., *The New Jerome*

Biblical Commentary (Englewood Cliffs, N.J.: Prentice Hall, 1990), 1157. For comparison see the fine article by Charles J. Scalise, "The 'Sensus Literalis': A Hermeneutical Key to Biblical Exegesis," *Scottish Journal of Theology* 42 (1988): 45-65. The *sensus plenior* depends upon the scholastic theory of instrumental relationship between the divine and human authors of Scripture.

5. Nigel M. De S. Cameron, *Biblical Higher Criticism and the Defense of Infallibilism in 19th Century Britain,* Texts and Studies in Religion, vol. 33 (Lewiston/Queenston: Edwin Mellen, 1987), 18.

6. R. Alan Culpepper, *Anatomy of the Fourth Gospel: A Study in Literary Design* (Philadelphia: Fortress, 1983), speaks to this polarizing assessment: ". . . our effort to set aside interest in the Johannine community or the historical Jesus should not be interpreted as a denial of any historical core or matrix of the gospel. Once the effort has been made to understand the narrative character of the gospels, some rapprochement with the traditional, historical issues will be necessary" (11).

7. For the rationale behind feminist hermeneutics, see the following articles: Mary Ann Tolbert, "Defining the Problem: The Bible and Feminist Hermeneutics," *Semeia* 28 (1983): 113-26; Katharine Doob Sakenfeld, "Feminist Uses of Biblical Materials," in Letty M. Russell, ed., *Feminist Interpretation of the Bible* (Philadelphia: Westminster, 1985), 55-64.

8. Among the works of the evangelical feminist scholars I mentioned are the following: Aida Besancon Spencer, *Beyond the Curse: Women Called to Ministry* (Nashville: Thomas Nelson, 1985); Ben Witherington III, *Women in the Earliest Churches,* Society for New Testament Studies Monograph Series 59 (Cambridge: Cambridge University Press, 1988); David M. Scholer, "Feminist Hermeneutics and Evangelical Biblical Interpretation," *Journal of the Evangelical Theological Society* December 30 (1987): 407-20; idem, *A Biblical Basis for Equal Partnership: Women and Men in the Ministry of the Church* (New York: The Ministers and Missionaries Benefit Board of American Baptist Churches, 1986); and E. Margaret Howe, *Women and Church Leadership* (Grand Rapids: Zondervan, 1982).

9. It is very important to distinguish between feminist *theology* (which may be distinctly Christian) and feminist *spirituality*. Writers often employ these terms interchangeably and thereby cause considerable confusion. Feminist theology can be either Jewish or Christian and is concerned with the history, sources, structures, and personal application of its respective tradition, anchored in a continuing relationship with the self-revealing God of Holy Scripture. Two recent examples of Christian feminist theology are Daphne Hampson, *Theology and Feminism* (Oxford: Basil Blackwell, Ltd., 1990), and the work of Eleanor Rae and Bernice Marie-Daly, *Created in Her Image* (New York: Crossroad, 1990). A groundbreaking monograph in Jewish

feminist theology is Judith Plaskow's *Standing Again at Sinai: Rethinking Judaism from a Feminist Perspective* (New York: Harper and Row, 1990).

Feminist spirituality, a term which covers many discrete emphases, is not explicitly theological in the sense just used (although it may reflect deep commitment to the Jewish or Christian tradition). It accents the distinctive biological and cultural experiences of women and often looks to alternative "deities" to worship—either the "divine within" or goddess figures. An extensive survey of feminist spirituality is available in the collection edited by Judith Plaskow and Carol P. Christ, *Weaving the Visions: New Patterns in Feminist Spirituality* (New York: Harper and Row, 1989).

See my recent article, coauthored with E. Glenn Hinson, "The Contribution of Women to Spirituality," in *Becoming Christian*, ed. Bill J. Leonard (Louisville: John Knox-Westminster, 1990), 116-30, which deals with Christian feminist spirituality.

10. Francis Schussler Fiorenza, "The Crisis of Scriptural Authority: Interpretation and Reception," *Interpretation* 44 October (1990), drawing from the work of Hans Robert Jauss, uses the term "reception hermeneutics" to describe the process whereby one can best understand a piece of literature. It requires that "one has to understand the expectation horizon of the audience as well as the expectation horizon of the author" (365).

11. Perhaps he has given too narrow a definition to theological thinking. According to a recent article by Stephen Toulmin, all serious questions are at bottom theological, for "issues of theology exist, and arise, at the base of all abstract academic disciplines equally." Stephen Toulmin, *Theological Education* 26 (Spring 1990): 60. I would supplement Toulmin's analysis by suggesting that issues of theology are indeed the ultimate questions that every human being asks. I have been assisted in this perspective by Clyde F. Crews' useful textbook, *Ultimate Questions: A Theological Primer* (New York: Paulist, 1986).

Very helpful in our attempt to understand and correct the absence of serious theological reflection in our age is the study by Joseph C. Hough, Jr., and John Cobb, Jr., *Christian Identity and Theological Education* (Chico, Calif.: Scholars Press, 1985), which examines at length the relationship of theological education to the ongoing life of the church. Cf. Edward Farley, *Theologia* (Philadelphia: Fortress, 1983).

12. See the fine article by Craig Dykstra, "Communities of Conviction and the Liberal Arts," *Bulletin: The Council of Societies for the Study of Religion* 19 September (1990).

13. Bill J. Leonard, *God's Last and Only Hope: The Fragmentation of the Southern Baptist Convention* (Grand Rapids: Eerdmans, 1990), 38.

14. Colin Gunton, "Used and Being Used: Scripture and Systematic Theology," *Theoloogy Today* 57 October (1990): 248-59, can help us think

about historical relativity without a thoroughgoing relativism. He writes: "To claim that all expressions and formulations are relative to their time does not imply an absolute relativism of the kind that treats cultures as totalities sealed off from one another. The point is one about the finitude, contingency, historicity, and fallibility of any place in the tradition, ours included. . . . That is not to deny that a formulation, theological or otherwise, may claim to be true" (252-53).

15. E. Glenn Hinson insists that Baptists have rejected the binding quality of the creedal statements of the Reformation and the principal works of seventeenth century Scholasticism. James Leo Garrett, Jr., E. Glenn Hinson, and James E. Tull, *Are Southern Baptists "Evangelicals"?* (Macon: Mercer, 1983), 166. For a different perspective, see especially Russ Bush and Tom J. Nettles, *Baptists and the Bible* (Chicago: Moody, 1980).

How to understand and employ "Baptist distinctives" is a critical concern on both sides of our current impasse. For assistance on this issue, see *The Takeover in the Southern Baptist Convention,* ed. Robison James (Decatur, Ga.: *SBC Today,* 1989).

16. John Donahue, "The Changing Shape of New Testament Theology," *Theological Studies* 50 (1989): 314-35. Cf. the helpful article by Patrick Keifert, "An Ecumenical Horizon for 'Canon Within a Canon?'" *Currents in Theology and Mission* 14 June (1987).

17. Darrell Jodock, "The Reciprocity Between Scripture and Theology: The Role of Scripture in Contemporary Theological Reflection," *Interpretation* 54 October (1990): 369-82.

18. Jane Dempsey Douglass, *Women, Freedom, and Calvin* (Philadelphia: Westminster, 1985), 9.

19. See my recent article, "Exercising the Priesthood of the Believer: Women Pursuing Ministry," *The Campus Minister,* 12 Spring (1990): 21-29. See also these two earlier articles, "Toward An Encompassing Theological Vision for Women in Light of Baptist Tradition," *Folio: A Newsletter for Southern Baptist Women in Ministry,* Autumn 1986, and "When Keeping Silent No Longer Will Do: A Theological Agenda for the Contemporary Church," *Review and Expositor* 83 (Winter 1986). Rather than allowing a lingering perception of women ministers as interlopers in Baptist life, we must lay appropriate claim to the Baptist belief that one's being called needs no authority other than the lordship of Christ to determine the viability of such a call. For this important point, Baptists are especially indebted to Martin Luther, "The Freedom of the Christian," in *Three Treatises* (Philadelphia: Fortress, 1960), 290*ff.* Robert K. Johnston offers helpful hermeneutical guidelines for exploring this issue in *Evangelicals at an Impasse: Biblical Authority in Practice* (Atlanta: John Knox Press, 1979), 69-75.

20. E. Y. Mullins, *The Axioms of Religion* (Philadelphia: The Griffith

& Rowland Press, 1908), 34-35. Cf. E. Glenn Hinson, *Soul Liberty* (Nashville: Convention, 1975).

21. Martin Luther clearly distinguished between a "theology of glory" and a "theology of the cross" in the Heidelberg Disputation of 1518. For him, the theology of the cross is not only the foundation for the Christian faith, but it is the only way to understand correctly the nature of God. A theology of glory, on the other hand, is more concerned with the triumphant, unambiguous exercise of power. See the fine work of Alister E. McGrath, *Luther's Theology of the Cross* (Oxford: Basil Blackwell, 1985), for a careful delineation of this aspect of Luther's theology. Cf. idem, *The Mystery of the Cross* (Grand Rapids: Zondervan, 1988).

22. James A. Sanders, "The Bible and the Believing Communities," in *The Hermeneutical Quest: Essays in Honor of James Luther Mays,* ed. Donald G. Miller (Allison Park, Pa.: Pickwick, 1986), 145. Cf. James Hopewell, "A Congregational Paradigm for Theological Education," *Theological Education* (Autumn 1984): 60-80.

23. John Robinson, *The Roots of a Radical* (London: SCM, 1980), 73.

24. C.H. Dodd, *The Apostolic Preaching and Its Developments* (New York: Harper and Brothers, 1936), 13.

25. James Barr, *Holy Scripture* (Philadelphia: Westminster, 1983), 14.

26. Ibid.

27. Ibid., 18.

28. Clark Pinnock, *Tracking the Maze: Finding Our Way Through Modern Theology from an Evangelical Perspective* (San Francisco: Harper and Row, 1990), 172.

29. A. D. R. Polman, *The Word of God According to St. Augustine,* trans. A. J. Pomerans (Grand Rapids: Eerdmans, 1961), 41. Cf. Jack B. Rogers and Donald K. McKim, *The Authority and Interpretation of the Bible* (San Francisco: Harper and Row, 1979), for a historical survey of the developing understandings in the church of the foundation, form, and function of Scripture.

30. Timothy George, *Theology of the Reformers* (Nashville: Broadman, 1988), 315. Rogers and McKim, *Authority and Interpretation* (73ff.) argue that the Reformers accented the "saving function" of Scripture; it serves to lead people to Christ.

31. John Macquarrie, *Principles of Christian Theology,* rev. ed. (London: SCM, 1977), 318f.

32. See Clark Pinnock's very helpful study, *The Scripture Principle* (San Francisco: Harper and Row, 1984), for a clear explication of the function of this principle.

33. J. A. T. Robinson employs this distinction in all of his Christological writings. See his *Roots of a Radical,* 72, and *The Human Face of God* (Philadelphia: Westminster, 1973).

34. C. F. D. Moule, "The Holy Spirit and Scripture," Valedictory Lecture, Cambridge University, 29 November 1980, Cambridge, England.

35. George Lindbeck, *The Nature of Doctrine* (Philadelphia: Westminster, 1984), 117. A further clarification of his proposal is found in his article "Scripture, Consensus, and Community," *This World: A Journal of Religion and Public Life* 23 (Fall 1988): 5-24.

36. Ibid.

37. Ibid., 118.

38. Hans Frei, *The Eclipse of Biblical Narrative* (New Haven: Yale University Press, 1974). Cf. Henning Graf Reventlow, *The Authority of the Bible and the Rise of the Modern World* (Philadelphia: Fortress, 1985), 9-31, for an extensive analysis of the cultural situation that led to the marginalization of biblical authority.

39. Pinnock, *Tracking the Maze,* 182*ff.* In his perceptive new book *Theology for the Third Millennium: An Ecumenical View* (New York: Doubleday, 1988), 4, Hans Kung characterizes postmodernity as a time of new global understandings of regions, religions, and denominations. I fear for many Southern Baptists it is a time of buttressing a sectarian or insular worldview, instead.

40. Lindbeck, 120.

41. David Kelsey, *The Uses of Scripture in Recent Theology* (Philadelphia: Fortress, 1975), 48.

42. Moule, Valedictory Address.

43. Rosemary Radford Ruether, *Sexism and God-Talk* (Boston: Beacon, 1983), 31. Harrelson's perspective that Scripture helps us discriminate its own levels of significance is quite helpful in this regard.

44. See Stanley J. Grenz's chapter, "Isaac Backus," in *Baptist Theologians,* ed. Timothy George and David S. Dockery (Nashville: Broadman Press, 1990), 112*ff.*

45. Elizabeth Schussler Fiorenza, *In Memory of Her: A Feminist Theological Reconstruction of Christian Origins* (New York: Crossroads, 1983).

46. Maurice Wiles, "The Uses of Holy Scripture," *Explorations in Theology 4* (London: Darton, Longman, and Todd, 1973), 81, urges that the Bible be viewed "as a common resource of life and spirituality" for the Christian community.

47. Paul Fiddes, *Past Event and Present Salvation* (Louisville: Westminster/John Knox, 1989), 190.

48. Basil M. Pennington, *Called: New Thinking on Christian Vocation* (New York: Seabury, 1982).

49. Augustine offered this insight about theology in his instructive work on the Trinity: "The only merit of this science is that from it a saving faith is born, nourished, defended, and strengthened." *De Trinitate,* 14.1.

8
Conflict and Identity in the SBC:
The Quest for a New Consensus
*Timothy George**

The internecine conflict in the Southern Baptist Convention can only be properly understood in the context of the wider struggle of American evangelicals to come to grips with the crisis of modernity. Future historians will probably treat the present controversy as the culmination of a thirty-year process of denominational reorientation extending from 1961 to 1991—from Ralph Elliott's *The Meaning of Genesis* to *The New American Commentary,* both products of Broadman Press. The battle for denominational control has now resulted in a decisive shift in direction for the SBC (called "takeover" by moderates, and "turnaround" by conservatives), a process not likely to be reversed in the foreseeable future despite continuing skirmishes between incumbents and insurgents.

Given this new political reality, the nature of the "impasse" in the SBC has changed even since the gathering of these essays began. The fond hope for a return to the *status quo ante bellum* is no longer a viable possibility. Moderates must decide whether they can find a place to stand in the new order or else seek alternative alignments. Conservatives have an even greater worry: Can they survive their own success? Can they forge a new consensus which will include

*Timothy George (Th.D., Harvard University) is founding Dean and Professor of Divinity at the Beeson Divinity School of Samford University. A prolific author, George has written over 40 articles for a variety of scholarly journals and reference works including *The Disciple's Study Bible, The Mercer Dictionary of the Bible,* and *The Dictionary of Christianity in America.* He is the author of the highly acclaimed *Theology of the Reformers, Faithful Witness: The Life and Mission of William Carey,* and *John Robinson and the English Separatist Tradition.* He has edited works on *John Calvin, Baptist Theologians, James Petigru Boyce* and a volume on *Continuity and Discontinuity in Church History.* He is a member of Shades Mountain Baptist Church in Birmingham, Alabama.

most, if not all, Southern Baptists without replicating the very system their movement was launched to reform?

These questions pose a profound crisis of identity for Southern Baptists in the last decade of the twentieth century. The first four essays in this volume deal with vital issues which must be faced in the quest for a new consensus. Following a brief overview of the developing rift in the Convention, I shall focus on three strategic areas of concern which press for clarification and restatement: Biblical authority, Baptist heritage, and theological renewal. With my colleagues as discussion partners, I shall examine how these three bases of the traditional body of divinity, long arenas of conflict within the denomination, may also serve as the crucible for evangelical renewal.

The SBC: From Synthesis to Schism

In 1900 the Southern Baptist Sunday School Board, then only nine years old, published a remarkable collection of essays entitled *Baptist Why and Why Not*. In the opening paragraph J. M. Frost declared: "Baptists are one in contending for the faith; one in their history and the heritage of their fathers; one in their purpose to preach the gospel of the grace of God among all nations."[1] The chapter titles of the book have a polemical ring—"Why Baptist and Not Campbellite," "Why Immersion and Not Sprinkling," "Why Missionary and Not 'Omissionary.'" The purpose of the volume was to be a "campaign book," a tool for the promotion of denominational interests such as Baptist schools, missionary endeavors, and benevolent concerns.[2] While recognizing diversity among themselves on many ancillary matters, the twenty-five contributors to this volume stood together on a common doctrinal foundation. "We accept the Scriptures as an all-sufficient and infallible rule of faith and practice, and insist upon the absolute inerrancy and sole authority of the Word of God. We recognize at this point no room for division, either of practice or belief, or even sentiment."[3] A "Declaration of Faith" was appended to the volume incorporating many of the articles which were later adopted in *The Baptist Faith and Message* of 1925. In that same year the Convention would also approve the Cooperative Program, thus providing both a confessional and organizational basis for its consolidation and expansion.

While there has never been absolute uniformity among Southern Baptist congregations, the denomination entered the twentieth century remarkably united in its basic mission and purpose. Three developments during the early decades of the century further solidified the Southern Baptist synthesis: the refusal to join the emerging ecumenical movement, the containment of the Fundamentalist-Modernist controversy, and the construction of an impressive denominational bureaucracy supported by a systematic plan of finance. These were not isolated strands but rather interconnected facets of the developing Southern Baptist consciousness. Each reinforced the other, and each provided a common enemy to oppose—the "bastard" Union Movement, as one denominational executive described it; theological liberalism, safely sequestered in the Northern denominations; and eccelesiastical separatism epitomized by J. Frank Norris whose guerrilla tactics against the denominational "machine" were more of a nuisance than a genuine threat.[4] All three factors entered into the report of a special committee, unanimously adopted by the SBC in 1951. While affirming the missions efforts of Southern Baptists outside the traditional "Southland," the report focused on the doctrinal deviation of many ecumenical leaders who deny "such scriptural truths as the Virgin birth, the deity of Christ, and the inerrancy of the Holy Scriptures."[5]

David Dockery, in an earlier chapter in this book, has pointed to two developments in the 1950s which portended ill for the gathering storms of the next three decades: the introduction of historical-critical studies in Baptist seminaries and colleges and the dominance of a program-centered approach to ministry. The success of the latter imbued Convention leaders with a heady sense of invincibility as they steered the denomination in an increasingly progressivist direction during the 1960s and 1970s. As early as 1963 historian Samuel Hill predicted that the denominational applecart could be upset by a populist, grass-roots reaction: "The convention's polity being as it is, wresting of control by the ultra-conservatives from the moderates is not impossible."[6] To some extent, the term "inerrancy" became the rallying cry for conservatives because other targets were too mobile to hit squarely. As Nancy Ammerman explains, the "actual moderate agenda" was camouflaged by an amorphous appeal to "freedom" because moderate leaders were convinced that "they could not rally majority support" for their progressivist ideas.[7] In both cases the underlying theological basis of the conflict was seldom explored—moderates largely denying that there was a theological rationale for the controversy; conservatives fixated so narrowly on inerrancy that doctrinal concerns in other areas were ignored or pushed to the sidelines.

The SBC stands today on the brink of schism. The next several years will likely witness the emergence of a splinter denomination guided by activist moderates who have abandoned their hopes for reforming the SBC in a mainline Protestant direction. Like Landmark Baptists and Independent Baptists who left the Convention in earlier generations, these "Free Baptists" (as they might like to be called) will continue to exist side by side with Southern Baptists, offering still another Baptist alternative on the religious landscape, much as PCA and PCUSA churches coexist today in most Southern cities representing two distinct variants of the Presbyterian tradition.

The conservative victory in the SBC will prove hollow, however, unless it is accompanied by genuine spiritual and theological renewal and a process of reconciliation with cooperating, Bible-believing moderates. The new consensus must embody the best scholarly insights of the evangelical renaissance of the past forty years, largely neglected in Southern Baptist academic circles until recently. The new consensus must also anticipate the questions of the third millennium and seek to answer them in the light of Holy Scripture, our Baptist heritage, and a theology which is faithful to the living God, its gracious and sovereign Object. Perhaps the greatest lesson of the past thirty years is this: We are able to understand the present and illuminate the future only to the extent that we do not forsake the warranted wisdom of the past.

Biblical Authority: Reclaiming Holy Scripture as the Word of God

Each of the lead essays in this volume has addressed itself to aspects of the central theological dispute in the SBC controversy, namely, the authority, inspiration, and proper interpretation of the Bible. In his chapter Dockery has reviewed various theories of biblical inspiration and restated the case for "a commitment to a completely truthful and fully authoritative Bible." Walter Harrelson has argued that a discriminating use of historical criticism is an indispensable tool in transmitting intact the Christian faith. John Newport has analyzed recent literary approaches to the Bible, showing both the promise and peril they pose for an evangelical approach to Scripture. Albert Mohler has called for the reclamation of biblical inerrancy as an essential element in a holistic theological framework.

The Baptist "battle for the Bible" must be set in the much wider context of the ambivalence inherent in biblical exegetical methodology for well over a hundred years now. Johannes Semler (d. 1791), one of the founders of the modern critical study of the Bible, already anticipated the relativizing of both the biblical canon and the classic dogmas of patristic Christianity.[8] There is more than a little irony in Wladimir Solowjew's depiction of the Antichrist, the very Man of Sin himself, as a famous scholar who held an earned doctorate in theology from Tübingen and had published a pioneering study in the field of biblical exegesis!

As Dockery has shown, historic Baptist confessions invariably express unquestioned confidence in the trustworthy character of the Bible describing it as *inspired, infallible, perfect, certain, true, without error,* and so forth.[9] For the most part, however, these statements were drafted in a pre-Enlightenment era prior to the rationalistic assault on the integrity of the biblical materials. We cannot here review the impact of this methodology on the use of the Bible in the life of the church. Suffice it to say that the doctrine of biblical inerrancy as set forth, for example, in the writings of Scottish theologians, such as Thomas Chalmers and William Cunningham, and the Princeton fathers, Hodge and Warfield,[10] was a deliberate response to the inroads of destructive biblical criticism. *The Chicago Statements on Biblical Inerrancy* (1978, 1981) are the most recent, and most carefully nuanced, articulations of this position.

The destructive potential of biblical criticism first became an issue of concern among Southern Baptists in the controversy surrounding the pressured resignation of Crawford H. Toy from the faculty of Southern Seminary in 1879. Enamored by advanced theories of "progressive" scholarship, Toy came to deny that many of the events recorded in the Old Testament had actually occurred. He also questioned the Christological implications of many messianic prophecies, including Genesis 49:9-10 which the New Testament (Rev. 5:5) specifically applies to Christ.[11] In the wake of

the Toy affair, Basil Manly, Jr., one of the Seminary's founders, drafted his *Bible Doctrine of Inspiration* (1888) as a deliberate restatement of the historic Protestant doctrine of Scripture. Without naming Toy, he reviewed the impact of "Higher Criticism," as it was then called, on biblical studies and made the following conclusion which has lost none of its relevance in the intervening century: "We have no need nor disposition to undervalue either the legitimate method or the fairly established results of modern critical research . . . a true "Higher Criticism" may be just as valuable as a false or misguided attempt at it may be dangerous and delusive."[12]

What is at stake in the present context is not the validity of chastened, "believing" criticism, which responsible conservatives allow, but rather the uncritical dissemination of postcritical presuppositions concerning the Bible, which some moderates have been reluctant to disavow. The doctrine of inerrancy, as defined by the Chicago Statements, precludes neither the recognition of various literary genres within the body of Scripture nor the investigation of sources and forms which were integral to the formation of Scripture in its present canonical shape. It does stand, however, as a check against the evaporation of biblical events and miracles into literary devices or imaginative constructs detached from their specific historical contexts. Thus we may agree with Harrelson that Genesis 1—11 is "a *theological* affirmation about the origins of the universe and its peoples at God's initiatives" without denying the historicity of Adam and Eve or any other feature of the received narrative. That Adam and Eve have symbolic and representative significance has never been doubted in Christian theology from the Christ-Adam analogy in Paul to the Reformed doctrine of federal headship. Genesis 1—11 can be "strictly" historical without being exhaustively so; it is *more* than an accurate record of what took place in space and time back then and there, but it is not less than that. Turning to the New Testament, we may make a similar claim for the account of Jesus' raising of Lazarus in John 11. Surely this narrative is about more than the resuscitation of a corpse: It is the manifestation of Jesus as the Resurrection and the Life. But it does not involve anything less than what John says took place in the village of Bethany during Jesus' earthly ministry. To interpret this pericope as a post-Easter story interpolated back into the Gospel of John is to do violence to the salvation-historical significance of the incarnation itself; it is to substitute a docetic reading of the text for the flesh-and-blood reality of Jesus.[13]

What is required of evangelical Bible scholars is not a wholesale rejection of all critical methodologies, but rather an even more rigorous criticism of the underlying assumptions of such approaches which frequently result in reductionistic and antisupernaturalist interpretations of Scripture. Many recent hermeneutical systems, including the various literary approaches which John Newport has described so ably, suffer from what might be called the "imperialism of the present." Peter Berger has characterized this modern malady which lies behind Rudolf Bultmann's program of demythologization and its various epigones:

> The present, however, remains strangely immune from relativization. In other words, the New Testament writers are seen as afflicted with a false consciousness rooted in their time, but the contemporary analyst takes the consciousness of *his* time as an unmixed intellectual blessing. The electricity and radio users are placed intellectually above the Apostle Paul.[14]

Guided by such hubris, the modern critical study of the Bible has become more and more detached from the life of the church. Rather than serving as a means of "passing on the faith intact," such studies tend toward a sterile specialization and show little if any interest in catechesis, worship, outreach, or spirituality.[15] In the early part of this century, Karl Barth, no stranger to biblical criticism, declared that the purpose of serious Scripture study was not to make the Bible "relevant" to our modern world, but rather to come to see how *irrelevant* the modern world—and we ourselves—have become in our rebellion against God. Only a reverent, believing scholarship, one which accepts without apology the total truthfulness of Holy Scripture, can point the church toward such an engagement with God's written Word.

Fortunately, Southern Baptist scholars need not start from scratch in this grand enterprise. The wealth of evangelical biblical scholarship over the past generation must be mined and extended through projects such as *The New American Commentary*. The great heritage of John A. Broadus, A.T. Robertson, and John R. Sampey must be reclaimed in continuity with the recent contributions of Earl Ellis, George R. Beasley-Murray, and Curtis Vaughan. Unnecessary critical concessions which weaken the objective truth and historical factuality of the biblical revelation must be opposed, but an open-minded interaction with promising trends such as the movement toward canonical theology fostered by Brevard Childs should be pursued with eagerness. Beyond the classroom, the library, and the word processor, specific steps must be taken to recover a sense of Holy Scripture as the Word of God in preaching, evangelism, counseling, education, and missions. Such a process involves not only correct belief about the Bible, but also a new and more vibrant place for the Bible in the life of the community of faith.

Baptist Heritage: The Future of Our Religious Past

The "conflict of visions" in the SBC encompasses not only differing views of the Bible but also diverse claims about relative degrees of fidelity to the Baptist tradition. Sometimes such claims are put forth in exaggerated polemical images. The moderate likens the Convention "takeover" to the rape of his mother; the conservative replies that at last his mother has been rescued from evil molesters. In the heat of the political struggle, both sides have sometimes depicted the conflict as a cosmic battle between the Children of Light and the Children of Darkness. Such apocalyptic language obscures the fact that the Baptist heritage can be described in various ways and that present differences are frequently echoes of earlier contentions. To see how the issue of Baptist identity is shaped by one's reading of the denominational past, we shall look briefly at an issue which has loomed large in recent debates.

Are Baptist a creedal people? On the surface it would seem that such a question is entirely gratuitous. It is like asking whether Baptist sprinkle infants. The phrase "Baptists are not a creedal people" has almost become an axiom within our tradition, and yet its meaning is not at all as univocal as some would imply.

Historically, the Baptist claim to be noncreedal has meant primarily three things: First, it was a protest against state-imposed religious conformity and the attendant civil sanctions associated therewith. From their earliest emergence in seventeenth-century England, Baptists of all theological persuasions have been ardent supporters of religious liberty. In this vein, Roger Williams opposed the Congregationalist ecclesiocracy in New England, and John Leland went to prison in Virginia rather than acquiesce to the Anglican state church. The doctrine of religious liberty required that there be no external political monitoring of the internal religious life of voluntary associations. However, it was this same cherished tenet which guaranteed the ability of such associations to order their own internal life, their doctrine and discipline, in accordance with their own perception of divine truth. Second, Baptist are not creedal in that they have never elevated any man-made doctrinal construct above Holy Scripture. As Baptist confessions themselves invariably declare, the Bible alone remains the *norma normans* for all our teaching and instruction, "the supreme standard by which all human conduct, creeds, and religious opinions should be tried."[16] Third, Baptist are not creedal in that no Baptist confession of faith has ever been promulgated as infallible or beyond revision. The multiplicity of Baptist confessions is witness to this distinctive trait. For example, William Lumpkin's anthology, *Baptist Confessions of Faith,* alone lists forty-five separate confessional documents.[17]

In these three major senses Baptists have never been *creedalistic.* However, the idea that voluntary, conscientious adherence to an explicit doctrinal standard is somehow foreign to the Baptist tradition is a peculiar notion not borne out by a careful examination of our heritage. During his lifetime and for many years thence, Andrew Fuller (d. 1815) was doubtless the most influential theologian among Baptists in both England and America. In an essay on "Creeds and Subscriptions," he declared:

> It has been very common among a certain class of writers, to exclaim against creeds on systems in religion as inconsistent with Christian liberty and the rights of conscience; but every well-informed and consistent believer must have a creed—a system which he supposes to contain the leading principles of divine revelation. . . .
> If the articles of faith be opposed to the authority of Scripture, or substituted in the place of such authority, they become objectionable and injurious; but if they simply express the united judgment of those who voluntarily subscribe them, they are incapable of any such kind of imputation.[18]

In this tradition James P. Boyce and the founders of Southern Seminary set forth the rationale for strict subscription to that institution's Abstract of Principles:

You will infringe the rights of no man, and you will secure the rights of those who have established here an instrumentality for the production of a sound ministry. It is no hardship to those who teach here, to be called upon to sign the declaration of their principles, for there are fields of usefulness open elsewhere to every man, and none need accept your call who cannot conscientiously sign your formulary.[19]

Similarly, E. Y. Mullins, the champion of soul liberty, outlined various basic Christian beliefs (e.g. biblical inspiration, the miracles of Christ, His vicarious atonement, bodily resurrection, literal ascension, and actual return) and declared before the SBC in 1923: "We believe that adherence to the above truths and facts is a necessary condition of service for teachers in our Baptist schools."[20] This statement served as an impetus for the formulation of *The Baptist Faith and Message* of 1925, of which Mullins was a principal architect.

The modern aversion to creeds, as opposed to the historic Baptist rejection of creedal*ism,* is related to several developments which have had a profound shaping influence on the contemporary Baptist consciousness. It was Thomas and Alexander Campbell who first raised the cry, "No creed but the Bible." The Campbellite campaign against creedalism led one Baptist leader, Robert B. Semple of Virginia, to declare, "Some of your opinions, though true, are pushed to extremes, such as those upon the use of creeds, confessions, . . . in short your views are so contrary to those of Baptist in general, that if a party was to go fully in to the practice of your principles I should say a new sect had sprung up, radically different from the Baptists as they now are."[21] Although Alexander Campbell was eventually excluded from the Baptist fellowship, he won a Pyrrhic victory when in time other Baptists incorporated his anticonfessionalism as their own view, and even defended it as the traditional Baptist position!

The Campbellite assimilation was congruent with another trend of major significance, namely, the development of individualism as the governing ethos of American culture. Baptists imbibed freely of the spirit of "rugged individualism" attenuating fixed norms of doctrine to a theology of radical subjectivism. W. S. Hudson, one of the most perceptive interpreters of Baptist history, has pointed to the devastating impact of this development on Baptist ecclesiology:

To the extent that Baptists were to develop an apologetic for their church life during the early decades of the twentieth century, it was to be on the basis of this highly individualistic principle. It has become increasingly apparent that this principle was derived from the general cultural and religious climate of the nineteenth century rather than from any serious study of the Bible. . . . The practical effect of the stress upon "soul competency" as the cardinal doctrine of Baptists was to make every man's hat his own church.[22]

As I have argued elsewhere, the priesthood of all believers (plural), a historic Reformation principle with corporate implications, devolved into the priesthood of *the believer,* a lonely, isolated seeker of truth, whose connection to the visible *congregatio sanctorum* was tenuous at best.[23] No doubt this development reflected, in part, a proper Baptist insistence on the personal element in faith over against the prevailing sacerdotalism and ritualism of other traditions. Still, this emphasis tended toward a religion of "every tub sitting on its own bottom," and accelerated a progressive disengagement from explicit confessional commitments.[24] Among Southern Baptists this mood was reflected in the intense debates surrounding the adoption of *The Baptist Faith and Message* in 1925. Among Northern Baptists the issue came to a head in 1946 when conservatives failed in their effort to persuade the convention to embrace even a minimal confessional standard.

The struggle for our religious past will likely continue in the SBC as disaffected moderates seek historical justification for new initiatives while conservatives also look to the heritage for precedents and vindication. How can such a "burnt-over district" serve as a basis for dialogue in the quest for a new consensus?

1. *The heritage as a critical principle.*—A better knowledge of the Baptist past will allow a more informed critique of present trends. What is naively assumed as the "historic Baptist view" may be shown to be a development of recent and perhaps questionable vintage. (I have tried to show that this is the case with the bias against confessions. Some moderates have leveled a similar charge against the doctrine of inerrancy.) Of course, the heritage may have been wrong at critical points! No one today defends the institution of slavery as did some of the ablest minds among the original founders of the SBC. Likewise, doctrinaire Landmarkism is rejected by article six of *The* (1963) *Baptist Faith and Message* which defines

the church as "the body of Christ which includes all of the redeemed of all the ages."[25] The heritage provides a vantage point from which we may gain perspective for evaluating our own theology and practice in the light of Holy Scripture.

2. *Baptist distinctives and evangelical essentials.*—A careful study of the Baptist past will reveal both distinctive features in our denominational history and wide areas of agreement with other evangelical Christians who stand with us as heirs of the Protestant Reformation.[26] Believer's baptism by immersion, congregational polity, the unique contribution Baptists have made to the struggle for religious liberty—these are distinguishing marks of our tradition. On occasion we have stoutly defended our "fences" while suffering the foundations to be shaken and destroyed. Robert Wuthnow's analysis of contemporary Protestant church life has led him to conclude that the fundamental religious divide is not among denominations but rather within them.[27] As Southern Baptists forge a new consensus in the 1990s and beyond, we must seek contact and alliances with evangelical believers outside our own tradition even as we reclaim those elements of special Baptist identity which have shaped and enriched our religious past. Along with other explicitly evangelical denominations such as the Assemblies of God and the Lutheran Church-Missouri Synod, Southern Baptists can play a major role in leading the wider evangelical community into the next century. To accept this challenge is not to betray our Baptist heritage but rather to enlarge it and to share it in the mission of world evangelization.

3. *Common roots?*—We have focused primarily on the Baptist heritage as a source of conflict and polemics in the present controversy. However, we should not forget that conservatives and moderates still hold much in common including the shared experience of divine grace in salvation. The rhetoric of conflict has frequently overshadowed underlying affinities. Both parties can learn from each other to affirm principles and ideals which are integral to the Baptist heritage, even though they have become associated with one or the other side in the recent conflict. The doctrine of biblical inerrancy, for example, is embraced by the majority of Baptists, moderates and conservatives alike. Similarly, religious liberty and the separation of church and state are valued by both groups, even if there is strong disagreement on how these principles apply to issues of contemporary concern such as prayer in public schools.

Just as the debate over biblical authority has refocused attention on the central document of the Christian faith, so too the struggle over Baptist heritage can have a healthy effect if it excites a new eagerness to unearth the hidden treasures of our religious past. Historian Walter Shurden put it well: "To fight over your heritage is not a good way to learn about it; but even that is better than ignoring it altogether."[28]

Theological Renewal: The Recovery of Christian Belief

John H. Leith has written that "the primary source of the malaise of the church is the loss of a distinctive Christian message and of the biblical and theological competence that made its preaching effective."[29] Albert Mohler has given a brilliant analysis of how this loss has impacted the SBC. His fourteen-point program of theological revitalization is worthy of further elaboration and implementation. In addition to the doctrine of Holy Scripture, biblical theism and salvific particularism are of paramount importance.

Carl F. H. Henry has said that the two basic axioms of the Christian religion are *the living God* and *divine revelation*.[30] Throughout our history, Baptists have been explicitly orthodox in our continuity with the Trinitarian and Christological consensus of the early church. Major exceptions to this tradition, such as the General Baptist defection to Unitarianism in the eighteenth century, have been met with swift repudiation. In recent years, however, accomodationist views of the reality of God, such as those put forth by process theology, have vied for acceptance under the banner of tolerable diversity. Baptist theologians must have the courage to say "no" to such views which, if carried to their logical extreme, would undermine the gospel itself.[31]

Mohler points to a second area of theological slippage which shapers of a new consensus among Southern Baptists must face squarely: the relativizing of the traditional Christian claim that personal faith in Jesus Christ is the only way of salvation for all peoples everywhere. Undoubtedly, this presupposition has undergirded the development of the Southern Baptist missionary enterprise from its humble origins to its present status as one of the leading forces of evangelical outreach in the Christian world. Yet it is challenged today by a host of competing ideologies and theories ranging from religious syncretism and unchecked pluralism to "anonymous Christianity" and schemes of "second-chance" salvation. Had such ideas prevailed among Baptists of an earlier era, William Carey would never have gone to India, nor Lottie Moon to China or, had they done so, they would have merely affirmed the values of the Hindu and Confucianist cultures they encountered rather than calling men and women "out of darkness into the marvelous light." That this topic was hotly debated at a recent meeting of the Evangelical Theological Society is evidence of its growing significance within all sectors of the Christian community.

As Southern Baptists confront these and other explosive issues in our efforts to move beyond the impasse toward a renewed framework of theological integrity, it will be helpful to keep in mind the following affirmations.

1. *Heresy is a possibility.*—The first generation of Christians found themselves confronted with a pattern of teaching which they could not countenance and remain faithful to their Lord (Gal. 1:9; 1 John 4:1-3). In the providence of God, heresy has sometimes served as useful purpose in calling forth a clearer definition of the true faith. For example, Marcion's rejection of the Old Testament as Christian Scripture accelerated the formation of the New Testament canon, while Pelagius's merit-based soteriology prompted Augustine's exposition of the doctrines of grace.

Surely we must be careful to distinguish the heresy from the heretic, and always reject censorious personal attacks against fellow believers, however serious their theological deviations may be. Still, the church of Jesus Christ must be willing to recognize and to reject gross perversions of the gospel when they crop up in its midst. A church which cannot distinguish heresy from truth or, even worse, which no longer thinks this is worth doing, is a church which has lost its right to bear witness to the transforming gospel of Jesus Christ who declared Himself to be not only the Way and the Life, but also the Truth, the only Truth which leads to the Father.

2. *Theological discrimination is a priority.*—It is crucial for Southern Baptists to learn to distinguish the central affirmations of the faith from the peripheral, adiaphorous issues which have become so divisive in our time. Mohler's image of "theological triage" is an apt metaphor for this process since it recalls an emergency setting of great stress such as a battlefield or shipwreck.

How could such a procedure work in the present context? Let us consider two issues which have been identified as potentially divisive among Southern Baptists, the revival of interest in Calvinism and women in ministry.

Over the past twenty years there has been a growing interest in the Reformed rootage of Southern Baptist life, prompted by the discovery that most early Southern Baptist theologians and church leaders were staunchly Calvinistic in their adherence to the doctrines of grace. One should not overestimate the size of this development; in sociological terms it resembles a special interest group rather than a "movement." Still, it has proved controversial in some areas since "Baptist" and "Calvinistic" are hardly regarded as synonymous, and because the antimissionary struggles of the last century have left deep scars and suspicious attitudes toward topics such as election, predestination, effectual calling, and so forth. Yet most Southern Baptist Calvinists are committed inerrantists; most have been sympathetic to if not politically active in the conservative resurgence. Southern Baptist Calvinists can contribute to the new consensus if they can show their theology to be a legitimate variant within the heritage, and if they can work cooperatively with others who may not ring all five bells quite the way they do. Their case for participation will be immensely strengthened if they show themselves to be aggressively evangelistic and missionary minded, thus dispelling the myth that Calvinism is antithetical to the promiscuous preaching of the gospel and the fulfillment of the Great Commission.

The need to distinguish first- and second-order theological concerns appears even more urgently in the controversy surrounding women in ministry in SBC life. Two entrenched camps have staked out opposing ground on this issue. One group sees any concession to the leadership of women in official church life as a flagrant violation of Scripture, comparable (nearly) to the denial of the virgin birth or the bodily resurrection. The other group sees the refusal of such roles to women as a heinous sin comparable to slavery, a matter to break fellowship over.

One way to refocus this issue would be to separate the question of "women in ministry" from the theology of feminism, with which it has been largely confused. For evangelicals committed to the authority of Scripture the question of whether women should serve as pastors and/or deacons cannot be decided on, "Well, isn't everyone else doing it?" but rather by, "What does the Bible say about it?"

Evangelicals outside of the SBC are divided on the latter question, and two groups, both advocates of biblical inerrancy, have been formed to promote opposing positions—the Council for Biblical Equality and the Council on Biblical Manhood and Womanhood. Regrettably Southern Baptists are only beginning to participate in this wider evangelical discussion.

The incursion of feminist theology into the life of the church is a problem of a different magnitude, one with far greater "life-threatening" dangers to historic Christian beliefs. The "depatri-archializing" of Scripture; the refusal to call God "Lord," since the later is seen as a term of oppressive domination; the insistence of gender-inclusive language for the Godhead; the quest for female deities to put alongside of, or in some cases in place of, Jesus of Nazareth; feminist hermeneutics which relativizes the authority of the biblical text—each of these views calls into question the fundamental reality of God and the integrity of His revelation. Elizabeth Achtemeier, herself a proponent of the full participation of women in ministry, claims that

> all these feminist errors—indeed, all this feminist rejection of God and its resulting idolatry—are built on *the theological misstep of identifying God with his creation*. And that misstep becomes inevitable when the feminists reject any notion of the inspiration of the canonical witness to God, make their own experience their authority, and use female language for God. As soon as God is called female, the images of birth, of suckling, of carrying in the womb, and most importantly, the identification of the deity with the life in all things becomes inevitable, and the Bible's careful and consistent distinction between Creator and creation is blurred and lost.[32]

This is not to say that all feminist theologies are equally destructive, nor is it to deny that there are "elements of truth" (Newport) in the feminist critique of sexism both in society and the church. However, it is to claim that the evaluation of feminist theology is a first-order priority which must be distinguished from the intraevangelical discussion of the proper role of women in the service of the church.

3. *The cultivation of a holistic orthodoxy is a necessity.*—In his *Commentary on Daniel* (9:25), John Calvin compared the work of God among His ancient people with the challenge of his own day.

But God still wishes in these days to build his spiritual temple amidst the anxieties of the times. The faithful must still hold the trowel in one hand the sword in the other, because the building of the church must still be combined with many struggles.[33]

The sword and the trowel were images chosen by one of Calvin's later admirers, Charles H. Spurgeon, to mirror two vital aspects of his own vocation as pastor and theologian. At the heart of biblical faith is the single-minded pursuit of truth, the precise shape of which becomes clear only in confrontation with competing loyalties and affirmations. Polemics cannot be divorced from dogmatics, as Barth's *magnum opus* abundantly demonstrates in large and small print! However, both Calvin and Spurgeon were more interested in edifying the faithful than in opposing the naysayers. Without omitting the latter when it is necessary, the task of theological renewal in the SBC must clearly concentrate now on the former.

The cultivation of a holistic orthodoxy embraces not only what is taught in our seminary and college classrooms, as important as that is, but also what is heard from our pulpits, taught in our Sunday Schools, experienced in our worship, shared with our neighbors, and passed on to our children. Nothing less than a theological revival, something of more substance than "a happy hour with Jesus," can bring about this kind of transformation in our denominational life. Orthodoxy has the dual connotation of both right thinking about God and praise which is worthy of God. The coinherence of warranted wisdom and sincere piety is both the goal of theological renewal and its source. *Theologia est scientia vivendo deo.*

Notes

1. J. M. Frost, ed., *Baptist Why and Why Not* (Nashville: Sunday School Board, 1900), 9.

2. Ibid., 14.

3. Ibid., 12.

4. J. S. Rogers *et al.*, "A Symposium by Southern State Secretaries on the Union Movement," *Southwestern Journal of Theology* 3 (1919): 23. On the role of the ecumenical movement in Southern Baptist life, see Timothy George, "Southern Baptist Relationships with Other Protestants," *Baptist History and Heritage* 25 (1990): 24-34.

5. *Annual,* SBC, 1951, 460.

6. Samuel Hill, Jr., "The Southern Baptists: Need for Reformation, Redirection," *The Christian Century,* January 9, 1963, 40. Apparently this is the first recorded use of the term "moderate" in the context of the SBC conflict. See Bill J. Leonard, *God's Last and Only Hope: The Fragmentation of the Southern Baptist Convention* (Grand Rapids: Eerdmans, 1990), 63-64.

7. Nancy Tatom Ammerman, *Baptist Battles: Social Change and Religious Conflict in the Southern Baptist Convention* (New Brunswick: Rutgers University Press, 1990), 179: "Moderate leaders were reluctant to hit the trail in open support of the agenda that had in fact guided their actions. . . . As a result, moderates were reduced to general calls for 'freedom' and to responding to the agenda defined by the fundamentalists."

8. See Gunther Hornig, *Die Anfänge der historisch-kritischen Theologie* (Göttingen, 1961).

9. See also L. Russ Bush and Tom J. Nettles, *Baptists and the Bible* (Chicago: Moody, 1980), and Timothy George, "The Renewal of Baptist Theology," in *Baptist Theologians,* eds. Timothy George and David S. Dockery (Nashville: Broadman Press, 1990), 20-21.

10. On the Princeton theologians, see Mark A. Noll, *The Princeton Theology, 1812-1921* (Grand Rapids: Baker, 1983). On the Scottish inerrantists, see Alec Cheyne, "The Bible and Change in the Nineteenth Century," in *The Bible in Scottish Life and Literature,* ed. David F. Wright (Edinburgh: Saint Andrew, 1988), 192-207.

11. On the Toy Controversy, see Billy G. Hurt, "Crawford Howell Toy: Interpreter of the Old Testament," (Th.D. diss. The Southern Baptist Theological Seminary, 1965), and Pope A. Duncan, "Crawford Howell Toy: Heresy at Louisville," *American Religious Heretics,* ed. George H. Shriver (Nashville: Abingdon, 1966), 56-88.

12. Basil Manly, Jr., *The Bible Doctrine of Inspiration* (Philadelphia: American Baptist Publication Society, 1888), 229.

13. See the important studies of Colin Brown, *Miracles and the Critical Mind* (Grand Rapids: Zondervan, 1985), and Craig Blomberg, *The Historical Reliability of the Gospels* (Downers Grove: Inter-Varsity, 1987).

14. Peter Berger, *A Rumor of Angels: Modern Society and the Rediscovery of the Supernatural* (New York: Doubleday, 1969), 41.

15. See the recent article by B. H. Throckmorton, Jr., "The Bible in the Church," *The Christian Century,* October 10, 1990.

16. Herschel H. Hobbs, *The Baptist Faith and Message* (Nashville: Convention, 1971), 18.

17. William L. Lumpkin, *Baptist Confessions of Faith* (Valley Forge: Judson, 1959).

18. *The Complete Works of the Rev. Andrew Fuller* (Philadelphia: American Baptist Publication Society, 1845), 3:449-51.

19. This quotation is from Boyce's inaugural address before the trustees of Furman University in 1856, "Three Changes in Theological Institutions," Timothy George, ed., *James Petigru Boyce: Selected Writings* (Nashville: Broadman Press, 1989), 56. Cf. William Cathcart's statement, "The extensive use of a creed in Baptist Churches should be encouraged by earnest Christians who love our Scriptural principles." He also cites with approval this comment from Charles H. Spurgeon: "The pretense that articles of faith fetter the mind, is annihilated by the fact that the boldest thinkers are to be found among men who are not foolhardy to forsake the old landmarks. He who finds his creed a fetter has none at all, for to the true believer a plain statement of his faith is no more a chain than a sword-belt to the soldier, or a girdle to the pilgrim." *The Baptist Encyclopedia* (Philadelphia: Louis H. Everts, 1881), 294.

20. *Annual,* SBC (1923).

21. Quoted, Robert A. Baker, ed., *A Baptist Source Book* (Nashville: Broadman, 1966), 78. For a recent Southern Baptist exchange on this theme, see both the article by Thomas J. Nettles, "Creedalism, Confessionalism, and the Baptist Faith and Message," and the editor's introduction to it in Robison B. James, ed., *The Unfettered Word: Southern Baptist Confront the Authority-Inerrancy Question* (Waco: Word, 1987), 138-54. James cites the writings of John Leland and the fact that the SBC adopted no formal statement at its founding in 1845 as evidence of "noncreedal inclination" among Southern Baptists. In the context of arguing for religious liberty against state-imposed conformity, Leland clearly warned against turning confessional statements into a "Virgin Mary" or "a petty Bible." He too, however, acknowledged confessions as "advantageous" and binding upon those who *voluntarily* embraced them, as did most Separate Baptists whose churches and associations adopted numerous confessions and issued disciplinary sanctions against those who violated such commitments. The 293 delegates (as they were called then, rather than "messengers") who gathered in Augusta to organize the SBC in 1845 were thoroughly united in their confessional adherence, the vast majority of them belonging to churches and local associations which embraced the Philadelphia Confession of Faith, called the "Century Confession" in the South because of its adoption by Charleston Baptists in 1700, some forty years prior to its promulgation in Philadelphia. See Robert A. Baker and Paul L. Craven, Jr., *Adventure in Faith: The First 300 Years of First Baptist Church, Charleston, South Carolina* (Nashville: Broadman Press, 1982), 80-83.

22. W. S. Hudson, ed., *Baptist Concepts of the Church* (Chicago: Judson, 1959), 215-16.

214

Beyond the Impasse?

23. Timothy George, "The Priesthood of All Believers and the Quest for Theological Integrity," *Criswell Theological Review* 3 (1989): 284-94.

24. Cf. the statement of Carlyle Marney: "It was a gross perversion of the gospel that inserted a bastard individualism here and taught us that the believer's priesthood meant that 'every tub must set on its own bottom.' " *Priests to Each Other* (Valley Forge: Judson, 1974), 12.

25. Hobbs, *The Baptist Faith and Message*, 74.

26. See Timothy George, "The Reformation Roots of the Baptist Tradition," *Review and Expositor* 86 (1989): 9-22.

27. Robert Wuthnow, *The Struggle for American's Soul* (Grand Rapids: Eerdmans, 1989).

28. Walter B. Shurden, *Not a Silent People* (Nashville: Broadman Press, 1972), 31.

29. John H. Leith, *The Reformed Imperative* (Philadelphia: Westminster Press, 1988), 22.

30. Carl F. H. Henry, *Toward a Recovery of Christian Belief* (Wheaton: Crossway, 1990), 68.

31. Cf. Karl Barth's ringing challenge: "If we do not have the confidence of *damnamus,* we ought to omit *credimus,* and go back to doing theology as usual." *Church Dogmatics* I/1, 630.

32. Elizabeth Achtemeier, "Female Language for God: Should the Church Adopt It?" *The Hermeneutical Quest: Essays in Honor of James Luther Mays,* ed. Donald G. Miller (Allison Park, Pa.: Pickwick, 1986), 114. See also the excellent paper by Roland M. Frye, "Language for God and Feminist Language," distributed by the Center for Theological Inquiry, Princeton Theological Seminary.

33. *Comm.* Daniel 9:25 in *Calvin's Commentaries* (Grand Rapids: Baker, 1984), 13:203.

PART II
Dialogue and Further Reflections

9

A Response
by David S. Dockery

Robison B. James asks, "Is there any way beyond the deadlock?" After reading the diverse perspectives represented in the
previous chapters one is tempted to answer negatively. I would,
however, hope and pray that a convergence from several sides might
take place in order to move us beyond the impasse. In this response I
will not attempt to interact with every chapter in the previous
section. Instead, I will focus my response on two chapters and then
suggest a confessional statement around which a new consensus can
possibly develop.

Walter Harrelson and John Newport offer carefully stated descriptions of the values of historical and literary criticism. While I
might quibble at points, there is much in these chapters that I find
beneficial. Paige Patterson's warnings concerning the weaknesses
of critical methodologies provide a balance for Harrelson and
Newport.[1]

I heartily affirm the clarion calls issued by R. Albert Mohler and
Timothy George for a historically informed and confessionally
grounded theological commitment. While there exists common
ground among all eight contributors, significant differences as well
as smaller nuances can be identified among us. Readers will probably be able to locate these differences on a continuum. Room for
some form of continuing fellowship and ongoing conversation obviously exists. I find, however, that the confessional minimalism
suggested by Rob James and the pluriform shape of theology offered
by Molly Truman Marshall's "large room" represent the greatest
difference from my own perspective. Thus I will respond to their
thought-provoking suggestions and will appropriately focus my primary attention on James's proposals.

First, let me say that I find my coeditor's proposal stimulating.
His desire to move "beyond old habits and onto new ground" is

most refreshing. I likewise heartily affirm his insistence that the Bible have its way with us. I would like to invite him to join me in seeking a new ground that distances itself from the legalism and rigidity of fundamentalism, the heterodoxy of modernism, and the outright pluralism and deconstructionism of much post-modernism, while remaining confessional, evangelical, biblical, and Baptist. Though James touches on all four of these points, his conclusions tend to be confessionally minimal, subevangelical, and (for me) inconsistently Baptist (though some other readers might see his work as the most consistently Baptist of all, which of course indicates that much of the impasse is involved with understanding what it means to be Baptist). My friend and colleague, Molly Truman Marshall, calls for a "large room" in which to do theology. Though neither Marshall nor James calls for an outright theological pluralism, his confessional minimalism and her "large room" theological constructions implicitly point us in that direction. My response to these two friends is to call for: (1) a full-orbed confessional theology, and (2) an evangelical biblicism that can pave the way for (3) a new consensus.

A Full-Orbed Confessional Theology

Theological controversy inevitably develops when claims for resolving specific theological conflicts cannot be reconciled in a manner that allows both parties to retain their integrity in the midst of the reconciliation. One way beyond this impasse is to embrace theological pluralism. Advocates of theological pluralism maintain that theological boundaries are superseded by other possibilities. Thus, no limits can long endure. In fact it is sometimes felt that endurance itself is suspect. Nothing that endures can therefore be affirmed. No contributor to this volume explicitly affirms this approach to pluralism, but implicitly a type of confessional minimalism, to which I earlier referred, points in the direction of a type of inclusivism (to distinguish pluralism from inclusivism). I wish first of all to reject outright all forms of theological inclusivism that reject historic Christian distinctives. The new inclusivism is distinguished by what it does not affirm, quite unlike the well-defined battle lines between liberalism and orthodoxy.

Theological inclusivism creates a persuasion that is evidenced by what one is not against rather than what is affirmed as essential to Christian faith. The challenge for all of us is twofold: (1) we must recognize the reality of modernity, and (2) we must simultaneously affirm what is essential to the Christian faith. Of course to affirm such essentials and fail to adopt some form of pluralism opens oneself to the charge of exclusivism. Thus to claim that a confessionalism rooted in historic orthodoxy is necessary for modern Christians can be perceived as divisive, haughty, and exclusivistic. Somehow, however, we must meet both challenges identified above. I commend both James and Marshall (especially Marshall) for helping us take seriously the challenge of modernity.

Just as scholastic orthodoxy and the rise of enlightenment thought were the seedbed out of which both liberal theology (Schleiermacher) and pietism (Spener) developed, so new opportunities possibly await Southern Baptists. I can envision a reactionary and rigid fundamentalism and the challenges of modernity as the soils out of which either a contemporary inclusivism or a renewed evangelicalism can develop. I wish to challenge my colleagues to consider seriously a renewed evangelical confessionalism that is rooted in the historic orthodoxy of the early church confessions, the Reformation, and pietistic renewals and is poised for the challenges of our modern context. As Baptists we can learn from our friends in other traditions who have called for a vibrant, confessional evangelicalism. We can look to Presbyterians like Richard Lovelace (*Dynamics of the Spiritual Life*), Methodists like Thomas Oden (*After Modernity*) and Paul Mickey (*Essentials of Wesleyan Theology*), and even charismatic-theologian J. R. Williams (*Renewal Theology*).

While these approaches affirm distinctives of their various traditions, they each also affirm an orthodox Trinitarianism, the full deity and humanity of Jesus Christ, the necessity of regeneration, strong declarations of justification by faith, an objective understanding of the atonement, a confession of the church as God's people, and the return of Jesus Christ. We could add certain Baptist distinctives such as a regenerate church membership, believer's baptism, and the importance of the priesthood of believers.[2] This full-orbed confessional theology, which gladly affirms the importance and priority of a vital relationship with Jesus Christ, must be grounded in exegetically sound and hermeneutically faithful interpretations and proclamations of Holy Scripture. This brings us to our second point: the need for an evangelical biblicism.

An Evangelical Biblicism

Both in his view of doctrine and Holy Scripture, James commendably suggests a "both/and" answer to the question of Spirit and/or Bible. Yet his creative suggestions seem to create an "either/or" dichotomy where he calls for a relationship with Christ *or* a doctrinal commitment. I applaud and gladly affirm the importance of the priority of a relationship with Christ.

When he articulates his position the way he does I certainly feel the press of such an argument and recognize that Scripture is a derived and secondary authority to Christ.[3] But what needs to be emphasized is that Christ is unknowable in any objective sense apart from the revealed word from God found in the Bible. I never want to imply that a salvific relationship with Christ is anything other than the ultimate aspect of Christianity, nor would I want to suggest that something other than *Jesus is Lord* is the basic Christian confession or the basic Baptist confession. But there is more to a Baptist confession than this basic belief (as evidenced by the numerous Baptist statements from the London confessions to *The Baptist Faith and Message*). Certainly Jesus is the final revelation of God, and it is to Jesus that we ought to appeal. But major questions remain unanswered. How do we know which Jesus is Lord? How do we know which Jesus to place our faith in apart from revelation about Him in Holy Scripture? Do we want a relationship with a "new age" Jesus? How does the shape of our confession that Jesus is Lord differ from a similar confession of a cultic or Gnostic group? I would suggest that James's dualistic option is not what it appears.

The Jesus whom we confess as Lord and with whom we have a personal relationship is the preexistent Word (John 1:1) who has become human in space and time (v. 14). The One who created the world (v. 3; Heb. 1:2) is also the One who was born of a virgin (Matt. 1:23) and grew physically, intellectually, spiritually, and socially (Luke 2:40, 52). He is the divine Son who was fully human, yet without sin (Rom. 8:3). He died for our sins and was raised for our justification (1 Cor. 15:3-4; Rom. 4:24-25), and having purified our sins He sat down at the right hand of God (Heb. 1:3) from where He will appear a second time to bring salvation to those who are waiting for Him (9:28). It is this Jesus who is Lord (Rom. 10:9) and with whom we have a salvific relationship. If that is James's contention, then I agree wholeheartedly. If not, I again ask how do we know apart from Holy Scripture?

The only other option is a type of mysticism, which is the kind of Christianity seemingly affirmed by James. In so doing he decries a "bookish faith" (p. 137). This seems very un-Baptist to me because if Baptists are anything they are a people of the Book. I do not know how to have a biblical faith apart from a bookish faith, which is not in any sense a type of bibliolatry (for I have already acknowledged that Scripture has a derived authority from God Himself, since it is a God-breathed book). To define ourselves as "people of the Book" does not in any way mean the Bible becomes the object of our worship—it means the Book points us to our Creator and Redeemer, the One truly worthy of our worship.

James's proposal for a nonbookish Christianity does not return us to an apostolic-type of Christianity as he suggested. In fact just the opposite is true. The English word *Bible* is derived from the Greek word *biblion* or *biblia*, which means scroll(s) or book(s). English-speaking Christians use three major titles to refer to this holy book. We call it the Bible, the Scripture(s), and the Word of God. These words, as we use them today, have a far more significant connotation than the Greek word *biblion*. While *biblion* could be used in a variety of ways in the ancient world, the word *Bible*, for believers today, refers to the Book *par excellence*, the recognized source of divine revelation for contemporary believers.

In Daniel 9:2 the Greek translation used *ta biblia* to refer to the prophetic writings. Paul used the word *biblia* when he made his request to Timothy (2 Tim. 4:13), by which he probably referred to some scrolls containing the Hebrew Scriptures. This usage passed into the postapostolic church (see 2 Clement 14:2). Sometime during this period a significant change occurred in the common usage of the plural *biblia* to the singular *biblion*. This change reflected the growing conception of the Bible as the one utterance of God.

Even before the canonization of the sacred books, importance was attached to the sacred writings. Moses wrote "all the words of the Lord" in the "book of the covenant" (Ex. 21—23; 24:4-7, KJV). Joshua's farewell address was written "in the book of the law of God" (Josh. 24:26, KJV). Samuel spoke words about the kingdom and "wrote them down on a scroll and deposited it before the Lord" (1 Sam. 10:25, NIV). Jesus repeatedly appealed to the

authoritative Scriptures (see Matt. 19:4; 22:29). Similarly, Paul and the apostles thought of the scrolls as the "very words of God" (Rom. 3:2, NIV).

The term *Scripture* is a rendering of the Greek word *graphe*. The plural form identifies the whole collection of sacred writings (see Matt. 21:42; 1 Cor. 15:3-4). The singular form can mean either a specific passage (see Mark 12:10) or the constituent body of writings (see Gal. 3:22). Paul characteristically used *gramma* (writing or Scripture) to refer to the Torah or the Law. Second Timothy 3:15 refers to the "holy scriptures" (*hiera grammata*), which Timothy had known since he was a child and which were able to make him wise for salvation. The divine author of Scripture is the Holy Spirit (Acts 28:25), who has breathed out Scripture as a function of His creative activity. This sacred Book's instruction is divine and authoritative for salvation and Christian living.

Baptists appeal to the authority of the Book because they have recognized Scripture as the written Word of God since the time of the Second London Confession (1677). It is very important to recognize that the designation *Word of God* is appropriately used in three distinct contexts. Primarily, the phrase refers to Jesus Christ. The phrase rightly points to the divinely disclosed message through God's spokesmen and this in principle to the biblical writings. The three usages are certainly related, lying within one another in concentric circles. So the phrase belongs to Christ, the ultimate, total Word; to the proclamation of Christ in the apostolic church; and to the truth of Christ embodied in written form in the Scriptures. The Word of God, which was first orally proclaimed, was finally embodied in written form in the New Testament.

Our Lord authenticated this usage by declaring that Scripture as the Word of God cannot be broken (see John 10:35). It is biblically and theologically right to acknowledge that the prophetic-apostolic word is God's Word written. Without this writing there would be no Bible, no Scriptures, and therefore no Word of God available to us. The Book (the Bible) is God's Word written. Contrary to James's suggestion, Baptists are in line with their prophetic-apostolic-postapostolic heritage when they claim to be a "people of the book"—for they have been, are, and should remain such a people. We must not create a dichotomy between Word and Spirit. We need the Holy Spirit who inspired Scripture to illuminate Scripture and enable us to understand and apply it today. I too want a "both/and" answer to Bible and Spirit—for it is the work of the Spirit who helps us live our lives individually and corporately according to the message of the Book.

A New Consensus: Confessional, Evangelical, and Biblical

In conclusion I would suggest a new consensus must develop if we are to move beyond the present impasse. While Marshall is correct in helping us see the changes in culture that have contributed to our present controversy, I still maintain that the impasse is primarily the result of a crisis of biblical authority. It is, however, even broader than that. It is also a crisis of piety (living out a commitment to biblical authority) and a crisis of theology (articulating the meaning and significance of biblical authority for our generation in the midst of a changing and post-Christian culture). Thus we need a renewed commitment to biblical authority, evangelical renewal, and a full-orbed confessional theology reflecting the whole counsel of God (see Acts 20:27). We need what R. Albert Mohler has, in another place called Baptist evangelicals and evangelical Baptists.[4] I would like to address the biblical authority crisis by suggesting a confessional statement that is biblical, evangelical, and Baptist, which possibly can serve as a foundation for the new consensus in Baptist life.

1. We believe all knowledge of God comes by way of revelation which is God's manifestation of Himself to humankind in such a way that men and women can know and fellowship with Him.
2. We believe God has revealed Himself to all peoples at all times and all places through nature, history, and in human consciences and experiences. He has revealed Himself specifically to specific people in specific places through redemptive acts and prophetic and apostolic words. Ultimately, he has revealed Himself in Jesus Christ, the Living Word of God. We believe this special revelation of God is given to us through Holy Scripture, an inspired Word from God. We believe that while God's general revelation is to be interpreted in light of His special revelation; they are not in conflict with one another, but are complementary and harmonious.

3. We believe these acts of special revelation have been interpreted by God's prophets and apostles and under the providential hand of God have been gathered together and recognized by the church to form the canon of Sacred Scripture, consisting of thirty-nine books in the Old Testament and twenty-seven books in the New Testament. We believe that God's revelation is personal in that God reveals Himself personally and redemptively, but His revelation is also propositional in that it reveals truths about God and His creation. This special revelation is progressive, which means in the witness of biblical history there is a developing disclosure of God, His will, and His truth in the Old and New Testaments. The development is not contradictory in any fashion, but is supplementary to what has been previously revealed.

4. We believe Scripture is inspired and is entirely and completely the Word of God as well as the words of human authors. It is inadequate to affirm that the Bible is only a human witness to divine revelation because the Bible is also God's witness to Himself. Through the superintending influence of God's Spirit on the writers of Holy Scripture, the accounts and interpretations of God's revelation have been recorded as God intended so that the Bible is actually the written Word of God.

5. We believe inspiration was the work of God in which God, by His Spirit through human writers, gave us His Word. The origin of Scripture is divine; and as such, the Holy Scriptures are the authoritative Word of God and are the supreme written norm by which God binds the conscience. While the process of divine inspiration remains largely a mystery, we believe that the work of inspiration can best be described as concursive and plenary. God, in His work of inspiration, utilized the distinctive personalities and literary styles of the human writers whom He had chosen and prepared.

6. We believe that the Spirit's work of inspiration results in a Bible that is God's Word written to all people for all times. We also believe this written Word of God properly interpreted in light of which culture and communication means had developed by the time of its composition will be shown to be completely true (and therefore not false) and reliable in all that

it affirms, to the degree of precision intended by the author, in all matters relating to God and His creation.

7. We believe in the Spirit's work of illumination that enables believers to interpret the biblical text in its original context in such a way as to understand the biblical author's meanings, as well as its canonical significance for our contemporary world. Ultimately, the Bible is to be interpreted in light of the centrality of Jesus Christ, who affirmed the complete veracity of the Bible and lived His life in fulfillment of Holy Scripture.

8. We believe the Bible is the ultimate standard of authority for God's people. We further believe the Bible is our only and all-sufficient rule of faith and practice. The Holy Spirit, who inspired Holy Scripture, leads believers today to recognize the authority of Scripture and to respond to and obey its message.

This confessional statement is not intended as a final word, but as a place to begin to develop a common consensus grounded in Holy Scripture.[5] While our differences are many as evidenced in this volume, we must begin at the heart of the problem: the crisis of biblical authority. This statement will no doubt appear too binding for some and incomplete for others. My hope, however, is that it can serve as a starting point for us to join together in affirmation of what we have in common in order to move beyond the impasse. It is not intended to address every issue or provide all the answers, but it does address the significant issues of our day in Baptist life while holding out hope for continued conversation and mutual understanding.

Notes

1. For a recent work that affirms the total truthfulness of Scripture and simultaneously sees the value of some forms of critical methodologies, see D. A. Black and D. S. Dockery, eds. *New Testament Criticism and Interpretation* (Grand Rapids: Zondervan, 1991).

2. See Timothy George, "The Renewal of Baptist Theology," *Baptist Theologians,* ed. Timothy George and David S. Dockery (Nashville: Broadman Press, 1990), 13-25; also cf. James T. Draper, Jr., *Foundations of Biblical Faith* (Nashville: Broadman Press, 1979).

3. A similar argument can be found in Richard Land, "The Nature of Biblical Authority: A Conservative Response," *Conservative, Moderate, Liberal: The Biblical Authority Debate,* ed. C. R. Blaisdell (St. Louis: CBP, 1990), 69-79.

4. See R. Albert Mohler, "A Call for Baptist Evangelicals and Evangelical Baptists," *Southern Baptists and American Evangelicals: The Conversation Continues* (Nashville: Broadman Press, forthcoming).

5. A full amplification of these points can be found in David S. Dockery, *The Doctrine of the Bible* (Nashville: Convention Press, 1991). I have borrowed key points of the "covenant agreement" adopted by the trustees, administration, and faculty of The Southern Baptist Theological Seminary (April 1991).

10
A Response
by Walter Harrelson

The chapters by Professors George, Marshall, Patterson, and James all go beyond the limited perspective found in my chapter dealing with the value of historical criticism of Scripture. It is right and proper that they do so. My objective was deliberately to register the point that faithful critical study of the Bible is essential for its interpretation. Historical criticism prepares the ground for the interpretation and is essential to interpretation. Historical criticism also demands interpretation. In different ways, George, Marshall, Patterson, and James make that point.

It is perhaps most graphically put in James's distinction between the two parts of my quotation from my Aunt Zora. Aunt Zora, James rightly points out, is a historical critic when she says that there must be "something wrong," when the Bible identifies certain atrocities as demanded by God. But Aunt Zora is a theologian when she says, ". . . because God is not like that." Historical criticism can place the biblical material in its presumed historical-social-cultural setting and can offer hypotheses as to the processes by which the material took shape over time. But historical critics do not affirm who God is or what God can do, not as critics. That is theological utterance, and it needs always to be so identified.

But theological utterances that are faithful to the Bible's central affirmations—and here I can only reaffirm that it is my experience and my considered judgment that the Bible itself continues, by the Spirit, to lead individuals and the believing community to recognize those central affirmations—have been developed in association with the biblical materials and continue to be in creative tension with those materials. The very process of handing on the biblical message, as I sought to show in my chapter, is a process that requires theological formulation and reformulation over time.

It is right and proper, then, for us to insist in face of the present impasse in Southern Baptist life that the struggle be focused in this never-ending and never-finished effort to reclaim for our own day the essential theological affirmations of the Bible and offer these affirmations to church and world as liberating and life-giving truth. If the struggle degenerates into power plays and efforts to control institutions and programs and ways of thinking, that is sad indeed. But as all four of the authors in chapters 5-8 point out, we cannot get away from the necessity to put the biblical message into theological terms and images on the basis of which we can present its truth-claims and its liberating power. The mere rereading of the Bible never sufficed in biblical times and it does not suffice today.

Our four authors of chapters 5-8, however, have nicely stressed different dimensions of this theological affirmation. Marshall has eloquently underscored the centrality of the theology of the cross, thereby pointing to the central New Testament affirmation of God's marvelous condescension in taking the side of sinful humankind, entering fully into the life of the world, but without sin, and in so doing standing with suffering and sinful humankind in their desperate need. Various doctrines of the atonement have developed, as we know, all of them seeking to portray this incredible love and mercy and condescension of God that led to God's ". . . [becoming] sin for us, so that in him we might become the righteousness of God" in the world (2 Cor. 5:21, NIV). A community of sinners, by God's condescending and suffering love, begins to partake of and embody that community of love and joy and peace and righteousness that God promised to Israel as its destiny.

Robison James chooses rather to stress the *relation* of God and people, God and believer, that is effected in the life of faith, realized supremely in Jesus Christ and in particular in the cross and resurrection of Jesus Christ. This theology of relations, says James, must take center stage, for it is of even greater import than the specialized doctrinal statements that develop from this central, relational reality. It is God's entering fully into human life, in the life of the believing community, that is the central meaning of the Word of God, and all our understandings of the authority of Scripture should be grounded in this primary affirmation that in Christ God was reconciling the world to the divine Self (2 Cor. 5:18). If we give adequate place to this relational understanding of Christian theology then we can best stave off doctrinal affirmations that easily become clubs with which to bludgeon our opponents into submission.

Paige Patterson concentrates on the danger that historical criticism may become destructive of the life of faith, destructive of evangelical Christianity. Whether some critics intend deliberately to deceive their hearers and readers, or whether they are perhaps unaware of the consequences of their labors, he claims that the application of critical scholarship often produces skepticism and reduces confidence in the truth of the Bible. He gives examples. Others could give examples of the liberating power of biblical criticism, rightly applied. None of us, I believe, needs to question the motives or the intentions of other interpreters, but we have every right to evaluate the adequacy and the consequences of our and of others' scholarly work and theological affirmations.

Timothy George stresses three basic needs. First, Baptists need to reaffirm the authority of the Bible as the Word of God. This point needs to be held in close relationship with the point made by Robison James about the central biblical meaning of the Word of God as a living message about God, a message affirming God's claim upon the world and its peoples and especially upon the people of the covenant. When the Word of God is understood in this sense, then inerrancy may become less a stumbling block for those who worry about the term. Surely, all faithful Christians will affirm that this disclosure of God, out of the mystery of the divine Trinity, in the form of a message delivered through agents of God, and then embodied and delivered in Jesus Christ the Word of God, is a disclosure without error, full of glory, grace, and truth.

Second, George speaks about the place of creeds and confessions in the life of Baptists throughout history, showing that Baptists have no inherent hostility to creedal statements or confessions that attempt to sum up for the life of faith those central affirmations of the Bible that the Christian community has arrived at through the centuries. As Albert Mohler stressed in chapter 4, George also underscores the appropriateness of the church's having such statements on the basis of which to order its life and to identify heresy.

It is essential here to recognize how pluriform the statements of Scripture are, what a rich tapestry it offers, what a "symphony" of voices (James) it provides. Even so, there is every reason to be grateful to our forebears who have sought to sum up the faith and enable us to place into fresh, clear, and cogent terms what the heart and center of God's Word, God's message, clearly is.

The problem lies in the uses to which these creeds and confessions have been put. Used as bludgeons to bring others into line, such statements are of course theologically and humanly damaging. Here, the biblical prohibition of all forms of idolatry comes into play, and the central affirmation of Christian freedom is compromised, as James and others have pointed out. But used as banners to placard the central affirmations of faith, as summations to call the faithful to confront again and again the central Mystery of God with Us, creeds and confessions are of tremendous power. And used too as means of gathering up the fruits of critical and constructive reflection on biblical faith, they are very important to biblical scholars, to historians, to ethicists, to systematic theologians, and to pastoral theologians, as well as to reflective lay members of the Christian community.

The question we have to ask is whether the demand for adherence to theological statements affirming the infallibility of the Bible and its literal historical truth can be responded to in ways that are genuinely constructive. We do not need to call into question the motives of those who demand adherence to such statements, though we certainly are entitled to recognize the temptation that we and others often have to impose our views on other persons. Can we find ways to recast these theological demands so that they are more affirmative, more like banners to be waved and hymns to be sung? If we can, then perhaps there are ways to move beyond our present impasse, and if so, Professor George's outlook on the future of the Southern Baptists may turn out to have been unduly pessimistic.

For years I have been convinced that in biblical exegesis and in theological and ethical restatement of the biblical message we regularly fail to give adequate place to one marvelous biblical resource. I am talking about the prophetic sketches of God's consummating work that God has purposed and that lies ahead, beckoning. These pictures of the fulfillment of the divine purpose, found scattered throughout the prophetic collections, are so varied, so eloquent, so powerful in both thought and poetic beauty, that they provide common ground, though of course contested ground, for dialogue between Jews and Christians and for constructive debate among Christians of all kinds and persuasions, I believe. They speak about a coming triumph of *God's* purpose, centered in this world, marked by the transformation of life on earth. Different texts stress different aspects of this transformation. Some speak of a coming agent of God who will provide God's people and the entire human community with authentic, peaceful, just, and humane leadership (Isa. 9; 11; Mic. 5; Zech. 9, etc.). Others speak of the centrality of Zion, God's holy hill, to which the nations are drawn to learn God's teaching (Isa. 2 and Mic. 4) or to worship God under new terms appropriate for all the nations (Zech. 14), or of Zion as place of renewal and fulfillment of life for all the scattered, oppressed, wounded, and despised of earth (Isa. 40; 35, etc). Some speak of a new heart and a new spirit planted within the hearts of God's people (Ezek. 36). Others speak of a new covenant made with the people of God, the character of which is God's placing the divine Teaching into the very inward being of all God's people, so that faithfulness to the will of God is as natural as breathing (Jer. 31).

Such passages, believed and held before the faithful community, offer a fresh set of images that might serve somehow *between* a Bible affirmed to be inerrant and theological statements believed to sum up rightly the Bible's truths. These images and metaphors of God's eschatological triumph are powerful motivators to mission and service. They bring judgment upon a faithless community. They lure all the faithful toward that day of consummation that beckons. And their moral depth and their sheer beauty and ring of truth give them immense believability, even for the skeptical and the scorners.

Might it be the case that we need to concentrate in these troubled times, Baptists from all branches of the tradition and of all theological persuasions, on how biblical eschatology might help us illuminate the *actual working authority of the Bible in the life of the believing community and individual*? I believe that it could be so. But we should note that this is *prophetic* eschatology, not apocalyptic eschatology; this is the eschatology of those who in faith know that God has not given up on a desperately evil and sinful world. May we not also believe that God has not given up on us who find ourselves in what appears to be an impasse?

11
A Response
by John P. Newport

With the exception of Molly Truman Marshall, the four respond-ers did not question my presentation of "The Challenge of Recent Literary Approaches to the Bible" and its relationship to the South-ern Baptist impasse. I hope that my chapter is an example of "believing criticism" which would commend itself to both funda-mental-conservatives and moderate-conservatives.

The Imperialism of the Present (Allegory)

I agree with Timothy George that some of the literary approaches to the Bible suffer from the "imperialism of the present." Instead of starting with the biblical perspective, there is a tendency to start with human experience and then seek a correspondence between this experience and the biblical teachings. In order to find this correspondence, this model seeks to identify and define a "deeper meaning" hidden "beneath" the literal sense of the biblical texts. Additionally, this model supposes that a text possesses a variety of meanings, all of which are connected to the interests or perspective of the interpreter.[1]

The interpreter who uses this method usually takes the biblical teachings and translates them into the categories of some other "more relevant" conceptual system such as existential or process philosophy. This new conceptuality is understood as the real mean-ing of these biblical texts. The Bible is thus emptied of its own reality and treated only as a symbolic expression of a deeper truth. This allegorical approach is evident in the theologies and sermons of Paul Tillich and Rudolf Bultmann and in the preaching and teach-ing of those whom they influenced.[2] This approach serves many Bible teachers and preachers who choose to avoid the difficult task of exegesis in favor of "sharing" reflections about what a text "means for them."

The Modification Emphasis of the Reader-Response Approach

In all fairness, as I indicate in my chapter, the reader-response view influenced by Hans-Georg Gadamer insists that the biblical texts and the contemporary interpreter should criticize each other. As with the allegorical approach, the reader-response view believes that common human experience illuminates Christian faith. However, along with neorthodoxy, it insists that the Bible must interpret and correct contemporary experience.[3]

A coalition of otherwise diverse theologians has begun to emerge around this approach. This group includes David Tracy and his colleagues at the University of Chicago. It also includes some process and feminist theologians, as well as leading Roman Catholic theologians such as Bernard Lonergan, Edward Schillebeeckx, and Karl Rahner.

The Self-Fulfillment Emphasis

Another example of the "imperialism of the present" in biblical interpretation and preaching is the growing dominance of the Western psychologized consciousness. This view has nurtured a tendency to view all institutions, even religion, as human creations designed to facilitate our self-fulfillment. From this perspective, the Christian faith is seen primarily as psychological wish-fulfillment. Such a view follows if the claims of the Bible must always be correlated with contemporary human experience in order that they be God's Word. The result is that the Word of God can never be said to stand unambiguously over against and criticize contemporary experience.[4]

The Possible Correction of the New-Critical and Biblical Narrative Emphasis

In order to correct this growing allegorical and critical correlation dominance, Mark Ellingsen suggests that we should turn to some of the new-criticism emphases which I discuss in my chapter. According to Ellingsen, if they are properly qualified, these techniques can be helpful in developing a proper evangelical use of the Bible.[5]

The new-critical approach emphasizes the autonomy of a literary text. This suggests the possibility of achieving a text's descriptive, normative meaning. It would preclude any endeavor (as allegory tries to do) to find the meaning of the biblical narratives by bypassing their literal sense. By providing a way to affirm the possibility of identifying the biblical text's normative, literal meaning as not contingent on the interpreter's perspective, new-critical suppositions offer a possible method of proclaiming the Word of God in face of the psychologized consciousness of our contemporary culture. On such grounds the Word will not be heard as a mere human creation. The Word of God and its meaning stands over against us, regardless of our own wants, desires, and states of mind.

A biblical narrative approach also provides a useful model for describing how the biblical faith shapes the lives of believers, and drives us to a deeper appreciation of the role of preaching and the sole authority of Scripture. Those who employ the method of allegory commonly interpret the Bible in the light of what they see as an intellectually credible worldview. They thus tend to derive the concepts of God and Logos from this worldview prior to the study of the biblical text. Tillich's notion of God as "Being-Itself," Bultmann's concept of the Christ as "Bringer of authentic existence," and Paul Ricoeur's presentation of Christ as "Martyr" all illustrate this tendency.[6]

If a person accepts this allegorical approach, the biblical accounts themselves provide nothing more than a particularity for these general ontological concepts. They witness to the particular way in which the biblical writers express these "deeper truths." This can be seen as another evidence of the fact that the proponents of this view are unwilling to allow Scripture to interpret itself. This bears serious, practical consequences. It has been noted that the piety of many Christians is deistic, and their view of Christ is markedly similar to the currently popular view of authentic existence. This result is probably because such piety has been nurtured by the post-Enlightenment, allegorical proclamation which we have described. The biblical narrative approach, by contrast, avoids these problems. It states that God can only be first known in relation to the biblical narrative. Consequently, the biblical narrative, as the source and norm for Christian piety, will, of necessity, be something distinct from and critical of the prevailing trends of Western culture.[7]

The Contribution of the "Bible as Culture" Approach

In many ways, the Christian community with its Bible functions like a culture. When Christians allow Scripture's authority to reign in them so that the stories become their own, then the truth of these stories begins to shape their lives. They become participants in the Bible's strange new world, the one true reality of God's interactions with the people through Jesus Christ. This biblical world has so formed their lives that they cannot but proceed with confidence in the truth of the Christian faith. They are confident and to a large extent have found their experience to confirm that the biblical world makes sense in helping them cope with present reality and gives them hope for the future.[8]

This approach to using the Bible does not preclude the possibility of a rational comparison and conversation between the Christian faith and other alternatives. It also allows for the possibility that certain features of Christian faith could be persuasive to non-Christians. The commitment of this approach to the possibility of discerning normative or descriptive meaning of biblical texts affirms that meaning and theological claims are public and accessible to all. This approach involves the claim that Christians will and may legitimately assume the truth of the narrative until it is disproven by relevant data.

It should be noted that this approach is not a more parochial presupposition than some that are pertinent to the scientific community. The evaluation of scientific truth is not just the domain of scientists. Reliable evidence from outside the scientific community which challenges the theories could falsify certain scientific claims. The biblical narrative approach concedes this same possibility with respect to the gospel's truth since this approach is no more a product of a ghetto than are scientific truth claims. Christians are open to a critical evaluation of the Bible's truth claims. For example, Wolfhart Pannenberg contends that the Christian faith is grounded upon historically verifiable events—especially upon the resurrection. Believers, in addition, know and experience these biblical

realities. In preaching and teaching, additional confidence in the truth of biblical realities is gained, as the Spirit causes the biblical text to overwhelm and convince its hearers.[9]

Objections to the New-Criticism Approach

Of course, as stated in my chapter, the objection to the new-criticism approach, that it tends to uproot Christianity from its historical moorings, stands. The new-criticism approach cannot do justice to Paul's statement about the resurrection: "If Christ has not been raised, then our preaching is in vain and your faith is in vain" (1 Cor. 15:14-19, RSV). From the evangelical perspective, the resurrection accounts are viewed as depicting a corresponding objective reality that occurs in ordinary space and time. For this very reason, they cannot be "special, salvation" events as defined within neoorthodoxy.

The Possibilities of a Believing Criticism

Paige Patterson sees promise for the exegete in the literary approaches to the Bible which recognize the value of the text in its present form. He states that my assessment of the contributions and limitations of the various literary approaches to the Bible is an excellent introduction to these literary developments.

Rob James agrees with Patterson that he has found help in the recent literary approaches to the Bible. James is also in agreement with my emphasis on Calvin's doctrine of "accommodation" as an important insight which should help us move beyond the impasse. It is helpful to remember that the Bible as historical testimony does not exhaust or even completely penetrate the mystery of ultimate power and meaning. Yet it does claim to reveal God as He would be known as our God.

Rob James calls for fundamental-conservatives and moderate-conservatives to move from two sides onto *new* ground. Hopefully, my chapter will help in such a movement. All of the writers in the book agree on the necessity of a *believing* criticism. One of the reasons why the six Southern Baptist seminary presidents projected the two Inerrancy Conferences at Ridgecrest was to attempt to establish agreed upon parameters of "believing criticism." A significant statement in this regard was made by Earle Ellis at the Inerrancy Conference:

> Historical criticism as such should not be identified with the rationalistic assumptions on which it has sometimes been pursued. There are encouraging signs today that it is moving beyond the "closed" world view of rationalism toward a renewal of theistic assumptions and an openness to transcendence in its analysis and interpretation of the scriptures.
>
> We historical-literary critics are, like all ministers, servants of the Word of God, not masters of it. We come to scripture to listen. Only in the context of listening in the Spirit, even as we do our historical-literary analysis, will the mysteries of the scripture both in its historical and present meaning be unveiled. Using the Bible apart from the Spirit, whether in the pulpit or study, will inevitably lead to aberrations. The Reformation symbol of the Spirit-Dove above the open scriptures should always be emblematic of our study.[10]

Evangelicals and Southern Baptists need both scholars and prophets; both cautious guardians and adventurous explorers.

The Contribution of Canonical Criticism

In her critique of my chapter, Molly Truman Marshall calls for more clarity and finer discrimination in certain areas. First, she suggests that the canonical approach needs to be included because it does justice to the diversity of the entire Bible and further demonstrates how earlier communities of faith understood and reshaped the texts as Scripture. Marshall contends that the utilization of Childs's hermeneutical approach does not set the text adrift but will allow the discovery of various levels of meanings held by the texts.

I agree on the importance of canonical criticism, especially the work of Brevard Childs. I did not give more attention to canonical criticism because Walter Harrelson suggested that this discussion would be contained in his chapter.

As Marshall suggests, canonical criticism maintains that the Bible gives considerable evidence of how "authoritative traditions encountered ancient cultural challenges, were rendered adaptable to those challenges, and thus themselves were formed and reformed according to the needs of the believing communities." And that evidence "gives indications of how to make again today the points originally made and then to move on in our contexts to further theological horizons (views of truth)." Such a use is possible because of several continuity factors: the Christians' covenant identity and their ability to remember the mighty acts of God, to find dynamic analogies with the ancient experiences of God's people, and to apply the biblical comfort or challenges to themselves.[11]

Childs maintains that the purpose of the canonical process is to ensure that "a tradition from the past be transmitted in such a way that its authoritative claims be laid upon all successive generations of Israel."[12] The interpreter who studies Scripture from the perspective of its canonical intentionality will be able to discern the text's function for the community of faith today and will also learn the boundaries in which exegesis should take place. Neither the historical-critical method nor any other will have absolute priority in the interpretation process because Scripture's nature as canon sets the limits within which these methods are practiced.[13]

In short, Childs seems to be opting for a certain descriptive, plain meaning in the biblical text which sets limits for interpretation. However, he does not foreclose the possibility of the interpreter's contribution to the text's interpretation in a given context, particularly with regard to finding a unity among various texts.[14]

The approach of Childs also appears to be congenial with the view of a number of evangelicals and the International Council on Biblical Inerrancy. They would allow that interpretation involves several stages. At the most basic stage, the sheer retelling of the biblical text, the literal meaning is descriptively ascertainable by all interpreters. However, this simple descriptive meaning is not adequate at the stage of applying the text. At this stage, the text functions to render Christ present to readers so that they come to identify with the world that Scripture portrays and to acknowledge its truth. At this stage the text is meaningful by appropriation.

However, the Bible itself furnishes some limits to its meaning and provides conceptions which are not dependent upon the interpreter's (human) experience of the Word. Also the descriptive or literal meaning of the text about which all may agree functions as a criterion by which to determine how the text legitimately can be appropriated. This means that one is not free to make the text say whatever one wants to make it mean.[15]

Canonical criticism also points out the effect of placing all the biblical books in a single canonical collection. Books like Luke, Jonah, Ecclesiastes, and Ruth, as well as countless smaller literary units, were originally written in a situationally oriented and independent way. But in the canon they have been placed in the company of many other compositions, which now impinge upon their subject matter, and vice versa. A book like Jonah, for example, is now read in relation to the total setting of the Old Testament, and even more important, in relation to Jesus and what He said about the sign of Jonah and His own resurrection. Mark and John, Romans and Hebrews, Galatians and James came together in the canon, and the result is a fuller picture than before. This placing of diverse texts alongside one another affects all of them, and the text can now say more than it did before. A new world of meaning is opened up by this process, and the collection is able to speak to countless different persons.[16]

We are compelled to look at the Bible as a whole, with all of its tensions and rich conversation. It is important, for example, that Job and Isaiah and Philippians should exist in the canon with Deuteronomy and Proverbs when the problem of evil and suffering is considered. The task of interpretation is to deal with the whole world of the text in its totality.[17]

Second, Marshall expresses surprise that I do not suggest that the reason for retaining the biblical authors' intents as primary has to do with an understanding of Spirit-inspired authority. I presume this and surely agree that the Spirit inspired the authors and the text at each step of the formation of biblical materials into the texts as we have them in the canon. This does not deny that the Scriptures are also human literary documents.

The Strength and Weakness of the Reader-Response Approach

Third, Marshall questions my statement that the various literary approaches are "contradictory." In my revised chapter, the word that I use is *imbalance*. I state that "Each of these (literary) movements has some truth. . . . but in each case the secular theory tends to lead to a new imbalance." A more complete statement of the wording in my chapter states that "Marxist and feminist readings have a *tendency* to distort the text by insisting that their themes are the primary interpretive grids.'' I immediately qualify this statement by noting that "it is possible to combine the better features of these approaches (liberation, feminist) so as to give an appropriately balanced emphasis to author, text, reader, and the spiritual reality or worldview that is presented in the biblical text.''

Marshall seems to imply that I do not recognize the contribution of feminist and liberation interpreters in correcting an imbalance. As indicated above, I do acknowledge this contribution. I state that *"theological* feminism has indisputable elements of truth.'' However, as Marshall notes, I am critical of those more radical feminist and liberation writers who tend to give experience or a preconceived perspective authority equal to that of the Scriptures. It is easy to allow the context to control the text. If the sociological approach is uncritically embraced, a view shaped by culture with its own intellectual and social history becomes the guide for interpreting Scripture and gospel. The sociology of knowledge determines the theology of knowledge. Evangelical Christians must firmly resist this reversal.[18]

Even Gadamer anticipates the charge that the reader-response model is a reversion to pure subjectivity. He insists that, though the understanding may be described in part as understanding oneself in the text, the proper stance is one of subordination. We open ourselves to the superior claim the text makes and respond to what it has to tell us. We do not take control of the meaning which the text affirms. Rather, we seek to serve the text, letting its claims dominate our minds so that a valid interpretation and application issue forth.[19]

In this connection, I would call for an openness to new and more intensive studies of the context of texts used by rigid patriarchal interpreters. An example of this type of work is found in the writings of Sharon Gritz in her new book *Paul, Women Teachers, and the Mother Goddess at Ephesus.*[20] The teachings of James I. Packer and Walter C. Kaiser at the 1988 Conference on Biblical Interpretation are also helpful as interpretations of the controversial texts on women in ministry.[21]

It is important to note that competent evangelical interpreters also call attention to the "analogy of faith'' principle of biblical interpretation. This principle emphasizes the importance of the broader biblical teaching on the equality of sexes in the New Testament. Evangelical theology will rightly accord ultimate normative authority only to Scripture as a whole and in its wholeness.[22]

I would agree with Timothy George that it is important to separate the question of "women in ministry" from the theology of feminism. In *The Battle for the Trinity*, Donald Bloesch has also called attention to the weaknesses of some feminist hermeneutics which relativizes the authority of the biblical text.[23]

The Importance of the Revelation of God in History

Fourth, I agree with Marshall that the literary emphasis on the "world within the narrative text" does not *necessarily* mean that the interpreter is arguing that there is no world outside the text. However, as I have suggested, there is a danger here because a number of prominent authors tend to neglect or ignore the cruciality of God's revelation *in history* for human salvation.

Since the Kantian era, philosophers, educators, and some theologians have tended to think of reality in terms of distinct points of view: "You have your perspective; I have mine." For Kant, nothing can be apprehended in itself; all objects are known only phenomenally on the basis of the experience and constitutive contribution of the knower. Normative meaning is an unintelligible concept on such grounds.

From the beginning the Bible contends that there can be no other God or Jesus Christ than the one depicted in the biblical text. This was the conviction of early church fathers such as Irenaeus and Augustine. For example, to say that Jesus has not risen is to manufacture a Jesus different from the one depicted in the biblical text. But faith implies acknowledgment of Scripture's authority and the church's interpretation that Scripture depicts the only Jesus there is.[24]

I noted in my chapter that recently there has developed a kind of literary analytic relativism (the idea that a text can mean anything to anyone because it is fundamentally inaccessible). The source of such literary analytic theory is the school of deconstruction, first developed by Jacques Derrida. In order to counteract this drift toward relativism, at least one of the prominent proponents of the reader-response model, Paul Ricoeur, has sought to introduce the idea that a text might have an "objective," presumably descriptive meaning distinguishable from and prior to its meaning by appropriation.[25] At this point Ricoeur seems to be in agreement with the biblical narrative approach. He acknowledges the possibility that at some logically distinct point in the process of interpretation the descriptive, normative meaning of a text functions as a norm for judging later phases pertaining to application. For the present, we must note that most proponents of the reader-response model do not accept Ricoeur's qualification. Consequently their theology and preaching flirts with Western society's relativism and narcissism.[26]

G. Ernest Wright contends that the Bible's historical grounding is unique among religions—that the Bible is the witness to the only religious movement in history that centers its case squarely in history and its inspired interpretation. According to the biblical worldview, a personal revelation through particular circumstances of time and space is the only way to become acquainted with the sovereign, free, and personal God and His purposes. Particularity, far from being a scandal, has the highest metaphysical credentials—for God Himself is a particular, a Person. So, for the biblical worldview, the starting point is in revelation which comes through particulars—not through philosophical reasoning, religious intuition, divination, or human religious consciousness.[27]

If Jesus Christ did not die *in history* for our sins and rise for our empowerment, evangelism, missions, and the teaching that personal faith in Jesus Christ is the only way to a saving knowledge of God for all peoples everywhere is undermined.

Notes

1. Mark Ellingsen, *The Integrity of Biblical Narrative* (Minneapolis: Fortress, 1990), 10; and Hans W. Frei, *The Eclipse of Biblical Narrative* (New Haven: Yale University Press, 1974), 29.

2. Ellingsen, 11; and Paul Tillich, *The New Being* (New York: Scribner's 1955), esp. 37; and *The Shaking of Foundations* (New York: Scribner's, 1948), esp. 93-103, 169-72.

3. Ellingsen, 13; and Han-Georg Gadamer, *Truth and Method*, 2d ed. (New York: Seabury Press, 1975), 107, 236-37, 263-67, 428-30.

4. Ellingsen, 27.

5. Ibid., 31, 32; and William K. Wimsatt, *The Verbal Icon* (London: Methuen & Co., 1954), xvi-xvii, 3-11, 22-38, 249-50; and George A. Lindbeck, *The Nature of Doctrine* (Philadelphia: Westminster, 1984), 33-34, 68, 101*f*, 119.

Dialogue and Further Reflections

6. Ellingsen, 32, 33.

7. Ibid.; Frei, 58*f*, 91-94, 102-5, 114-16, 118.

8. Ellingsen, 39-40.

9. Ibid., 40, 59, 60; Lindbeck, 68, 131; and Wolfhart Pannenberg, *Jesus—God and Man*, trans. L. L. Wilkins and D. A. Priebe (London: SCM, 1968), 27-28.

10. E. Earle Ellis, "Historical-Literary Criticism—After Two Hundred years: Origins, Aberrations, Contributions, Limitations," *The Proceedings of the Conference on Biblical Inerrancy 1987* (Nashville: Broadman, 1987), 415-18.

11. William J. Larkin, Jr., *Culture and Biblical Hermeneutics* (Grand Rapids: Baker, 1988), 55.

12. Brevard S. Childs, *Introduction to the Old Testament as Scripture* (Philadelphia: Fortress, 1979), 78.

13. Larkin, 55-56.

14. Ellingsen, *The Evangelical Movement* (Minneapolis: Augsburg, 1988), 370.

15. Ibid., 370-71.

16. Clark H. Pinnock, *The Scripture Principle* (San Francisco: Harper and Row, 1984), 187-88; cf. Robert K. Johnston, ed., *The Use of the Bible in Theology* (Atlanta: John Knox, 1985), 35-55.

17. Pinnock, 189; cf. James Barr, *Holy Scripture* (Philadelphia: Westminster, 1983), 130-71.

18. Gabriel Fackre, "God the Discloser," *Christian Faith and Practice in the Modern World*, eds. Noll and Wells (Grand Rapids; Eerdmans, 1988) 107-8.

19. Larkin, 58.

20. Sharon Gritz, *Paul, Women Teachers, and the Mother Goddess at Ephesus* (Lanhan: University Press of America, 1991).

21. Cf. *The Proceedings of the Conference on Biblical Interpretation* (Nashville: Broadman, 1988), 103-15, 212-14.

22. Cf. D. A. Carson, ed., *Biblical Interpretation and the Church: The Problem of Contextualization* (Nashville: Nelson, 1984), esp. Carson's own essay, 20-24.

23. Donald Bloesch, *The Battle for the Trinity* (Ann Arbor: Servant, 1985).

24. Ellingsen, *Integrity*, 37.

25. Paul Ricoeur, *Interpretation Theory: Discourse and the Surplus of Meaning* (Fort Worth: Texas Christian University Press, 1976), 75, 78-79; and idem, *Essays on Biblical Interpretation*, ed. Lewis S. Mudge (Philadelphia: Fortress, 1980), 68-69.

26. Ellingsen, *Integrity*, 59.

27. G. Ernest Wright, "Archaeology, History, and Theology," *Harvard Divinity Bulletin*, 95.

12

A Response
by R. Albert Mohler, Jr.

Can Southern Baptists move "Beyond the Impasse?" That question is even more problematic now than it was when this volume was first envisioned and the contributors began their struggle with this project. The events of 1990 and 1991 represent a seemingly insurmountable obstacle to the removal of the impasse.

The most significant of these recent events is the establishment of the Cooperative Baptist Fellowship, which is—though it is often denied—a rival denominational body seeking support from Southern Baptist moderates. The establishment of this Fellowship has required a case to be made for its existence. The *Address to the Public* broadcast by this body to the wider world, sets forth clearly the theological distance between the SBC and the progressives leading the CBF.

Though preaching a gospel of inclusiveness and diversity, the Fellowship's *Address* explicitly rejects the concept of biblical inerrancy with the statement that "The Bible neither claims nor reveals inerrancy as a Christian teaching." Though the *Address* claims that differences with the conservatives are "not at the point of the inspiration or authority of the Bible," it later states that "We also, however, have a different understanding of the nature of the Bible." That "different understanding" is not articulated in the document, but a clear and unmistakable rejection of inerrancy is made plain.

The existence of the Fellowship and the message of its *Address to the Public* make clear the increasing distance between the polarities within the Southern Baptist spectrum. Should any miss this point, John Hewett, the newly elected moderator of the Fellowship provided instant clarification. He stated in an interview that theological differences separated SBC moderates and conservatives from the onset of the denominational controversy. Moderates were unwilling to concede the existence of these differences, however, "Because they felt that to admit theological differences was to invite massive defeat.''[1] And thus the impasse looms.

Hewett also stated that "Southern Baptists weren't willing to debate theology."[2] That is, in many cases, unfortunately true, for this atheological age has produced a generation virtually disarmed for theological debate or dialogue. Theological issues are often reduced to the level of individual preference or whimsy, with little regard for the most basic issues of truth and falsehood.

This project has offered an alternative to that muddle, and the participants have engaged one another with mutual respect and a spirit of collegiality. The result has been genuine dialogue. This means that differences of conviction are not denied or soft-pedaled, but set out with charity and clarity as true respect for dialogue partners demands.

Rob James and Molly Truman Marshall have honored me by the serious attention they gave my proposals, and I will respond in kind. First, I will respond to specific points they raised concerning my chapter, and then I will turn to respond to their own creative proposals.

James suggests that none of my fourteen imperatives "is distinctly Baptist." This is generally true, for my primary concern is the integrity of what is "distinctly Christian"—issues which must be settled before moving onward to denominational distinctives. Those "distinctives" are themselves subject to debate, but space does not allow that discussion here.

Let this statement suffice: There is no contradiction between a stalwart and fulsome Baptist confessionalism with doctrinal parameters and the traditional Baptist distinctives of soul competency, congregational church government, and the priesthood of believers (all of which, of course, have received distinctive emphasis among Baptists, but none of which can be claimed for Baptists alone). If this contradiction is claimed with seriousness, any genuine theological dialogue collapses of its own weight, and Baptists should simply accept individualism and latitudinarianism as part and parcel of Baptist identity. Southern Baptists should then apologize to a host of saints including Basil Manly (Sr. and Jr.), B. H. Carroll, James P. Boyce, E. Y. Mullins, and Herschel Hobbs.

Marshall raises a similar concern, noting "a marked inattention to religious liberty and the priesthood of all believers" in my proposals. That inattention is conceded, for, as stated above, those issues were not the focus of my most basic concern in that essay—issues which are foundational to those worthy Baptist tenets.

James questions whether I would concede that the reduction of doctrinal studies in the SBC has been the result of an increasing attention to biblical studies. My answer is "no," for I reject the dichotomy. I do agree, as he requests, with his statement that "getting doctrines right is not an end in itself." But I would insist that it is an end to which every genuine disciple must aim, and without which that discipleship is endangered, if not misunderstood.

In her response to my call for "theological triage," Marshall recalls my suggestion that among the issues which should be held for second- or third-order significance was the ordination of women (p. 178). She asks if I would place "qualifications for ministry in general" in that category. I am pleased to respond in the affirmative, yet my suggestion was not that these issues should be considered as *adiaphora* or "indifferent" matters, but that they should not rank as first-order concerns with the essential *kerygma* of the Christian faith. The real issue is what I have described as the range of "convictional cooperation" with fellow Baptists.

Marshall also questions my suggestion that seminary faculties have responded more adequately to the concerns of the academy than those of the church (p. 176). The academy, I maintain, has been addressed by theological faculties more than the church—*as publics of theological attention and address*. This is not to question the churchly discipleship of seminary professors nor is it a reckless broadside for employment in controversy. It is a diagnosis of the extent to which the norms, expectations, and worldviews of the academy have shaped the conception of theological formation, even in confessional seminaries.

The academy is growing increasingly hostile to even the most anemic theological truth-claims. We should expect our seminary professors to exercise and maintain scholarly research and writing which represent the highest quality of academic rigor. But the academic situation as it now exists will require confessional theologians, biblical scholars, and all other seminary professors to *confront* the academy's hostility to truth-claims and assure the church of its priority in establishing norms, expectations, and parameters.

In her thoughtful and interesting chapter Marshall presented a call for seeing denominational life in terms of a "large room" or a "broad place" (pp. 179-80). I welcome her emphasis on the cross and on the story of Jesus of Nazareth. Nevertheless, I do not have a clear understanding of what she means when she appears to call for the priority of the story of Jesus over Scripture as the later codification of that story. I would argue that we are not members of the apostolic community and we have no prior access to the Jesus story other than Scripture.

This same concept appears when she cites *The* (1963) *Baptist Faith and Message* statement on Scripture which avers that "the criterion by which the Bible is to be interpreted is Jesus Christ." This can be a meaningful statement if it is intended to point to Jesus Christ as the supreme focus of the biblical message. On the other hand, the statement can be quite problematic if it is employed with the presupposition that we have some other source of revelation for the story of Jesus itself, or that we should employ some form of "internal critique" within Scripture with freedom to deny the truth status of selected passages within the Bible.

Scripture witnesses to Jesus Christ. It is sufficient to reveal the truth concerning the Savior who is alone sufficient to save. Scripture is not the agent of salvation but it is the vehicle of revelation God has granted to us, without which salvation would be unknown. It is the Word of God for us, and we have no other means of authoritative revelation at our disposal.

This is, however, precisely what is suggested by Rosemary Radford Reuther in her promotion of the "prophetic-liberating tradition." It is not merely a matter of Christological passages having priority, for the truth status of other passages is effectively rejected. This is also the pattern of Elizabeth Schussler Fiorenza, who allows the norm of liberation to have priority over the biblical text itself. Thus she suggests that the later epistles demonstrate the marginalization of women and slaves for the sake of the political interests of the early church. The integrity and truth status of those passages is thus impugned.

Jesus Christ stated clearly that He came to *fulfill* Scripture, and He never rejected any passage of the Jewish canon. His disciples should see in this a rejection of any interpretive methodology which would do so. *The Baptist Faith and Message* statement that Scripture is "truth, without any mixture of error" does not settle all interpretive issues, and Baptists will join all other Christians in an earnest struggle with difficult passages. But that statement does exclude any methodology which explicitly or implicitly denies any passage of Scripture its full authority and truthfulness.

The references to Reuther and Fiorenza raise the issue of feminist hermeneutics, a form of liberation theology which now holds sway in many Christian communions. The interpretive history of biblical texts should always remain open for debate and respectful critique. But many feminists, these representatives included, have progressed beyond this to interrogate and hold under judgment the text itself. This is simply not an acceptable evangelical option, as it is a direct abrogation of the Scripture principle. Those who claim identity as *evangelical* feminists must demonstrate observable exegetical controls which prevent this abrogation and truly honor the text.

As it stands, radical feminist theologies represent but one variant of the multiple ideological temptations which confront the contemporary church. Nevertheless, it poses what may now be the greatest danger to the orthodox Christian tradition, attacking theism itself at the doctrine of the Trinity. This should not be assumed of all who would employ aspects of feminist thought, but it does call upon them to make their evangelical affirmations clear and plain.

Marshall's chapter is helpful in raising many of these issues, and her winsome and thoughtful proposals deserve the most careful engagement. The limits of this short chapter do not allow adequate interaction with her essay, but perhaps it may afford an opportunity to continue the discussion.

The same limitations apply to the encyclopedic and far-ranging essay offered by James. James cries "foul" at my call for theological dialogue, for I also proposed no less than fourteen imperatives for the denominational future. He is concerned that the "procedure could create the impression that the results of the dialogue are being laid down before it starts." He is correct, at least in part, for I do not think that any genuine dialogue is possible, or could be profitable, if there is no established common ground. Just what that common ground might be is the basic contention between my essay and that of James.

James's most basic concern appears to come in his early section on the Bible's concern with doctrine and relation. He states that "doctrine is to conform to our ongoing relation with God in Christ, not the other way around. . . ." My most basic concern with this statement is its assertion of what I see as a false and ultimately fatal dichotomy.

There is no faith relation with Christ free of doctrinal content. The knower must have some knowledge of the known, or no relation exists. That seemingly redundant and self-evident statement should underline the issue. Jesus Christ and our knowledge of Him are not in any sense coextensive. But one cannot have a relation with Him without knowledge, and that knowledge represents incipient doctrine. James is clearly correct in his assertion that "the whole purpose of biblical doctrine is to bring about that living relationship," but I must take strong issue with his later statement that "God's revelation in the Bible is not basically a matter of doctrinal truths so that in the first instance, we are to believe them. Rather, God in the first place reveals *Himself* to us in Christ. . . ."

If one does *not* believe the truths concerning the Christ as revealed in Holy Scripture, one *cannot* have any authentic relationship with Him. Doctrine, we eagerly concede, does not in itself save. There is a measure of truth in what I think James means to say. One may worship orthodoxy more than Christ. But, on the other hand, one cannot truly worship Christ and seek to live as an authentic disciple and deny, denigrate, or neglect in any sense the biblical teachings concerning Him.

James also demonstrates a most interesting interpretation of Protestant fundamentalism and one of its most famous archetypes, J. Gresham Machen. I simple do not recognize much of Machen in James's treatment of him. Machen is presented, and not without graciousness, as a foil for Edgar Y. Mullins. According to this, Machen is the scholastic (with whom James argues that SBC conservatives should identify) while Mullins stressed individual Christian experience.

Here again the dichotomy raises its now familiar head. I do not believe that either Machen or Mullins would recognize himself in James's exposition. Machen was most assuredly a scholastic in the sense that he was an eager heir of the Reformed scholastic tradition associated with "Old Princeton." But he would never have stressed this scholasticism over the faith relationship. The thought would never have crossed his orthodox Presbyterian mind. In *Christianity and Liberalism*, Machen sought to argue against those who openly rejected biblical truth. The line of Machen's argument James cites does not relate to ontological claims at all, but to the noetic dimension of faith. Machen's basic argument is this: There is no relationship with the crucified and risen Savior without some true knowledge of the cross and resurrection, "the blessed theology of the cross." Can any genuine argument be made against this point?

That argument would most certainly not come from E. Y. Mullins. The man S. Parkes Cadman once called "The Saint Francis of the Baptists" certainly placed a distinctive and undeniable emphasis on the priority of Christian experience. Mullins and Machen represented different traditions and theological methodologies. But Mullins was no less interested in affirming Christian truths as essential to faith.

The author of *Christianity at the Cross Roads* and *The Axioms of Religion* was no less concerned about doctrinal deviation and neglect. His 1923 address to the Southern Baptist Convention included a recitation of essential Christian truth-claims ranging from the virgin birth to Christ's physical ascension. "We believe," stated Mullins, "that adherence to these truths and facts is a necessary condition of service for teachers in our Baptist schools."

Mullins, who has been claimed by both parties in the present SBC conflict, is notoriously difficult to label. Nevertheless, his vocal defense of doctrinal fundamentals is undeniable, and he saw no inherent conflict between concern for doctrine and his famous defense of soul competency and personal religious experience. He represented a significant shift from the Reformed paradigm of James P. Boyce and Basil Manly, Jr., but his was not a shift from theological legalism to latitudinarianism.[3]

From Mullins and Machen, James moves onward to propose a psychological basis for preoccupation with doctrine. He identifies a "trauma-reaction syndrome" which produced a tendency toward "heightened supernaturalism" (pp. 129-30). I would suggest that we should avoid such psycho-babble as fundamentally unhelpful in the current debate. James is by nature a gracious individual, and yet I think he would take legitimate offense at the notion that Baptists of his stripe are so because of what I may term a "trauma-avoidance syndrome," which produces anti-supernaturalism. That is a form of contemporary condescension we can well do without.

James's suggestion of a "heightened supernaturalism" (pp. 130, 146) is most interesting. Just what does this mean? What other kind of supernaturalism exists as an alternative? "Heightened" according to whose standards? The bottom line is that the doctrinal issues James identifies have not been "heightened" by evangelicals, but *highlighted* within Scripture. The evangelical tradition has simply stated the biblical truth-claim.

Just what would Professor James hold to be a proper supernaturalism? It was none other than E. Y. Mullins who identified a hearty and undiluted affirmation of Christian supernaturalism *as part of the mission of the Southern Baptist Convention*! As he stated in his 1924 presidential address to the Convention:

> The mission of the Convention is to interpret and demonstrate to a world of modernism that true relation between spiritual cause and effect. You cannot water down the missionary motive and accomplish the missionary aim. Christ's deity and His atonement and His resurrection from the dead are the dynamic forces behind the missionary enterprise. Christianizing the social order is good. Uplift movements are good. *But the power of it all is in the supernaturalism of the Gospel* (emphasis his).

A survey of the history of doctrine indicates clearly that heresy has most often preceded orthodoxy. That is, statements of orthodox faith have customarily resulted from the challenge of heterodox assertions. The Council of Nicaea met to deal with Arius's heresy, not to exult in "heightened supernaturalism." Likewise, the fundamentalists of the 1920s did not emerge from a vacuum; they were responding to explicit denials of biblical truth and classical Christian doctrines." The *rejection* of truth preceded their concern.

I do not believe that James has taken this with full seriousness. The historic fact is that fundamentalists were, in the main, responding to unmistakable rejections of biblical truth. While contemporary fundamentalism has taken on connotations of negativism, separatism, and militancy with which I cannot identify, we must reclaim an authentic Baptist evangelicalism which shares a deep and credible concern for the doctrinal integrity of the Christian faith, without the negative baggage of modern separatistic fundamentalists.[4] We must also raise a complaint at this point concerning James's constant habit in this chapter of identifying those concerned with doctrine as "fundamentalists." This word can be employed in the current discussion only as an epithet.

The most troublesome section of James's essay relates to his discussion of whether God is "uptight" (pp. 142-43). James wishes to employ the word as "a term of art," by which he means that "[God] does not have a legalistic mind-set and a meticulous, hyperscrupulous nature." As evidence he cites the "nonconformity [of] Jesus" and the judgment Jesus directed toward the older brother in the "parable of the prodigal son" (who must, we might surmise, have had a hang-up on doctrine). We must pause here to reflect that not even the most eager allegorist has yet extended the identity of the elder brother to God, uptight or otherwise.

God is not uptight, but that "does not mean that He is a picture of laid-back indifference, however." James points to God's passionate will to encounter us and establish a relation with us "if we will have it so."

James suggests that "there may be something wrong with fundamentalist religion, because fundamentalists tend to be uptight, and God is not." He continues: "Something about their view of God makes it hard for God—the real God who is not uptight—to get through to them."

This conclusive statement causes me much grief, for it lays bare the magnitude of the impasse which looms before, above, and all around us. The God of those James identifies as fundamentalists is nothing more than a projection of their own "uptightness."

Yet, they are in good company, for the vast tapestry of biblical faith has been woven from the lives of those who have been claimed by the grace of a God who took human sin with full seriousness and yet willed to provide a means of redemption and reconciliation through the life, death, and resurrection of His Son.

Completely absent in the notion of a God who is not "uptight" is the essential category of holiness. Scripture clearly, repeatedly, and straightforwardly reveals a God who is jealous of His holiness, will abide no other gods, hates sin, and punishes the wicked. He is a "consuming fire" of holiness and righteousness. What does it mean to propose that God does not have "a meticulous, hyperscrupulous nature"? In light of the biblical record, can this be a description of the God of Abraham, Isaac, and Jacob; of Rebecca, Rachel, and Ruth; the Father of our Lord Jesus Christ?

Conclusion

Can the impasse be overcome? This project has provided a unique and unprecedented forum for genuine theological dialogue. The project has required courage, candor, and perseverance, but it has never produced boredom. The contributors came together in mutual respect, and I deeply appreciate the opportunity to struggle together with David Dockery, Rob James, Timothy George, John Newport, Molly Truman Marshall, Paige Patterson, and Walter Harrelson.

Can consensus be achieved? That is the underlying issue which frames this project. The chapters collected in this volume reveal that the impasse facing the Southern Baptist Convention now looms even larger than it did when this project was first envisioned. The differences are basic and foundational and are now set forth with candor.

What lies ahead? That question cannot be answered within this volume, but the outlines of the future can be traced in the development of the Cooperative Baptist Fellowship and other recent events. The future course of the Southern Baptist Convention is unclear, but the denomination must have learned *something* in the past twelve years of struggle. At a bare minimum, the denomination should now recognize the impossibility of any attempt to forge consensus by the course of confessional minimalism.

This is why I must take issue with James when he suggests:

> Your doctrines and my doctrines may differ at some significant point, perhaps in our doctrine of Scripture. Even so, we can share leadership in missions, evangelism, and theological education *if* the crucial question . . . is whether you and I are mutually related to Jesus Christ as Savior and Lord, living faithfully in Him and for Him (p. 128).

This has the seductive power of such minimalism. The problem arises when the full significance of doctrinal differences comes to light. At the extremes, the differences are so great that partisans do not share common conceptions of theological education (What is to be taught?), missions (What is the substance of the missionary message?), and evangelism (What is the nature of biblical evangelism?). No one should expect total consensus on all theological issues, but the absence of a confessional consensus on foundational issues is fatal to any body serious about the tasks of missions, evangelism, and theological education.

The cultural, ideological, and theological divide which runs throughout American Christianity now runs through the Southern Baptist Convention. Yet, I believe that the vast mainstream of this denomination does share an evangelical consensus on these issues

and will move forward. The future will require that consensus to be nurtured, matured, and boldly attested.

Any consensus based on a lowest common doctrinal denominator will be insufficient to protect the theological integrity of the people called Southern Baptists. The Southern Baptist Convention desperately needs comprehensive theological recovery and genuine renewal in Baptist hearts. We must pray that the sovereign grace and limitless love of Almighty God will bring about what human effort cannot alone produce.

Notes

1. Norman Jameson, "Fellowship Lets Moderates Get on with the Task," *Associated Baptist Press*, May 13, 1991, 3-4.

2. Ibid.

3. See R. Albert Mohler, Jr., "God's Grace the Effort Will Succeed: Southern Seminary in Historical Perspective," an address to the Board of Trustees of The Southern Baptist Theological Seminary, September 24, 1990.

4. See R. Albert Mohler, Jr., "A Call for Evangelical Baptists and Baptist Evangelicals," in *Southern Baptists and American Evangelicals*, ed. David S. Dockery (Nashville: Broadman Press, forthcoming).

13
A Response
by Robison B. James

In this chapter, I respond briefly to the main chapters by Paige Patterson and Timothy George, and at greater length to the one by Molly Truman Marshall. A final rejoinder follows, in which I comment on the way these contributors and others have responded to my earlier chapter. At the beginning of that rejoinder, a "detective story" explains what makes this chapter longer than the other "responses." (Also, Walter Harrelson generously turned over to me more than half the space he could have claimed for his response.)

Paige Patterson and Biblical Criticism

Beginning three-fourths of the way through his chapter, Paige Patterson allows more room for the historical-critical study of Scripture than the earlier parts of his chapter suggested he would. True, he believes any such study would have to proceed believingly, and under several limitations, which he sets forth.

Nevertheless, Patterson says explicitly in the last two sections of his chapter that the historical-critical method, reverently used, should not be *rejected*. And by repeated implication he says such scholarship should be *pursued* (on certain conditions, to be sure).

Obviously, I agree with those statements, as far as they go. I also agree with many, though not all, of Patterson's cautions and guidelines. In particular, I would second his opening principle, which he quotes from Millard Erickson, as a good statement: Biblical criticism is appropriate if it is "carefully used and based upon assumptions that are consistent with the full authority of the Bible."

I further call attention to the important proviso that Patterson states in his fourth guideline: "Historical-critical scholars must be held to the same standards of probability and certitude which govern all legitimate inquiry into history.''

So far as Patterson's chapter as a whole is concerned, I believe his readers are justified in reading the worried things he says earlier in his essay in the light of where he comes out. When that is done, much of what he says earlier in the chapter seems to me to boil down to this proposition: Biblical criticism can derail faith and reshuffle someone's sense of mission in life, especially if it is presented without pastoral skill or concern.

But to that we must surely reply that the broadened horizons that come with *any* education can do that to people. Furthermore, if theological education of a moderate stripe produces some casualties, what about conservative and fundamentalist schooling? Do they not produce their share of casualties? Of course they do. And sometimes they run a lot of people away from Christianity, as well.

As a final point in response to his chapter, let me urge that we make a clear distinction between critically historical scholarship on the one hand, and theological judgments on the other hand. Usually Catholics, Jews, and various kinds of Protestants can agree on a wide range of historical conclusions. But not in their theology.

In general, English-speaking scholars do a better job making the distinction I am talking about than the Germans do. This distinction is important at no less than two places in Patterson's chapter. Both places involve German speakers.

(a) When I said Gerhard Maier's *The End of the Historical-Critical Method* was ''very bad scholarship,'' I not only cited Peter Stuhlmacher's incisive critique of Maier. I also explained that Maier's book blackens the water of our discussion ''like a great squid'' because Maier assumes that picking out a canon within the canon is something historical criticism is supposed to do.[1]

I think that is a mistake, even in German. Picking out a canon within the canon (certainly in the ideological way that some of the early historical critics went about it) is a *theological* judgment.

(b) The woman who wants us to burn her books, Eta Linnemann, had a dramatic conversion out of a drug-damaged life into evangelical Christianity. But the intellectual thing she was converted away from was not historical criticism, certainly not in our English-language sense. She was converted away from a theological position, a faith position, namely, the closed-universe, historicist perspective of the Bultmannian school[2]—which she regularly refers to as "historical-critical *theology*," I might add. If some of Linnemann's more histrionic statements were on target, Patterson would not be giving historical criticism the cautious "go ahead" that he gives it in his chapter.

We may take heart from the helpful things Patterson has done in his chapter without being blind to our many serious differences.

Timothy George and Creeds

Timothy George's gracefully written and thought-provoking chapter deserves more, but I can comment only on "creedalism." On that issue, I find George's position not only to one side of the majority of Baptist views, but also at one end of what is acceptable according to those "definite doctrines that Baptists believe, cherish, and with which they have been and are now closely identified."[3] I suspect George would agree with me that his views on creedalism need to be checked and balanced by views from the other end of the Baptist spectrum. We have a model for such "checking and balancing" from the late 1700s, as I will explain.

Meanwhile, I emphasize something I have several times explained: Our Baptist hostility toward binding creeds, though it obviously makes room for freedom, is driven by a concern for *authority*. Why must we remain free in relation to what George calls "man-made doctrinal constructs"? So that we can believe anything and everything? No, but because that is the only way the Bible, the Word of God, can be our authority, rather than someone's interpretation of it.[4]

We might all do some fresh reading in the Separate Baptists. These aggressive, evangelistic people brought the fire of New England's Great Awakening into the South after 1754. They got modest help from Regular Baptists, who had been in the South for eighty years. But, for the most part, it was the Separates who won the South for Baptists. And they did it in fifty years! In the process, they stamped Baptist religion with many of the features it still has among Southern Baptists, *including our skittishness about creeds*.[5]

It is misleading to imply, as George does, that our Baptist bias against creeds derives from outsiders such as the Campbells. No doubt the later Campbellite controversy intensified our anti-creedalism. But it was already there. And it was very Baptist.

What about the fact George points out, that many of the 293 persons who formed the SBC in 1845 came from churches using the Philadelphia Confession? One answer, as George acknowledges, comes in the public statement they issued at the time. "We have constructed for our basis no new creed," they said, "acting in this matter upon a Baptist aversion for all creeds but the Bible."[6]

But something happened fifty-eight years earlier that George does not mention. When the Separates in the South agreed to use the Regular Baptists' Philadelphia Confession, they did so *on certain conditions.* The action in Virginia in 1787 was recorded at the time in this way:

> After considerable debate, as to the propriety of having any confession of faith at all, the report of the committee was received with the following explanation:
> "To prevent the confession of faith from usurping a tyrannical power over the conscience of any, we do not mean, that every person is bound to the strict observance of every thing therein contained; yet that it holds forth the essential truths of the gospel. . . . Upon these terms we are united, and desire hereafter, that the names Regular and separate be buried in oblivion . . ."[7]

How Baptist! We acknowledge that our confessions hold forth the essential truths of the gospel, and we affirm those truths with glad conviction; yet our brothers' and sisters' *statement* of those truths lies somewhat lightly on the mind—its yoke is easy—lest our conscience be captive to their words, rather than to the mighty Word of Him who is alone the truth.

Speaking of the 1787 action in Virginia, the great Separate John Leland said in 1790, "perhaps it would have been better" if Virginia Separates and Regulars, like their counterparts in Georgia, had united *without* any confession of faith. Leland then launched into his classic "Virgin Mary" warning about confessions (see below).

Misleadingly, George says Leland issued this classic warning "in the context of arguing for religious liberty against state-imposed conformity." Whatever George means by that, people will read it to say, if the state *moves out* of the picture, a confession is fine.

Leland is saying almost the opposite. He is saying that if the state has *moved into* the picture, then there may be some excuse for a confession. In that case, a religious body might put its beliefs in a

confession to show that those beliefs fall within the bounds of what
the state will tolerate. But, Leland continues,

> in a government like that of Virginia, where all men believe and
> worship as they please . . . what need of a confession of faith? Why
> this Virgin Mary between the souls of men and the scriptures? Had a
> system of religion [a confession] been essential to salvation, or even
> to the happiness of the saints, would not Jesus, who was faithful in
> all his house, have left us one? If he has, it is accessible to all [i.e., in
> the Bible]. If he has not, why should a man be called a heretick
> because he cannot believe what he cannot believe, though he
> believes the Bible with all his heart? Confessions of faith often check
> any further pursuit after truth, confine the mind into a particular way
> of reasoning, and give rise to frequent separations. . . . It is some-
> times said that hereticks are always averse to confessions of faith. I
> wish I could say as much of tyrants. But after all, if a confession of
> faith, upon the whole, may be advantageous, the greatest care should
> be taken not to *sacradize*, or make a petty Bible of it.[8]

In his last sentence, Leland makes the best of a bad situation—a situation he has just declared dubious, if not dangerous, in incandescent
prose. How does George read this? He says Leland "acknowledged
confessions as 'advantageous' and binding upon those who *voluntarily* embraced them. . . ." Though it is unintentional, George thus
squelches a Baptist hero and obscures the way the Separate legacy
provides a check-and-balance landmark from our Baptist past.

Molly Truman Marshall and Her Narrative Theology Proposal

In her main chapter, Molly Truman Marshall offers a number of
fresh theological insights, including what I see as a major conciliating proposal. In the process, she affirms a resounding body of
orthodox beliefs. I deal first with those beliefs.

Orthodox beliefs.—Says Marshall, "we look to a possible theological consensus that might lead our denomination beyond the
present . . . impasse." Could that consensus include doctrinal parameters? "To my knowledge," she writes, "the moderates of our Convention have never contended that there is no need for such. They simply
have protested such a structure being imposed in a creedal way."

As for sin, she calls it a "moral affront" to God, "a costly and violent rebellion." And what does God do about it? "The truth about God is that God suffers in our place in the death of the Son in order to change us from 'enemies into friends.' " In so saying, she aligns herself firmly with objective views of the atonement.

How are the Father and Son who are involved in this atoning work related to each other? "Christian theology is properly concerned with the One God whom we confess as Trinity," says our author. As to the incarnation of the Son, she speaks of "the eternal Word of God enfleshed as the Christ." She also pulls David Dockery back from what she thinks is a too-strong analogy between Christ and the Bible. "Christ is the Incarnate Word and Scripture the written Word," she reminds him.

"That Scripture is wholly trustworthy is not at question among us," Marshall writes. Related is her belief in inspiration, or, as she expresses it, "the Bible as God's Word clad in human words." On that doctrine she corrects another of the book's contributors, John Newport. It is surprising, she remarks, that he failed to urge that the reason we take the biblical authors' intended meaning as the primary meaning of a text "has to do with an understanding of Spirit-inspired authority."

An intratextual approach.—I see it as an important conciliating proposal when Marshall recommends George Lindbeck's postliberal idea of an "intratextual" approach to the Bible (pp. 184-85).

According to this approach, we are to take our bearings from "within the text"—that is, from inside the biblical story of creation-fall-redemption-consummation. We do not locate the biblical world inside secular world history, as though it was the concoction of some earnest scribblers in the Ancient Near East. Rather, the reverse. We understand our fellow human beings, ourselves, our duties, our careers, our civilization, and our future, *according to how these things fit into the overarching biblical narrative*, from creation to consummation.

The result, in Lindbeck's vivid prose, is that the "scriptural world is thus able to absorb the universe. It supplies the interpretive framework within which believers seek to live their lives and understand reality."[9]

As this makes clear, an intratextual approach gives the Bible a kind of life-shaping authority that is hard to come by otherwise.

A historic split.—David Kelsey and Hans Frei have argued that an intratextual approach of this kind has the potential to overcome a historic split in the way the Bible has been interpreted.

For two reasons, I want to explain the thinking of Kelsey and Frei on this point.[10] First, their thinking will show precisely *why* the approach Marshall is recommending has major, conciliating possibilities for the Southern Baptist situation.

And second, these Frei-Kelsey ideas clarify something that is not sufficiently clear in my earlier chapter, namely, that the Bible subordinates "right doctrine" to "ongoing relation to God in Christ."

Kelsey and Frei point out that, according to Luther and Calvin, when we rightly read or rightly interpret the Bible, we are met and grasped simultaneously by the history the Bible relates *and* by the transforming grace it brings. More recently, however, and especially since about 1750, the Reformers' integrated way of reading the Bible has broken apart into subjective and objective components.

Some people are objectively focused. They grasp the Bible's propositions—its historical, doctrinal, or moral propositions. They then seek to apply the propositional content they derive from Scripture. (They may believe the Spirit illumines these truths, but the objective truths are still the point.) Protestant scholasticism illustrates this focus. The same objectivist tendency is visible in the way Protestant liberals reconstruct the historical Jesus and try to follow Him.

In these two cases, the meaning of Scripture is found in something external to it. That is the opposite of an intratextual approach, of course. For both scholastics and liberals, the meaning of the Bible is the doctrinal truths, the moral principles, the historical events, or a person from the past, that scholastics or liberals derive from the Bible.

By contrast, some people are subjectively focused. Tarrying little with the Bible's propositional content, but responding with immediacy to the Savior, these people receive the impact of Scripture into the subjective inwardness of their personal lives. This is true of Pietism. With differences, it is also true of existentialist interpretations, as in Rudolf Bultmann.

Here again we have the opposite of an intratextual approach. The meaning of the Bible is found in something outside the Bible. This time its meaning is thought to be one or another kind of human subjectivity that we are supposed to derive from the Bible.

The result of this historical development is a twofold split. Not only are the subjective and objective poles of our intercourse with Scripture split apart. It is also true that Christian is set against Christian, depending upon which of these approaches a given Christian takes.

Overcoming the split.—According to Frei and Kelsey, in the Reformation period the meaning of the Bible was seen as not external to the Bible in any of the ways I have discussed, scholastic, liberal, Pietist, or existentialist. Rather, the meaning of the Bible was understood to be internal to it. That is, its meaning was the Bible's unfolding drama of God's dealings with the world.

I should point out that the biblical drama I am talking about is very real. It is no mere fiction inside our heads. As I view it, this drama is more real than either the visible universe or the reconstructed past that we learn about from scientific and historical investigation.[11] The biblical drama is quite simply the truth about who we are and what we are, in our concrete reality. (At least some narrative theologians agree with that.)[12]

We human beings, then—what are we in our concrete reality, according to such narrative views? As Augustine would probably agree, each of us is an unfolding story. We *are* the individual life story that we are acting out. Of course, we do not enact our story all by ourselves. Our story is constantly intersected by the stories of others, especially by the embracing story of God's dealing with us and all His creation.[13]

When we opt into the biblical story as the story of our life, our inner subjectivity is brought into the action that is going on in that narrative, of course. But our inwardness does not become the focus of attention (as it would for a thoroughgoing Pietist, for example). Rather, our subjectivity is tied into a network of unfolding interactions *with others*—interactions with the characters who are rendered for us in the biblical story, especially the chief "actors," God and Jesus Christ, His Son.

As this makes clear, a narrative focus is not a purely subjective focus. On the other hand, it is not a purely objective focus, either. If we wanted to pin down one of the *characters in* this story "all to himself" or "all to herself"—that is, objectively—or if we wanted to analyze some structural *feature of* the story ("the nature of saving faith," for example), we would have to tease that character or that feature out of the flow of interactions, and analyze its nature, attributes, or "laws" (how it works).

That is what doctrinal systems tend to do, given their focus on objective truths. (It is both interesting and revealing, however, that doctrinal systems do less of that when they deal with "the work of Christ." That subject almost forces them to use narrative, or to "tell the old, old story.") When we look at typical doctrinal systems from inside the biblical drama, we can see that they often leave out or soft-pedal the main thing, namely the *ongoing relationships* in the biblical drama. Calvin knew better. He was clear that we do not have authentic knowledge of God in a detached, objective way, apart from our relatedness to Him, or apart from our pious, subjective involvement with Him.[14]

These observations make it clear, I trust, that a narrative kind of intratextual reading of the Bible brings back together the subjective and objective sides of our intercourse with Scripture. The two sides are united in those "storied interactions" that take place within the unfolding biblical drama—the drama in which God gives us a bit part to play, if we accept His casting.

That is the way the Reformers read the Bible, as we saw. It also has considerable promise for our situation. Many of the divisions among us, at least on the subject of the Bible, are polarized around a clash between "objective and subjective." This is true of the way an emphasis on doctrinal propositions can lord it over religious experience, or vice versa. An intratextual narrative approach is almost uniquely equipped to mediate such a conflict.

Redeeming is liberating.—How is the prophetic-liberating strand in Scripture related to the narrative ideas that Marshall employs?

The Bible's story of redemption becomes concrete for different Christians in different ways. For Calvin, the key—the "plot," as it were—appears to be giving glory to the God of sovereign grace. For Luther, the plot seems to be our finding the God of forgiving grace who reveals Himself by justifying the sinner through faith in Christ.

Anyone who takes the Bible seriously *as a unified story* will do the kind of thing Luther and Calvin did. They must. No plot, no unity! When Marshall does this, she settles upon the prophetic-liberating theme as the key to the plot. That theme is involved more or less throughout the Bible's story of salvation, and it is also a goading, aching concern among men and women today. Not a bad basis for choosing a central theme!

Or is it a choice? I do not think Marshall is "picking and choosing." The Bible is not limp or lame. It lives. And if it lives, it has the power to *center itself* around "the weightier matters of the law" (Matt 23:23). It has the capacity to press certain things upon you, or upon me, "as of first importance" (1 Cor. 15:3, RSV).

If that is what the Bible has done to Molly Marshall, who are we to be surprised, much less offended? The word *redemption* means liberation and release. It means "deliverance and freedom in matters of ultimate destiny and the meaning of life."[15] Woe to us if we do not also preach the gospel of redemption—which is, at the same time, the gospel of liberation!

Final Rejoinder

Although my fellow contributors have been generous in the time they spent with my earlier chapter, the responses from several of them reveal a curious fact. As I will explain, I do not fault Mohler, George, Dockery, and Patterson, but, for those readers, the main point I made in my chapter does not seem to have come across, while other points, including some points I disagree with, did come across.

A detective story.—In figuring out what happened, I have felt like an investigator in a detective story. I will weave into the early parts of my narrative a few scenes from that detective story. Those scenes are not just entertainment, I should add. I find them illuminating as to the kinds of thing that can happen when intelligent people from different sides of the fence talk, as we have talked, about moving "beyond the impasse."

One of the reasons this rejoinder is so extended—here I give one of my first discoveries—is the fact that I took on more than I could handle in chapter five. Patterson compliments the "lucid style" of that chapter, and I thank him; but whatever lucidity the chapter has belongs to the "micro level" of the chapter. That is, people tell me that the flow of the argument, from paragraph to paragraph, is easy to follow.

At the "macro level," however, the chapter is something else. It kept trying to be a book, and I kept cutting it down. Among the things that wound up "on the cutting room floor" were several "macro signals," that is, explanations about the overall nature and goal of my argument. I can see now how very much they were needed.

Main point of the former chapter: Biblical authority.—Marshall speaks of the "refrain" of my former chapter. I call it the "main point." She is the only respondent who seems to have recognized it. I want to restate the main point of the chapter now in a seven-sentence paragraph, as follows.

Especially when our fundamentalism gets the better of us, we keep the Bible from being fully authoritative. (We do this unwittingly and unintentionally, of course.) We resist its authority in at least seven ways. These "old habits" are enough to continue our impasse, that is, to keep us "in the wilderness." If we could shake them off and adopt seven opposite attitudes that the Bible mandates, however, we might find our way to a "new land." (I called the seven good attitudes "seven features of the new biblical land.") In that "new land," the Bible could be more truly authoritative—it could have its way with us—and we could work together in mutual acceptance of one another's leadership.

Contrary to George's analysis, my earlier chapter does not diagnose our impasse as fundamentalism squelching Baptist freedom. The focal issue is authority, not freedom. In the chapter's conclusion I said, "I have mainly argued for authority—for the authority of the Bible." Following that statement, I summarized the seven bad habits as seven ways in which the fundamentalism that is in all of us is resistant to Scripture.

The major misunderstanding: Was the anchor there?—In my former chapter, I emphasized the first of the biblically mandated good attitudes because I thought it had special importance for getting beyond the impasse. Here it is, somewhat rephrased:

> According to the Bible, our ongoing relation to God in Christ is basic and central, rather than the doctrinal statements that give an account of it, so we should conform our doctrines to our ongoing relation to God in Christ, rather than vice versa.

Just at this point, a major misunderstanding entered between my readers and me. They looked at this "ongoing relationship with Christ" and thought, *That thing could drift off anywhere. There is no anchor. Yet, here James is telling us we should conform Christian doctrine to whatever newfangled experience some person comes up with in his or her ongoing relation with Jesus.*

But I *saw* an anchor there, namely, the Bible. Thus it was only after musing for quite a while on the various responses to my chapter that it sank in. The anchor (which is also a dynamo, I might add) was completely invisible to my respondents.

In order to supply a *visible* anchor-dynamo, I will add to the first attitude the material I emphasize here below:

> According to the Bible, our ongoing relation to God in Christ is basic and central, rather than the doctrinal statements that give an account of it, so we should conform our doctrines to our ongoing relation to God in Christ, rather than vice versa; *and that makes sense because this is an ongoing relation to the living Lord who is wed—in the Spirit and by His own live speaking—to the Bible, the written Word.*

Put in this way, I do not think this first attitude sounds anchorless or mystical, as Dockery feared it was. This attitude is merely one version of the Baptist-Protestant insistence that we continue to relate to the Bible as authoritative above our formulated doctrines or creeds.

There are two reasons why this anchor-dynamo was visible to me, but not to my respondents. First, my *entire argument* was aimed at getting the Bible to really have its way with us. That argument was, or was meant to be, located inside the biblical world. It was "intratextual." But, except for Marshall, none of my respondents recognized this, so far as I can tell.

And second, I knew that, when my chapter got to the point of discussing "good attitude 3," I was going to talk concretely about how the Bible is the written Word of God, and how Christ the living Word adopts and speaks the words of those texts as His live Word to us. And I knew that, when the chapter reached "good attitude 4," I was going to explain that the New Testament idea of inspiration means the Spirit is there, *in* the God-breathed text, accosting us repeatedly in our ongoing intercourse with the Bible.

But, since most readers missed the biblical-authority thrust of the chapter, by the time I got around to discussing good attitudes 3 and 4, it was too late. They had settled into viewing this "ongoing relation with Christ" as though there was no anchor-dynamo there—as though the Bible was not structurally and constitutively *right in the middle* of that ongoing relationship.

"Bookish" religion and Dockery.—I used the term "bookish" in

a good sense and a bad sense. The good sense never took on weight or mass for Dockery. All he really heard was the bad sense. That is not surprising, because I put most of the rhetorical energy of the chapter into warning against bookish religion in the bad sense of "bookish." But I stated the good sense when I said

> there is an important sense in which I am urging that we be very bookish indeed. I am urging that we "go by the book," the Bible. But I am pointing out that if we do that, the book itself makes us alive to the Spirit [because of the book's God-breathedness]. The book itself keeps us away from bookish religion [in the bad sense of "bookish"]. . . .

That said, it should sound sincere, because it is sincere, when I tell Dockery I agree with him. Yes, Baptists should be a "people of the book." I state my theological basis for this agreement where I say, in my former chapter, "I believe God uniquely binds Himself, in the ongoing work of his Spirit, to these sixty-six books."

That could only mean that, if we neglect or wander from those books, we neglect the Lord, the Spirit, and the salvation with which He meets us in those texts (2 Cor. 3:16-18).

Dockery's analogy.—In his original chapter, Dockery proposes an analogy between Christ and Scripture. In her response, Marshall expresses reservations. She cautions, "Scripture does not bear the life of God as Jesus did." That is true. But the life of God bears Scripture. The living God is there, *under* those written words, and *in* them. God's Son, the risen Lord, the Spirit, meets us there and speaks through the written words. That is the point of the "here and now" half of the New Testament doctrine of inspiration, as I explained it in my former chapter. The Spirit is very attached to the Bible.

A narrative approach.—As a basis for the rest of this rejoinder, I hark back to the "intratextual, narrative approach" to the Bible that I explained in my response to Marshall above (pp. 260-63).

Roughly speaking, my "new land" proposal is built around that narrative approach, though I said little about it in my former chapter.[16] That chapter's main category, "ongoing relation to God in Christ," was chosen in order to bring out the way we human beings are enfolded—through our faith and by God's grace—into the unfolding drama of God's saving interactions with humankind.[17]

That unfolding drama, with its chief "characters," the Father and the Son, is the overarching biblical story. It is the biblical story, or the Story, as I will label it. Even more real than the physical universe, the Story of God's interactions with us is *the reality in which we live and move and have our being.*

This Story is heavenly and earthly, and (in a different cross-section) it is natural and supernatural. It is "bodied forth" in solid historical persons and events, including even us, by the grace of God. But this Story, turning as it does on the death of a Jew upon a bloody piece of wood, also reaches into transcendent heights we cannot scale, stems from a past we cannot fathom, and reaches into a future we can but poorly imagine.

It is *that Story*—rather than a structure of doctrinal propositions that gives a theological account of it—that provides the "interpretive framework within which believers seek to live their lives and understand reality" (Lindbeck's phrase, previously quoted).

Importance of doctrine.—This does not mean the propositional truth of doctrines is unimportant. It is important. I said that at least five times in my chapter (pp. 121 [twice], 123, 126, 128). For example—and here I respond especially to Patterson—I said a person's doctrines could be "confused enough" that those doctrines do not orient the person to do the kingdom work at hand. And I said "your doctrines and mine may be so diverse that we cannot work together, practically speaking."

For these reasons and more to come, I disagree with George that I "radically subordinate" doctrine to relation. I respond similarly to Dockery's fear of my supposed "confessional minimalism." Neither man may have noticed how fully my chapter is focused on the Bible, leaving doctrinal-confessional issues for later.

Doctrine: What is it?—But what do I mean by this "doctrine" that is to be subordinated to our ongoing relation to God in Christ? Marshall and George raise that question, at least by implication. I intended my language to convey the idea. My basic term was "right doctrine." I went on to speak of "doctrinal system" (twice), "a system of doctrine" (twice), "theological doctrines," "formulated doctrines," "formalized doctrines," "an ironclad system," and "a neat bundle of teachings we have put together."

As these expressions indicate, the "doctrine" that I believe the Bible tells us to keep subordinate to our ongoing relation to God in Christ is something that is (a) formulated, with at least a bit of systematic character to it, and (b) invested with some claim to be "right," or to be something we are expected to believe. Doctrine in this sense is often stated in a creed or a confession, but it is not limited to things found in creeds or confessions.

The link with inerrancy.—What do my "two cheers" for systematic doctrine have to do with inerrancy? I think some Baptists become less Baptist by trying to impose upon other Baptists an authoritative doctrine *about* the Bible.

But when one gets down to "the *actual working authority* of the Bible in the life of the believing community and individual" (Harrelson's phrase, from his "response," my emphasis), I think those Baptists may be outwitting themselves. Instead of encasing the Bible in a hard cocoon, instead of wrapping the Bible in exactly the right doctrine and telling people, "Believe that," I think it is time to say about the Bible what Jesus said about Lazarus: "Loose him, and let him go" (John 12:44). That is what I am trying to help happen when I explain what it will take if we are going to "let the Bible have its way with us."

When doctrines become cocoons for the Bible.—It may help my cause if I appeal to sentiments such as those expressed by our great Separate Baptist father, John Leland: "I never saw a defence of a religious system [of doctrine], but what a great part of it was designed to explain away the apparent meaning of plain texts of scripture."[18] I might also invoke some lighthearted words of the best biblical scholar among the founders of Southern Seminary, John Broadus. Teasing his fellow-founder, J. P. Boyce, he said Boyce was one of those "dreadful theological people, who know beforehand what every passage ought to mean, in order to suit their creeds and systems, and who have not a proper respect for philology and criticism."[19]

Those two quotations are "warm ups" toward confronting a criticism of my "new land" proposal by Timothy George, a criticism that I found startling. But I must first state a major assumption on which my proposal is predicated. It is an "intratextual, narrative assumption." Please note that it utilizes three categories, namely, (i) doctrinal propositions, (ii) religious experience, and (iii) the biblical story, or our ongoing relation to God in Christ.

Now the assumption: Neither our propositional formulation of doctrinal truth nor our subjective religious experience is absolute. Both of those things are relativized by being included within a "third," namely, the mothering reality in which the first two inhere,

the biblical story, the story in which the living, acting, speaking God relates to us ongoingly.

I believe those who have been good enough to criticize my new land proposal, including at points Marshall, have worked with only two decisive categories, namely, doctrinal propositions and subjective experience. Thus, when I say our doctrinal formulations should conform to our ongoing relation to God in Christ, some of my critics hear me to be saying that our doctrines should be the plaything of someone's subjective experience. That is not what I am saying. I am saying our doctrines must *conform to reality*—to that mothering reality vouchsafed to us in Holy Scripture in which we live and move and have our being.

In the light of what I have now said, I hope George will wish to back off his criticism, which I found startling, that my proposal is a revamping of theological liberalism—as though I would peel off the outer husk of *the Bible's own doctrine* to get at "the essence of Christianity" (p. 302).

A sure sign that something went wrong in George's assessment is the way he invokes my image of the cocoon. He thinks it is a picture of the husk made up of the New Testament's *own doctrines*, such as Paul's supposedly scholastic doctrine of justification.

But I explained that my image works in exactly the opposite direction. Our cocoon is what *we make* of the Bible in our religious life—for example, the way we or Adolf Harnack might make Jesus into a Victorian gentleman. A cocoon is precisely *not* what the Bible is, objectively, in itself, as God gave it.

The trouble with the kind of system-builders whom Broadus teases and Leland lambastes, is that a lot of them are so caught up in the webs of their own systems that they cannot tell their cocoons from the Bible.

That leads me to say, however, that having a cocoon is not all bad. In fact, it is inevitable. We all grasp and construe the Bible *somehow*. But—and this is important—all cocoons are not created equal. We should continually be cutting and trimming our cocoons as we go back again and again to the Bible itself, not without devout historical-criticism, I would hope.

Patterson and James find an agreement.—Patterson launches an articulate attack on a key step in my argument, but shows, I believe, that he and I are not far apart on the particular points he raises.

Patterson believes I am saying that first one thing happens, and then another thing happens; and that there is a dichotomy between these two things. First, we have an "experience of encountering" Christ, as Thomas did when he met the glorified Jesus and said, "My Lord and my God!" (John 20:28). (I speak of real "relation" to Christ, not "experience of" Him.) Then, subsequently, we come up with some doctrine or theology. Thus, between these two things there is an "unnecessary dichotomy"—a dichotomy between doctrine *about* Christ, and personal relationship *to* Christ.

Why did Patterson believe the preceding ideas state my view? When I said our relation to Christ has "priority" in the sense of being *basic, central, and formative*, Patterson seems to think I was saying it comes *first in time*, "prior" to any doctrines. The same applies to Mohler, who tracks Patterson closely at this point.[20]

I wonder whether Patterson and Mohler thought through the Thomas example I supplied. Thomas's encounter already involves his recognizing Jesus, *and Jesus' speaking first to him*. Tons of theological content are built into that! So the three of us agree (and my *context* hardly implied otherwise): Some cognition of Jesus Christ, at least at the level of childlike knowing, is *always* involved when people relate to Him in Christian faith, and this knowledge has much theological content implicit in it, whether a given believer can state that content in doctrinal terms or not.

Which Christ?—Patterson and Dockery believe we must have agreement on a considerable body of doctrine about Jesus Christ if we are to be sure we are proclaiming the same Lord. (It *can* help.) Since they think I downplay doctrine too much, they believe no one can know which Christ I am talking about. This may assume our doctrines are the key way we identify which Lord we are relating to.

I do not think the Bible agrees, not in the sense of "formulated doctrine," anyway. The Bible sometimes identifies Jesus Christ in terms of formulated doctrine, true. But not very often. Its over-whelming emphasis is upon identifying our Lord *through narrative*.

We get a hint as to why this is the case when we consider how we know other persons. We come to know them when their life story intersects ours, as they relate to us in what they say and do. So it is with God the Father and Son. We come to know God when our story is intersected by the Story in which God gives himself to be known by us in Jesus Christ. In that Story, God bears down upon us, *as who he is*, through the deeds and words in which He relates to us in Jesus Christ His Son.

This should make it clear why there is no ambiguity in my "new land" proposal as to which Jesus we are to relate to. It is not the "new age" Jesus, nor the Jesus of Islam. It is the God, the Christ, whose character, identity, person, and gracious self are rendered to us *in the biblical story*. He and no other.

Supple or stiff?—The biblical story is supple. It lets itself be told in many ways. By contrast, doctrinal statements tend to be rather stiff. Which do we need if we are at an impasse?

But if we moved toward story, especially a supple story, would we lose control? Would we wind up saying that anybody, just anybody, can come to the party and be chosen a leader?

No. The category of "story" may be supple, but it is not a fog or a mist. It allows us to make distinctions. All we have to do is recognize that not just any way of telling the story will do, and that there are a lot of competing stories around, stories that are untrue, or unsaving, or even soul destroying.

For example, 2 John calls certain people "antichrist" because they "do not confess that Jesus Christ has come in the flesh" (v. 7, NRSV). "[Coming] in the flesh" is a crucial part of the saving story. It is literally "crucial." No flesh, no death on the cross.

Commenting on this passage, George says New Testament Christians excluded these people from both fellowship and leadership, even though they claimed to have a "relation with Christ." They were excluded because they "denied the reality of the Incarnation."

George is right. But "denying the reality of the incarnation" is nicely ambiguous. It could mean these antichrists had bad systematic doctrine (they rejected the doctrine of the incarnation), or it could mean they were telling the wrong story, or both.

My strong recommendation is that, in dealing with our impasse, we stick as much as possible to a "storied" understanding of who we are, and of what we shall confess together, *and* that we let the suppleness of the Story work its charm upon our sometimes uptight spirits. That would not only be less stiff, it would also keep us closer to the Bible—closer to the spellbinding virtuosity of God, who tells His story to us in such marvelously pluriform ways.

Inclusiveness, Patterson, and Mohler.—Patterson adroitly raises the question, by implication, whether my words about accepting people despite doctrinal differences are not a little hollow. At the

University of Richmond in 1990, I gave tacit consent when he said the old SBC leadership systematically excluded inerrantists. I suggested then that this was probably a good thing, but not in the way that sounds. My point was that if we are to have relatively inclusive institutions that work—we must take care not to have too many exclusivists on the governing boards.[21]

Mohler, whom I esteem, speaks of my "constant habit," in my chapter, "of identifying those concerned with doctrine as 'fundamentalists'" (p. 251). If I implied that, it was only once in my conclusion. But long before that, I carefully explained that according to the most knowledgeable scholars (including evangelical George Marsden), we are not fundamentalists because we are concerned with doctrines, nor because we hold certain characteristic doctrines, but because of the *militant way in which* we hold our doctrines. Some other problems Mohler finds with my chapter may resolve themselves upon a more leisurely reading.[22]

Conclusion.—I believe it is important that the kind of dialogue undertaken in this book continue, given respect for differences, the independence of the parties, and the provisos noted in my former chapter (knowledgeable discussants, and written, researched exchanges over time). Many Southern Baptists, who may be more or less divided at the national level, will continue working together in various state Baptist conventions. Exchanges in some cases would not represent the necessary respect for differences, but in other cases they would.

Is the Cooperative Baptist Fellowship a barrier to such dialogue? If Mohler thinks so, I disagree. A parallel may show what I mean. During the 1970s, a kind of "shadow denomination" came to flower on the SBC's right flank. This fundamental-conservative realm served several functions. It allowed its adherents to consolidate a distinctive outlook, to project that point of view into the broader SBC, and to mobilize the organizational and ideological resources to take over the SBC's agencies.

Moderate-conservatives' fledgling institutions will do the same things for them, except for any possibility of takeover. The ground is thus being prepared for dialogue of an interesting "ecumenical" kind, if the parties can avoid fundamentalisms of both the right and the left. We are yet to see how much theological vitality is in the moderate-conservative movement in this new situation. How winsomely will it be able to project its point of view into the local, state, and national life of Southern Baptists? It may play the role of ancient Greece in relation to triumphant Rome.

In any case, we have the makings of an "ecumenical dialogue," if the parties want to pursue it. I put forth my "new land" proposal as a contribution to such a dialogue, although I need to explain that, in one respect, my proposal was only *indirectly* ecumenical.

I refer to the fact that my critique of the fundamentalism that is in all of us employed some strong language. (No offense was intended.) A good many strict inerrantists are convinced that only those who take their view *believe the Bible*. Although they are willing to be polite about it, they believe that there is only one basic subject under discussion when they discuss the Bible with a noninerrantist, namely, how far they can tolerate unbelief.

(As I have made plain, I think that is not only wrong, but that at least the seven attitudes I describe as "fundamentalist"—including the fundamentalist kind of inerrancy—are obstacles the Bible has to overcome as it seeks to have its way with us.)

How can there be ecumenical dialogue with someone who thinks every whisper is a step toward unbelief? Clearly, the hope is that such a person might come to greater *humility* about his or her position. My critique of fundamentalism was intended to help that humility come about. (I say that sincerely.) Thus it was "indirectly ecumenical."

I agree heartily with such essentials of historic Christian faith as Dockery presents in his sketch of a "full-orbed Christian theology" (pp. 218-19). And I grant that a properly Baptist, noncreedal confession of such essentials may well be a part of some moves toward rapprochement. I have focused on the prior question, How shall we deal with the Bible, the basis of confessions?

Of course, Dockery has done that, too. He has proposed "eight points on the Bible," as we might call it. But here, once again, though I agree substantially with what he offers, I have been grappling with a still more basic question, a "paradigm" question.

Whereas Dockery frames an eight-point confession to show how we might understand the Bible—how we might construe it, or "cocoon" it in a doctrinal statement—I have been asking, How does the Bible cocoon our doctrinal statements? That is, What kind of force and significance does the Bible assign to any doctrinal statement whatsoever, if the *Bible* wields plenary authority, or if we let *it* have its way with us? Good Baptists must find the best answer to that question. (A good answer at the level of a *confession* is the preamble of *The Baptist Faith and Message*.) This is a paradigm question.

Whereas most use of the Bible since the Reformers has been controlled by a two-category paradigm, as we saw, I believe we need a three-category paradigm. We must attend not only (i) to propositions, or to the way the Bible "informs" us, and (ii) to religious experience, or to the way the Bible "transforms" us, but also (iii) to the Bible's eminently real story of our ongoing relation to God in Christ, which includes the first two categories and assigns them their point and purpose.

The preceding paragraph may look like one more way of cocooning the Bible, but it is something else, both in purpose and result. It offers a three-category paradigm to place us "inside the Bible." Only from that *ancient, intratextual vantage* can we understand, in an authentically Baptist way, the purchase that a doctrinal statement properly has on us, including a statement about the Bible. I believe we should try for consensus on this paradigm issue—or at least for "equipoise," or a mutually accepted "check and balance"—before proceeding to confessional statements, short or long.

Notes

1. Rob James, "Historical-Critical Study of the Bible," *Theological Educator* 37 (Spring 1988): 64, 72.

2. In his own preaching and faith, even Bultmann, whom I am not defending, was not as confined within that perspective as his disciples often are.

3. Preamble, *The Baptist Faith and Message*, 1963.

4. R. B. James, "Militant Inerrancy Violates Authority Principle of Faith and Message Statement," *SBC Today*, February 1986, 8; idem, *The Unfettered Word* (Waco, Tex.: Word, 1987), 142, 143.

5. William L. Lumpkin, *Baptist Foundations in the South* (Nashville: Broadman, 1961), 147-62. Cf. H. Leon McBeth, *The Baptist Heritage* (Nashville: Broadman Press, 1987), 231.

6. Robert A. Baker, ed., *A Baptist Source Book* (Nashville: Broadman Press, 1966), 120.

7. H. Leon McBeth, *A Sourcebook for Baptist Heritage* (Nashville: Broadman Press, 1990) 166.

8. John Leland, *The Writings of John Leland*, ed., L. F. Greene (New York: Arno Press, 1969), 114.

9. George Lindbeck, *The Nature of Doctrine* (Philadelphia: Westminster, 1984), 119.

10. What follows is based largely on David H. Kelsey, "Protestant Attitudes Regarding Methods of Biblical Interpretation," in Frederick E. Greenspahn, ed., *Scripture in the Jewish and Christian Traditions* (Nashville: Abingdon, 1982), 134-61. Cf. also Hans W. Frei, *The Eclipse of Biblical Narrative* (New Haven: Yale University Press, 1974), and *The Identity of Jesus Christ* (Philadelphia: Fortress, 1975).

11. This is not to say that nature or human history is unreal. These two continuums are (for one thing) the basis and vessel for human personal life. Also, in His Son, God dignified them by fusing the reality of each with His own life in the incarnation.

12. That is the way I read Stephen Crites's influential little classic, "The Narrative Quality of Human Experience," *Journal of the American Academy of Religion* 39 (September 1971): 291-311, reprinted in S. Hauerwas and L. G. Jones, eds., *Why Narrative?* (Grand Rapids: Eerdmans, 1989), 65-88.

Crites argues that when we envision ourselves as physical bodies, or as minds, or as minds encased in bodies we are seeing ourselves only partially, only as we abstract our sensations or our thoughts out of our full, concrete reality. (Our concrete reality includes both of these, and more, in an unfolding drama or "story.") Across the centuries—especially in the languages in which we say what we are—we construct ourselves as bodies, minds, etc. We do that as we interact with each other, talk to each other, write books, hear and tell stories, read texts, teach children, and otherwise maintain the cultures and traditions that shape us.

13. Ibid. Cf. especially Hauerwas and Jones, 85.

14. Hans Frei nicely interprets *Institutes*, I, 2 thus: "Calvin insisted that a merely historical or doctrinal faith . . . would not do. The proper knowledge of God must be personal (as we would put the matter today); it must be correlated to self-knowledge, and it has to be of a religious or pious nature." Frei, *Eclipse*, 23.

15. John E. Alsup, "Redemption," in Paul J. Achtemeier, ed., *Harper's Bible Dictionary* (San Francisco; Harper and Row, 1985), 857.

16. I only use explicit narrative language where I discuss Pietism in that chapter. My reserve is due to the fact that I employ such ideas as those from George Lindbeck *selectively.* For people in the believer's church tradition, Lindbeck's cultural-linguistic understanding of religion needs adjustment (Lindbeck, *The Nature of Doctrine*, 35). Also, I do not take seriously his idea (nor does he, in some cases) that religions, understood along cultural-linguistic lines, are noncognitive (Lindbeck 16-19; cf. 66).

17. The summer 1990 versions of my chapter, to which Patterson and Dockery made responses in Richmond and Louisville, respectively, only spoke of "relation to Christ." Because of their criticisms, and because I took a second plunge into narrative theology, I added the adjective in order to speak of "*ongoing* relation to Christ." This changed little in my basic concepts, but it "freed up" my thinking by giving it a far better vehicle to sally forth in.

18. Leland, *The Writings of John Leland*, 123.

19. John A. Broadus, *Memoir of James Pettigru Boyce* (New York: Armstrong, 1893), 307-8.

20. Both quote two sentences where I say "in the first place," and "in the first instance" (pp. 283, 249). The context makes it clear that I am not talking about precedence *in time*, however (pp. 122-24).

21. Should we have inerrantists on seminary faculties? Prior to 1986, I thought we should not in the biblical areas, because I thought all inerrantists reject critical scholarship. I still believe scholars must be able to employ scholarly methods honestly.

22. Two examples among others: (a) Mohler's question "what other kind of supernaturalism exists" other than the "heightened" variety (pp. 250-51) is answered in the next sentence after I use that term: the biblical kind of supernaturalism (p. 130). (b) If holiness "is absent in the notion of a God who is not 'uptight,'" as Mohler says (p. 252), then Paul did not believe God is holy, because Paul's preaching was based on the revelation that God does *not* have "a legalistic mind-set and a meticulous, hyperscrupulous nature," that is, God is not uptight in the sense I defined (Rom. 3:23-26; 4:4-5).

14

A Response
by Paige Patterson

The experience of contributing to this project has been for me one of delightful fellowship with the colleagues involved. I have learned much and profited from the exchange.

Nevertheless, my own conclusion is that the book would perhaps more accurately have been entitled *The Nature of the Impasse*. Though proceeding beyond the impasse is a worthy goal and always appropriate, these pages demonstrate that the scholars involved have not entirely succeeded. However, this lack of agreement should not be construed as failure. Sincerely held convictions cannot be jettisoned for the sake of a sort of mechanical, makeshift union. Absence of agreement does not mean that we cannot regard one another as brothers and sisters in Christ or that we are unable to cooperate in certain kinds of enterprises. However, Amos was surely inspired when he observed, "Can two walk together, except they be agreed?" (Amos 3:3)

The differences among Southern Baptists today are sometimes trivial and frivolous. We must move beyond these. Others, such as certain eschatological questions, are significant but still no cause for an impasse. But these essays will also demonstrate that there are other issues which, if answered incorrectly, threaten the vitality of Baptist churches and institutions. In some cases, these issues may even impinge upon the eternal destinies of the lost. Proponents on all sides of these issues ardently believe that their own conclusions are correct. The right of each thus to believe and thus to propagate must be both endorsed and guarded. A concomitant to that liberty is the right of the community—whether that be a local assembly, an association, a state convention, or the national Convention—to chart its direction while attempting to discern the will and purpose of God and, as a part of that decision, to determine what a particular community of Christians will or will not support. Perhaps the most wholesome result of the essays compiled here will be a demonstration of how to disagree charitably while providing an introduction for thoughtful readers into the nature and extent of the impasse in Baptist life.

The essays submitted by Timothy George, Al Mohler, and David Dockery represent the articulation of positions with which I am in almost total agreement. In these chapters I find little with which to take issue. The same can be said of John Newport's assessment of recent literary approaches to biblical hermeneutics. Newport's survey is a helpful introduction to literary approaches, and he also notes the weaknesses of these and goes on to describe ways in which literary approaches to understanding the Bible may prove useful and legitimate. Although I could not agree about reducing Job to mere drama or dropping Solomon as the author of Ecclesiastes, most of Newport's conclusions appear to me to the helpful.

This response will be directed primarily to the essays by Walter Harrelson, Molly Truman Marshall, and Robison James. Of the three, the majority of my comments will be devoted to an interchange with the ideas presented by Robison James. But first, a response to Walter Harrelson is in order.

Harrelson wants to advance the thesis that historical criticism has been helpful for Christian theology. He even insists that historical criticism is essential to the passing on of the faith. This concern to preserve and pass on the faith is certainly legitimate for all Christians. Furthermore, gratitude may be expressed to Harrelson for his warning about theories such as those of Wellhausen, whose hypotheses attempt to demonstrate evolutionary development of the text of Scripture. In order to substantiate his claim that historical critical methodology is crucial, Harrelson cites dual authorship of Isaiah and the multiple sources for the accounts of creation, as well as the absence of historicality in these stories.

There are three problems associated with this perspective. First, enormous assumptions often lie at the root of these reconstructions, assumptions for which little, if any, evidence is provided. For example, Harrelson informs us concerning the priestly origin of one of the creation accounts that "this priestly tradition almost surely drew upon many sources, including the old Babylonian creation story, *Enuma Elish*." No evidence for this is cited. Even when historical critical scholars remember to provide evidences, these evidences often prove highly unsatisfactory, but Harrelson gives us

none. We are just supposed to trust the scholars, even though they do not agree among themselves. These unproven assumptions abound among practitioners of the historical critical method.

The second problem is the customary practice of representing historical critical studies as though they were little more than efforts to discover the ancient milieu of the text, including the identity of both its readers and author, together with his concerns. A much more forthright approach is taken by R. P. C. and A. T. Hanson in their recent monograph, *The Bible Without Illusions*.[1] First, they admit that a belief in "inerrancy" of the Scriptures is the view of the authors of the New Testament and of historic Christianity.

> Again, as we have seen, the writers of the New Testament certainly believed in the inerrancy of the Old Testament, which constituted for them the scriptures. The Christian Fathers and the mediaeval tradition continued this belief, and the Reformation did nothing to weaken it. On the contrary, since for many reformed theologians the authority of the Bible took the place which the Pope had held in the mediaeval scheme of things, the inerrancy of the Bible came to be more firmly maintained and explicitly defined among some reformed theologians than it had ever been before.[2]

Then the Hansons allege that historical criticism rendered this view untenable.

> Historical criticism demolished his view: Moses had not written the Pentateuch nor David the Psalms nor Solomon the Books of Proverbs and Ecclesiastes, nor Matthew and John the Apostles the Gospels attributed to them, nor Paul the Epistle to the Hebrews, nor the Pastoral Epistles. The book of Daniel was not written by a mystic predictor in the seventh century BC, but by a commentator on contemporary history in the second. The Bible was divided up among a host of anonymous sources. Apparent history was in many cases discovered to be fable or saga or myth. Samson disappeared into a sun-myth. The historical existence of Abraham, of Joseph, of Esther became highly precarious. Evidence for miracles recorded in the Old Testament was completely discredited. Joshua had not stopped the sun nor Balaam conversed with his ass, nor Jonah had the remarkable experience with the whale. It became completely impossible to regard the Bible as an infallible or inerrant book in any meaningful sense.[3]

The Hansons concluded appropriately that if historical criticism has been right in most of its conclusions then it is no longer possible to speak of the inspiration of the Bible.

> The question can of course now be asked, "What has become of the doctrine of the inspiration of the Bible?" The only honest answer must be that it has disappeared. The doctrine of inspiration in its traditional form was always unreal and unworkable. It was a compliment paid to the Bible rather than a serious estimate of its nature. Any other definition of the inspiration of the Bible, e.g. that it is inspired because it is inspiring, either does not apply to the whole book or is so different from the traditional doctrine that it is dishonest to call it by the same name.[4]

In light of the above, let the reader be warned that the usual exercise of the historical critical method is nowhere near as innocent or constructive as James, Harrelson, and Marshall would have us to believe. On the contrary, it is most often destructive to faith and cavalier and irreverent in its handling of the biblical documents.

Finally, it is not the case historically that the church has been encouraged to faith by historical critical studies. The gradual and often rapid quiescence of numerous denominations whose leaders have largely opted for historical critical interpretation, the loss of evangelistic and missionary vitality in churches invaded by this kind of thinking, and the tragic roll call of hundreds who virtually forfeited their faith as a result of such studies remain a startling and frightening testimony to the devastating effects of historical critical thinking among the people of God.

Molly Truman Marshall has reminded us that Baptists must always focus on the theology of the cross in contradistinction to a "theology of glory." She is right, although for Paul, the theology of the cross becomes a theology of glory. Also, Marshall has twice invoked the emphasis of the radical reformers or the so called "left wing" of the Reformation for its theology of the cross and its experiential Christianity. Again she is correct, and I am grateful that she has reminded us of the Anabaptists. One would be pressed to find many of these Anabaptists who differed with the other Reformation leaders about the total trustworthiness of the Scriptures. Classical liberalism, neoorthodoxy, and historical critical scholars could never claim the Anabaptists, such as Hubmaier, Marpeck, Blaurock, Grebel, Manz, Sattler, or even Menno Simons, as being

sympathetic with their approach. These were men who accepted every affirmation of the Scripture as absolutely true and hazarded their lives on those very certainties.

Robison James proposes that both conservatives and moderates attempt to move together to new ground. He accurately detects that this would have to be a work of God's grace. I appreciate his sincere effort to find a solution, and I especially admire the fact that James's lucid style leaves no doubt about the nature of his proposals.

James suggests that Mohler's fourteen imperatives do not deal sufficiently with Baptist distinctives and that this inadvertently suggests that "being Baptist is our problem." Though Mohler is perfectly capable to answering for himself, let me add confirmation to the fact that James has misread Mohler completely. Mohler has absolutely no problem with the Baptist principles listed by James. Neither do other conservatives. In fact, one additional principle should be added, namely, the autonomy of each democratic Baptist entity to determine whom it will support or employ and with whom it will maintain fellowship. Mohler's fourteen imperatives are stated precisely because these are the points at which serious erosion has occurred in Southern Baptist life. In short, there is little hope of rapprochement unless these critical features are constructively addressed.

Also, James cites the superb sociological study by Nancy Ammerman but only mentions the portion of Ammerman's analysis that seems to explain the failures of moderates in Convention life by poor organization rather than because of their relatively small number of adherents. This fails to take seriously the overwhelming evidence for the general support of the conservative resurgence among Southern Baptists. This is evidence which is derived directly from Ammerman's extensive sociological surveys. As a matter of fact, the conservative resurgence began and progressed with the strident opposition to every effort conservatives attempted by the entire establishment, including Baptist Press, the state papers, and the chief executive of almost every state and national agency. Both the theological concerns and the numerical majority had to be there for this turn ever to have succeeded.

James' first major proposal for resolving the impasse is to change the emphasis from right doctrine to a focus on our ongoing relation to God in Christ. Doctrines are "to conform to our living, ongoing relation to God in Christ," rather than the relationship to Christ conforming to doctrine. This proposal sounds noble, even pious. But in the final analysis, it is not only in error, but also James himself fails to follow his own proposal. For example, James says our situation is like that of Thomas, who upon confronting the risen Christ said, "My Lord and my God." By this James means to suggest that it was the experience of encountering the glorified Christ and submitting to Him that takes precedence over the theology of the moment. But Thomas's statement, "My Lord and my God" is theological to the core. In fact, it was the inescapable theological conclusion which led Thomas to the profound personal confession and experience.

Or again, James says,

> I conclude that God's revelation in the Bible is not basically a matter of doctrinal truths so that, in the first instance, we are to believe them. Rather, God in the first place reveals *Himself* to us in Christ, encountering us and offering us the chance in Christ to participate in His life and relate to Him now and eternally.

But the fact that God reveals Himself to us in Christ is also intensely theological. For example, I do not honor just any man I meet on the street by saying, "Mr. President." But, if I walk into the Oval Office and realize that the man standing before me is, in fact, the President, then based on my recognition of this fact, I would greet him and honor him as my President. Ontology and, therefore, theology must always provide the basis for legitimate religious experience. The confession and experience of Thomas resulted from the nature and person of the God-man, Jesus. The faith-experience and the intellectual cognition of the reality demanding the faith-experience are frequently simultaneous. Nevertheless the faith-experience, to be valid and eternally beneficial, must be based on reality and truth.

Just as an unnecessary dichotomy is proposed by James on the issues of the doctrine of Christology and of one's relationship to Christ, so he makes the same mistake in attempting to raise the question of whether Baptists are Pietists or scholastics. Why should they not be both at the same time? Furthermore, James is missing in this discussion the fact that for years conservatives were sometimes held in derision by moderates and liberals in Southern Baptist life precisely because they were deemed too dependent upon experiential religion and largely untutored in the skills of academia.

Throughout my days in school, conservatives were criticized as being ignorant, emotional enthusiasts who had not done their homework. They sang boisterously, confessed sin with a proliferation of tears, ranted in the pulpits, and shouted "Hallelujah" and "praise God" from the pew. The criticism found its mark and stung. So conservative Southern Baptists began doing their homework. Now we are painted as arid scholastics. I entirely agree with James on the importance of a living, experiential faith. Relationship to Jesus is everything. But this experience is not a relationship with, for example, the Jesus of Islam but with the incarnate God who died a substitutionary death for us on the cross and who was literally raised again on the third day (i.e., the Jesus revealed in Holy Scripture).

This question about theology and relationship also arises in another portion of James's essay. He says,

> Let me explain. Your doctrines and my doctrines may differ at some significant point, perhaps in our doctrine of Scripture. Even so, we can share leadership in missions, evangelism, and theological education *if* the crucial question (other than ready competence) is whether you and I are mutually related to Jesus Christ as Savior and Lord, living faithfully in Him and for Him.

But what if our doctrines differ precisely on the point of our Christology? Or suppose we differ over the nature of how persons are actually saved? What if some are Universalists? Can these Universalists share leadership in missions, evangelism, and theological education with those who believe that the lost spend eternity in hell? If one posits a merely human Jesus or advocates universal salvation, then one's definition of missions and evangelism will differ radically from historic Baptist convictions.

If our differences revolve around debates such as dichotomy and trichotomy in anthropology, then leadership can be shared. But this is precisely why Mohler's demand for theological consensus on major doctrines is a necessity. For example, James accuses fundamentalists of "subbiblical supernaturalism" (p. 131) regarding Jesus. He alleges that this drives them into Apollinarianism, Nestorianism, Monophysitism, or Docetism. "Subbiblical supernaturalism" is a puzzling phrase. Is James implying that the incarnation of Jesus is not supernatural? Probably he only means that the emphasis of "fundamentalists" (a pejorative term) on the Deity of Christ tends to overlook His humanity. But the truth is that virtually all conservatives insist on the full humanity of Jesus in a hypostatic union. And besides, if conservatives are to be accused of Apollinarianism, etc., then moderates could often be charged with Arianism, which is no better.

James also accuses fundamentalists of being militant, intolerant, cantankerous, and sometimes mean. Undoubtedly, this is regrettably true on occasion. However, it is only half of the truth. The rest of the story is that moderates and liberals are sometimes guilty of those very traits. Many conservatives attempting to negotiate the boisterous seas of academic life have often discovered some of these same attitudes in our Southern Baptist seminaries and universities. The same thing obtains for James's charge that fundamentalists exclude people because they are not true to the Bible. In an exchange at the University of Richmond, James not only did not protest when I suggested that inerrantists were systematically excluded from some seminary faculties and other leadership positions, but also he suggested that this was probably a good thing. So, exclusivity is apparently a practice for moderates and liberals as well. And, besides, it must be remembered that ''meanness'' or ''sweetness'' may be a crucial index to consistency in the life of the witness, but it has little to do with the truth or the falsity of the testimony given.

Again, James suggests that Paul warned against a '''bookish religion,' or the habit of fixing on the Bible as a written text and making the book decisive as a book rather than meeting the living God *in* the text.'' James invokes Paul's words in 2 Corinthians 3, indicating that ''the Bible as words written in a book kills and condemns us.''

But Paul's concern in 2 Corinthians 3 is surely not a reference to Scripture as such but to the law which, due to human failure, does condemn. This mistaken exegesis leads to another unnecessary dichotomy between the living word and written word. Certainly the living Word saves us, but we learn of that possibility only in the written Word.

This point is vividly illustrated by James's statement that,

> Accepting biblical authority in that way is not a question of whether I accept this or that doctrine about Scripture. It is a question whether I believe God is addressing me there. It is a question whether I am ready to hear in these texts the speech of the Holy One who holds the destiny of all things in His hand. (pp. 140-41)

Does this mean that as long as one hears the "Holy One" in Scripture one may interpret that "Holy One" as finite? Can one understand the "Holy One" to be mutable, in process, perhaps even vulnerable to mistake? Is any kind of experience with any sort of a "Holy One" acceptable as long as this experience arises out of the reading of the Bible?

And if, as James elsewhere argues, there are "healthy differences" between the Christologies of Luke and Acts on the one hand and Paul and John on the other, then which, if either, is true, and with whose Christ shall we have an experience? If James means that these "differences" are in perspective or emphasis only, that is one thing. But, if he intends to suggest that these Christologies have substantive differences, then most conservatives will insist that the varied emphases of the New Testament authors are complementary and cohesive, never contradictory.

Finally, my general response to Marshall, James, and Harrelson is to cite a similar group of essays recently published under the title *Conservative, Moderate, Liberal: The Biblical Authority Debate.*[5] The response of Charles W. Allen caught my eye, since I had been Charles's pastor when he was in high school. Although I grieve about his position, I do commend him for his honesty. In his brief response he says the following: "I call myself a Christian because the Christian witness to God's good news in Jesus Christ seems to claim me just as insistently as anything else I take to be true."[6]

But Charles Allen is also a liberal Christian.

> I call myself a *liberal* Christian, broadly speaking, because I see no need to exempt any part of that traditioning process from the usual perplexities—the errors and atrocities—of human history. Therefore, my trust in the process as a whole does not rule out a healthy dose of suspicion as well, extending all the way to scripture itself. I see no reason to resist the conclusion that the writers of both testaments frequently lost track of the message they were called to proclaim.[7]

And finally,

> As a liberal, if I identify some portion of theme of scripture as hopelessly disordered, I do not pretend to stand above scripture's traditioning process. I am instead playing a minor part in that very same process, which is the only way I know to be faithful to its most basic demands. I still find myself obliged to converse even with

those portions of scripture I presently find most appalling. But just as I confess Jesus as the Christ because I finally cannot help myself, so do I also frequently find myself unable to keep from acknowledging that there is much in scripture that runs counter to that confession.[8]

Here is a young man who went to a Southern Baptist seminary and learned from historical critical scholars that portions of the Bible were "hopelessly disordered."

Some of the Bible is "appalling." There are "errors" and even "atrocities" in human history and, therefore, also in the Bible. The Bible writers themselves frequently lost track of the message they were to proclaim. How could such an attitude inspire confidence in the authority of the Bible? Even Charles Allen acknowledges that he continues to confront Jesus and the Scriptures only because these seem "to claim me just as insistently as anything else I take to be true."

Southern Baptists are not prepared to find errors in the Bible, much less atrocities. They likely will not agree that the Bible is hopelessly disordered and certainly not appalling. The only way out of the impasse is to agree together that the Bible is God's authoritative word without error in any area of reality and the sole rule for both faith and practice.

A Final Word

In the responses of Robison James, Molly Truman Marshall, and Walter Harrelson to my own thoughts as provided in this book, there are conclusions with which I simply cannot concur. Molly Marshall suspects that my assessment that something has gone wrong in Baptist higher education seems "greatly overdrawn." Robison James follows along the same line by suggesting that just as historical-critical methodology has been hurtful to some, so there are casualties resulting from conservative and fundamentalist schooling. The implication here is that there must be about as many of one as there are of the other. The further implication is that these casualties occur for essentially the same reasons. All of these conclusions are, in my persuasion, erroneous.

One must only survey the deleterious effects of historical-critical methodology, together with the presuppositions which guide it, on the entire religious life of Europe and on those denominations in America which have largely embraced it. No argument can be set forth which will save historical-critical scholarship from its role as one of the culprits in rendering evangelistic and missionary programs of many modern denominations stillborn. Schools are lost from the control of the faithful constituencies which gave birth to them and sustained them. Opinions advocated by those institutions fly far afield from those of the founding fathers and the supporting churches. This is all documented to such an extent that it seems strange to me that anyone would question it any further. This is, of course, precisely what Eta Linnemann was seeing that in part caused her to reject historical-critical methodology.

In Robison James's critique of Gerhard Maier's *The End of the Historical-Critical Method*, he still has not told us why it is very bad scholarship. First, he refers us to Peter Stuhlmacher's critique of Maier, but he fails to tell us what there is about that critique that impresses him. As a matter of fact, I found it a singularly unimpressive critique of Maier. In the second place, James suggests that Maier makes a mistake in pointing out that the historical critics attempted to find a canon within a canon. But whether this was a formal effort (as even James admits it initially was) or whether it is simply an informal result of historical-critical studies, the fact remains that this is exactly where we end up. Historical-critical methodologists most often determine that certain segments of Scripture simply are not true and, hence, in that sense can no longer be considered canonical. Yes, they belong literally to the canon of the Old and New Testaments, but, no, they are not in any substantive way authoritative for us. So, what we have left is a material canon consisting of sixty-six books, but a theologically valid canon consisting only of those portions so designated by the critics. This remains totally unacceptable, precisely as Maier has pointed out.

Marshall wants us to believe that the Bible never claims inerrancy for itself, but surely this is her interpretation. Any cursory reading of a text such as Matthew 5:18, where Jesus specifically says that "not a jot or a tittle shall pass from the law till all be fulfilled," would seem to readers, both common and advanced, a relatively straightforward claim for the full accuracy of every syllable of Scripture. Indeed, it is hard to know just exactly how one would justify any other interpretation of those words by Jesus, to say nothing of many other texts.

But the most important thing that Marshall says in her response to me is her avowal that we are able to "discern that there are portions of the text which receive prophetic self-criticism because they reflect a betrayal of the true foundations of covenantal faith" (p. 293). She further suggests that I may want to "bracket out" a problematic text. To begin with, I never spoke of "bracketing out" anything. Rather, I suggested that we needed to take, first of all, those texts with a clear message and understand and obey them. While we are doing that, we might temporarily bracket others as we wait and search for greater knowledge to help us understand them. To bracket them does not mean to bracket them out.

As for Marshall's statement that we are able to discern that portions of the text receive prophetic self-criticism because they reflect a betrayal of the true foundations of covenantal faith, I can only reply that this is precisely what causes the impasse. Evangelical Christians simply cannot concur in the judgment that various portions of the Scripture contradict or criticize one another. This is a presupposition on the part of Marshall which she then needs to demonstrate. Once again, what Marshall has done is to determine that a part of the canon is reliable and a part is not. Maybe it all belongs to the same material canon, but some of it is theologically acceptable and some is not, and, in effect, we jettison what is not theologically acceptable based on the decisions of the scholars.

Once again, I repeat. If historical-critical methodology means determining all that we can about the milieu of a particular passage, the genre of the literature, and other beneficial historical insights, we then may affirm the method as being absolutely essential. But, if it means a rejection of some portions of Scripture as not really belonging to a reliable revelation from God (and this is precisely what most historical-critical methodologists pursue), then we have no other alternative except to reject the method as damaging to our understanding of biblical theology, devastating to world missions and evangelism, and certain to create an impasse that can never be bridged.

Notes

1. R. P. C. and A. T. Hanson, *The Bible Without Illusions* (Philadelphia: Trinity Press International, 1989).

2. Ibid., 51.
3. Ibid., 39-40.
4. Ibid., 124.
5. Charles R. Blaisdell, ed. *Conservative, Moderate, Liberal: The Biblical Authority Debate* (St. Louis: CBP Press, 1990).
6. Ibid., 82.
7. Ibid., 82.
8. Ibid., 83.

15
A Response
by Molly Truman Marshall

The purpose of this brief essay is to respond to the substantive
and provocative chapters of three of my dialogue partners, Paige
Patterson, Robison James, and Timothy George. In our writing and
conversations together, we have attempted a clear articulation of our
perspectives and an appreciation of (if not agreement with) the
viewpoint of others participating in this collegial venture. We have
endeavored to engage the possibility of getting past our present
impasse in Baptist life. Each of us laments the current malaise, but
because we diagnose the cause of our dis-ease in different ways, our
"cures" are, as might be expected, concomitantly varied.

Many precipitous events of the life of the Southern Baptist
Convention have occurred since the beginning of this project which
contribute to a more tentative outlook concerning a shared future.
Thus my response will reflect, on the one hand, my idealistic
yearning for a rapprochement between contending parties that will
tolerate the obvious diversity in our ecclesial life and, on the other,
an anticipation of the emergence of different forms of Baptist
cooperation.

Patterson warns of the misuse of critical procedures in biblical
studies, asserting the threat to a reverent, believing approach to
Scripture that such might occasion. His resistance to a methodology
which has, at times, been employed by some scholars as an exercise
in intemperate skepticism, is warranted. Yet his conclusion that
"something has gone wrong in Baptist higher education" because
some professors use the historical-critical approach to biblical studies seems greatly overdrawn.

The guilty ones, in Patterson's analysis, are Baptist professors,
ostensibly little interested in the life of the church or the cultivation
of responsible discipleship in their students, who launch deliberate
attacks on the reliability of the Bible. My own experience as a

student in Baptist higher education at the university and seminary levels contrasts sharply with his description. It was not marked by professors trying to undermine the confident faith of fledgling ministers, but by godly men and women encouraging our faith to seek understanding. Their judicious use of critical methodology was intended to encourage an enlarged understanding and personal application of the text being studied. Investigating Pentateuchal criticism or the redactional work of the Gospel Evangelists spurred further engagement with the biblical materials, through which the Word of God comes to human beings in particular historical contexts.

Adducing Clayton Sullivan's recounting of the inadequacy of his seminary preparation for his beginning work as a pastor as further evidence of the wiles of historical-critical studies, Patterson asserts that imbibing this method puts the minister at a distance from those whom she or he is called to serve. No responsible biblical critic ever argued that technical issues were immediately relevant to humans caught in a gripping crisis. Yet the assistance in more fully understanding the truth of a biblical text provided by this approach can contribute greatly to the minister being "thoroughly furnished for every good work" (2 Tim. 3:17). When one is ministering to another in the deep griefs of life, a sure word of comfort drawn from the Scriptures is the pastor's best resource; moreover, dwelling on the critical problems of a text before a hungry congregation is offering a stone instead of bread. It is the shepherding responsibility of the proclaimer rather to explore the biblical text with all the tools available in order to let the written Word "dwell richly" within the pastor's own life, and then to offer it in nourishing and relevant ways to the gathered church.

Clarifying the point of contact between specialist and novice is necessary in any field; however, the distance yawns even greater when the preacher (who is hopefully a specialist in biblical studies) fails to acknowledge the critical questions carried in the hearts of those who hear the sermon. The chasm can be bridged when both the pastor and the people commit themselves to attentive study and listening to God's self-revealing in the Bible. As Harrelson has so eloquently argued, historical-criticism is necessary for this enterprise in every generation.

While I agree with Patterson's assessment that certain uses of historical-critical methodologies can result in a disparagement of the

Scriptures, his roll call of examples only serves to underscore that his hermeneutical presupposition of the inerrancy of the Bible (which the Bible never claims of its own witness) provides his grid for interpretation. He does not demonstrate, however, that the truth of the gospel has been seriously challenged by these critical studies. Further attention to the rich oral and literary background of the Holy Scriptures can engender a deep gratitude that God has guided both the hearing and written reflection through the vivifying presence of the Spirit.

Finally, I concur with Patterson's concern to preserve the unity of the Bible, eschewing any hermeneutical truncation that gives a privileged status to a "canon within the canon." Indeed, the ancient church's hermeneutical decision that the Testaments are a unity must continue to guide contemporary biblical studies. But affirming the unity of the canon which narrates the story of the one God who deigns to interact in history with a particular people for the purpose of redemption does *not* mean that we cannot discern that there are portions of the text which receive prophetic self-criticism because they reflect a betrayal of the true foundations of covenantal faith.[1] Whereas Patterson might want to "bracket out" a problematic text, I want to urge that we look at the internal resources within the unity of Scripture that can prompt proper interpretation.

James's lively essay is the most explicitly Baptist of the eight chapters collected here. He accents the foundational features of Baptist identity and warns moderate-conservatives of the peril of abdicating these. As a positive note, he does not simply address one side of the controversy; instead, he offers exhortations to both sides about the "old habits" that keep us circling in the wilderness. He enjoins us to move forward in the hope that we might converge on the "new ground" to which God might be beckoning us.

This chapter provides a trenchant criticism of the failure of moderate-conservatives to articulate in a coherent manner what they stand for, not what they are willing to wage battle against. I would acknowledge a significant measure of truth to his analysis. Few SBC congregations are theologically formed in the distinctive features of Baptist faith. Perhaps this myopia has been due to an extended "dogmatic slumber" that allowed the program statements of the SBC agencies and institutions to carry the burden of expressing their theological and doctrinal beliefs. Thus the moderate-conservative agenda was attending to these healthy (though not perfect) frameworks of our cooperative efforts, assuming that what their churches believed and lived out was obvious. As we have learned throughout this protracted struggle, this assumption contributed to what Mohler and George have called a "collapse of theological responsibility." I share their concern.

Professor James believes that the Bible places a priority on right relation to God in Christ rather than on doctrine, and it functions to make that possible. One's beliefs, therefore, must conform to one's actions—primarily to this ongoing relation to God. The distinction between "believing in" and "believing that" (as Martin Marty distinguishes them in his introduction to Luther's meditations on the Beatitudes in *The Place of Trust*) is quite constructive and, in my judgment, follows the *ordo salutis* of the Bible. Few would doubt that his position is thoroughly Baptist. E. Y. Mullins, whom James certainly wants to claim as a forebear, argued for the centrality of Christian experience and used it as the interpretive category for his constructive theological work, *The Christian Religion in Its Doctrinal Expression*. A more contemporary interpreter of Baptist self-understanding, Herschel Hobbs, underscores this perspective in his 1971 exposition on *The Baptist Faith and Message* that Southern Baptists "have a living faith rather than a creedal one."

But do we need stronger connections between doctrine and praxis (i.e., relation) than James allows? Apparently the measure of sound doctrine is whether or not one is "abiding in Christ" in the manner he suggests, but what can adjudicate that it is a "right relation"? Is he relying on another Baptist tenet, the "liberty of conscience," for this role?

Perhaps my question is due to an ostensible discrepancy in the way that James and George are using the word *doctrine*. Does it simply mean instruction or teaching in Christian faith? Or does it hold the more formal meaning of *regula fidei*, by whose parameters it could be determined that one is outside the faith? James seems to prefer the former use, while George's chapter is suggestive of the latter.

I agree with James's tacit assertion (which echoes the delineation of Oxford theologian, Maurice Wiles) that Scripture is a source for Christian doctrine, without being the sole source. Obviously the writing of the New Testament and the development of doctrine were not successive stages in the life of the church, rather the two could not help but shape each other as they were emerging. Consequently, if Christian experience is given its proper place, then it, too, forms doctrinal understanding—and continues to do so. Yet James was strangely silent about the character of doctrinal development.

Can we be content to say that within the Bible there are "apparent reasons" to support the role of women in ministry and also "apparent reasons" against such support? This approach suggests that there is unresolved dissonance in the "symphonic pluralism" of the Scriptures. Could we not argue, instead, that doctrinal development works toward a coherent resolution of this and other vexed issues? Surely the unity of Scripture is not a doctrinal system, as he rightly judges, but is grounded in certain foundational theological themes of an ongoing redemptive drama which serve as interpretive clues to the less clear passages. Perhaps, then, we can speak of the doctrinal unity of the Scriptures—without sacrificing the Bible's rich diversity.

The refrain of James's chapter is the invitation to serious engagement with the Bible, accepting its authority as the way to get past our impasse. He notes the priority that Baptists have placed on biblical rather than doctrinal study, but intimates that the "official" literature has been adept at "cutting the Bible down to size." Have we not seen even more of this in recent years as the conservative resurgence wants not only its theological but its political agenda to be reflected in the Convention literature? Of course, this observation could be countered by saying that the gestalt of Southern Baptist literature was dictated by the so-called "progressivist" denominational direction of the 1960s and 1970s. In my estimation, however, the earlier enterprise attempted to allow us to take more of the Bible seriously, especially with regard to race relations, the historical character and context of the Scriptures, Christian peacemaking, and the role of women in church and society, to mention some of the more prominent issues. An avid concern for these critical and timely matters needs no defense.

If Rob James wants to revivify the Mullins wing of our Baptist heritage, Timothy George aligns himself with the theological vision of James P. Boyce. The differing emphases of these two streams in Baptist life replicates the larger tension between the Reformed and Pietistic heritages of the family called evangelical.

George avers that Southern Baptist academic circles have neglected the scholarly insights of the evangelical renaissance; however, this assertion may not take in the full sweep of contemporary

Southern Baptist scholarship which can surely be identified as evangelical. Evangelicalism is an expansive movement with great diversity, as Robert K. Johnston observed in his address "Varieties of American Evangelicalism" during the 1990 Denominational Heritage Week at The Southern Baptist Theological Seminary. While some Baptist professors may demur about the term "evangelical"—believing it to be less descriptive of our tradition than of other denominational groupings—they would not hesitate to embrace the center of evangelical faith, which Johnston describes as commitment to: 1) the authority of Scripture; 2) personal faith in Christ; and 3) a spiritually transformed life that communicates the gospel through evangelism and social reform.

Over against the contentions of many moderate-conservative Baptists, George argues (in agreement with Dockery) that our confessional tradition carries forward "the historic Protestant doctrine of Scripture" which he determines to be biblical inerrancy (although he does not believe that this is the most important thing to say about Holy Scripture). Thus, his approach toward Scripture stresses its trustworthy character rather than belaboring specific interpretations, which is a helpful step in the direction of the new consensus which he seeks. It is a nuanced posture that can be affirmed by many moderate Southern Baptists.

George enjoins biblical scholars to employ critical methodologies, but with full cognizance of the presuppositions or underlying assumptions these entail. He is particularly critical of feminist theology for the "life-threatening danger" it poses to Christian faith. As I mentioned at length in the notes to my chapter, there are many fully evangelical feminists who labor under the authority of Scripture, yet probe it with pressing questions about the patriarchal culture in which it was written and the way in which this heritage has been used to denigrate the dignity of women. Yet, I will heartily concur that there are currents in some feminist theologies which we must denounce as nonbiblical and non-Christian. A recent work likens the atonement of Jesus Christ to "divine child-abuse." Not only does this comprise heresy; it is also blasphemy! Hence, I welcome his call to make an evaluation of feminist theology a first-order priority among us.

A key issue for feminist theologians, noted by George, is the problem of exclusively masculine language for God. Perhaps James's metaphor of the Bible's "symphonic pluralism" can help us toward a more balanced way of addressing and speaking about our Sovereign God. The Old Testament speaks of God in both motherly (Ps. 92:2: Deut. 32:18) and fatherly ways and in the New, Jesus' reference to God as "Father" speaks about the intimacy of His relationship with God rather than God's masculinity or literal paternity.[2] (We acknowledge that the virginal conception of Jesus is cloaked in the language of mystery, i.e., "the power of the Most High will overshadow you," Luke 1:35.) Of course we must retain gender-specific language about Jesus Christ; calling Him "Lord" is an important confession of our biblical faith and obedient discipleship. But to require all references of God to be cast in the masculine gender or with male attributes is to verge upon "linguistic idolatry" (Rosemary Radford Ruether's term). Important reflection on the fundamental reality of God has come out of the persistent questions posed by feminist theology. Elizabeth Achtemeier's summation of the "feminist error," which George cites at length, forgets that the fully orbed biblical witness to the being of God includes the very imagery of birthing, nursing, and carrying in the womb, that she criticizes. The theological misstep, in my estimation, occurs when one concludes that female imagery for God necessarily connotes pantheism, the identification of the Creator with the creation, and that "male transcendence" preserves the distinction.

Most enlightening is George's discussion of contemporary Baptists' aversion to *creedalism*; in his judgment this is due more to the influence of the Campbellite movement and the hyper-individualism which has come to full flower in American Culture, as Robert Bellah's *Habits of the Heart* has demonstrated. Baptists have a rich heritage of confessions, but they have stoutly resisted any of these being elevated above the Bible, which would sanction creedalism. George believes that a corporate adherence to an "explicit doctrinal standard" could direct us toward a more fully *congregational* ecclesiology, and I agree. Our churches should embrace new ways of cultivating doctrinal awareness and unity, whether through catechetical methods, the use of confessions of faith in worship, or forms of discipleship training that nurture a deepening confessional commitment.

George's astute acquaintance with our Baptist heritage is commendable. He has reminded us of parts of that legacy that moderates have neglected. If we move with him toward a new consensus, "holistic orthodoxy" will require that voices of dissent can still be heard.

Our shared commitment is to be Christians and to be Baptists. May God lead us beyond this impasse which has squandered energy and resources which our churches and our world so need.

A Final Word

My colleagues and I have sustained a courteous and constructive conversation for nearly a year now. Rather than following Augustine's example of writing his *Retractions* (i.e., a compilation of "all those things which displease me in my works"), these final responses constitute a strengthening of our positions put forward in our main chapters. While each of us has sought to find substantive areas of commonality, we find that genuine differences remain although we share a strong commitment to biblical authority and, I believe, the essentials of Christian faith. I am grateful that we have not used our differences to question the Christian integrity of our partners in dialogue, but have pressed for a deeper understanding of the contours of each theologian's perspective.

Dockery suggests that my chapter offers a "pluriform shape of theology" which, he contends, is to be expected from a posture of "confessional minimalism." This criticism hardly seems warranted; my chapter not only affirms the historic doctrine of the Trinity, but also the sinfulness of humanity, a robust objective doctrine of atonement, the evangelistic mission of the church, the irreducibility of the incarnation (which I take to mean the full Deity and humanity of Jesus), the uniqueness of God's revelation in Christ and in Scripture, and the necessity of confessing Jesus Christ for one's redemption. This is hardly confessional minimalism! Nor is it an attempt to "reject historic Christian distinctives" through some vague "inclusivism."

My own understanding of "theological pluralism" is a process that discards and relativizes key aspects of biblical faith. Indeed, I want no part in such a reductionistic enterprise, as I believe my contribution to these essays demonstrates. Because I was not attempting to write an abstract of Christian doctrine (Baptists have several good ones already!), many areas of Christian doctrine were not addressed. For example, I did not include the virginal conception through the power of the Holy Spirit or the return of Christ, the ordinances of the church or the process of the believer's sanctification; however, this does not mean that I do not affirm these or am without theological boundaries as the charge of ''pluralism'' implies.

The approach of my chapter, rather, was to argue that the reconciling cross provides the common ground for all Christians and that primary attention and obedience to God's self-revealing there can bind even factious parties together, as Paul's Corinthian correspondence demonstrates. Of course, Holy Scripture relates many other theological concerns to this foundation, and our task is to interpret them faithfully in our confession and witness.

David Dockery has called us to embrace an evangelical biblicism and has guided us toward a sturdy confessional theology with his clear statement of the articles of such a perspective. I find his understanding of the nature of revelation particularly helpful, for it offers a balance between personal and propositional revelation and acknowledges the various media God uses to reveal God's own self and desire for human living.

Mohler is concerned that I accentuate the priority of the story of Jesus over Scripture, which is the later codification of that story. Of course, we do not stand where the apostolic community stood, having personally witnessed the life, death, and resurrection of Jesus. We are ineluctably dependent upon their written testimony. But we must remember Scripture receives its authority from Christ; thus, we believe in Jesus the Christ, and we trust the faithful witness of Scripture.

This distinction between whom we believe in for our redemption and the source we plumb to direct us toward that Savior reminds us of the servant role of Scripture. Like the ministry of John the Baptist, it points beyond itself. Yet the inerrancy debate seems to reverse the order; unless we believe in the Bible's inerrancy, we are in danger of being misled about Jesus, as Dockery's response to James's chapter suggests. Surely I agree with my colleagues' strong affirmation of Scripture as God's authoritative vehicle of revelation and would add that it interprets and critiques other forms of God's revelation through nature, conscience, and varied religious strivings.

Mohler further warns against the proposals of Rosemary Ruether and Elizabeth Schussler Fiorenza, contending that they allow contemporary feminist or liberation concerns to denigrate the ''truth status'' of the biblical texts. He is correct in noting their goal of bringing contemporary ethical issues into dialogue with Scripture; and, indeed, they find within Scripture—most notably the ministry and message of Jesus Christ—those resources that galvanize work toward liberation. Some passages are simply more relevant for their questions than are others, but that is very different from his allegation that these authors have impugned the integrity and truth status of certain passages. Specific injunctions directed toward unique historical circumstances make a transposition into another discrete historical epoch problematic; yet within the collection we claim as the Christian canon there are enduring principles and historical examples which provide apt instruction. Article six of Dockery's proposed confessional statement concerning Scripture can provide a helpful guideline (guardrail?) for appropriating more difficult texts. He suggests that the reader interpret ''in light of which culture and communication means had developed by the *time* of its composition. . . .'' This is sound instruction and can move each of us toward responsible hermeneutics.

A respected professor of homiletics once declared, ''every good sermon has both warning and encouragement.'' These essays and scholarly discussions have provided both. God grant that we might all benefit as we have need.

Note

1. In view of the way Patterson, on page 289, has read this sentence, I see that I have not been clear. In this place (first full paragraph, p. 293) I am agreeing with him about the unity of the Bible and about not chopping off parts of the Bible to derive a ''canon within the canon.'' My point is that Scripture is a living unity, and if we cut ''portions of the text'' off from the larger body of Scripture, then, yes, those texts *may* ''reflect a betrayal of the true foundations of covenantal faith''—for example, the spirit of Jonah who wants God to destroy the Ninevites rather than for them to repent or the narrowness of Peter when he refuses to eat with Gentile Christians in Antioch (Gal. 2:12). When such things are ''reflected'' in certain texts, we can ''discern'' that they are criticized by Scripture as a living hole. But this is not criticism from outside. It is internal. It is the ''prophetic *self*-criticism'' that belongs to the inner dynamics of the living Word.

2. Patrick D. Miller, Jr., offers us much help in contrasting the ways in which the Bible speaks of God in parental images which refer to God's maternal and paternal character. See his article ''Ministry Practice: Theses on the Gender of God,'' *Haelon Journal* 6 (Fall 1985): 4-8.

16
A Response
by Timothy George

The purpose of this brief chapter is to respond to the earlier essays of my colleagues Robison James, Paige Patterson, and Molly Truman Marshall. Each has raised numerous issues which cannot be dealt with in the short compass of this review. Therefore, I shall focus on what I take to be the more salient themes in their essays related to the impasse in the SBC.

Before turning to this task, however, I wish to commend the editors of our volume for their vision and statesmanship in convening our study group and steering us through treacherous waters to the conclusion of this project. If, as I believe, the controversy within our denomination was spawned in part by the collapse of theological responsibility, then perhaps, *deo volente*, some new light can emerge from a panel of scholars attempting once again to take seriously their vocation as Christian theologians.

Christian theology is marked by the single-minded pursuit of truth, the precise shape of which becomes clear only in confrontation with competing loyalties and affirmations. Our meetings have been both cordial and candid. We have not tried to paper over the very real differences we had, and still have, concerning both the past and future of our common life as Baptists. We have stared at one another across the table of dialogue and have discovered on the other side neither angels nor demons but rather sincere believers struggling out of passion and hurt and sometimes anger to be faithful to that from which none of us can run away. Some of us have come to this encounter with deep scars and old wounds. Yet I think we would all agree that our meetings have been marked by a sense of solidarity and mutual respect which befits a company of scholars who are also *ministri divini verbi*. We have not solved the problems of the Southern Baptist Convention, but we have talked *to* one another, not just *about* one another, and perhaps that is our greatest achievement.

1. James believes that the impasse in the SBC has resulted from the dominance of doctrinaire fundamentalism which with its "uptight God" and insistence on theological conformity has squelched that true evangelical freedom which is the birthright of every Baptist. Unlike many moderate apologists who only decry the motives and tactics of their opponents, James offers a positive solution to the dilemma he describes. He wants us to "let the Bible have its way with us," that is, to read the Bible in such a way that its theological content, what he calls "doctrine," is radically subordinated to our ongoing relation to Christ. Thus our mutual relation to Christ, rather than our common confession of Him, would become the basis for shared leadership within the denomination.

While James does not himself deny any of the classical dogmas of the Christian faith, his devaluation of doctrine is really a revamping of a line of argument put forth by liberal theologians of the nineteenth century in their efforts to consign much of the orthodox tradition to irrelevance. Their assumption was that if we could peel off the outer husk of doctrine (cf. James's image of the cocoon), then we would arrive at the inner core of biblical religion, at what Adolf von Harnack called "Das Wesen des Christentums." This project marched hand in hand with the so-called quest for the historical Jesus, which in the end produced a Jesus without myth, a Jesus without miracles, a Jesus who bore a striking resemblance to a late Victorian gentleman out for a walk with his dog on a Sunday afternoon, in other words, a Jesus who was little more (shades of Feuerbach) than the sum total of our dreams, fantasies, and self-projections.

Of course, James is surely correct that the *purpose* of sound doctrine is not primarily to produce correct theology—even the demons believe and tremble—but rather to build up believers in their love for and submission to the living Lord Jesus Christ. No one has expressed this principle better than John Calvin: *"Omnis recta cognitio Dei ab obedientia nascitur"* (*Institutes* 1.6.2).

The problem with James's approach is that the New Testament nowhere present a "relation with Christ" apart from a theological *Vorverständnis* of His person and work. When Paul said to the Philippian jailer, "Believe on the Lord Jesus Christ" (Acts 16:31), he was indeed making a profound doctrinal claim about the One he believed could deliver him from his sins. "Christ" was not Jesus' last name, nor "Lord" His first! These were messianic titles fraught with rich theological meaning. The essence of Christianity, according to the New Testament, is knowing and trusting Jesus Christ, not *in abstracto* but precisely as Lord, the incarnate Son of God, as Prophet, Priest, and King, as Savior, Redeemer, and Victor. To be sure, one can respond to Jesus in simple faith without exploring in depth all that these and other biblical ascriptions mean, just as the disciples still had much to learn after they had obeyed the Master's first command, "Come, follow me." However, a major part of their preparation for future leadership was a matured understanding of who Jesus was and what He had come to do. Thus the earliest portrayal of the New Testament church depicts a band of committed believers who "continued steadfastly in the *apostles' doctrine*" (Acts 2:42, emphasis added).

In the church of the New Testament doctrinal unity on evangelical essentials was not only a test of leadership but also of fellowship. The Johannine community excluded as Antichrist those Proto-Gnostics who denied the reality of the incarnation, although we know from the recently discovered Nag Hammadi writings that many such could boast a personal "relation with Christ." Paul went further consigning to perdition even angels who pervert the gospel, this in the very epistle in which he championed Christian freedom (Gal. 1:8; 5:1).

The question today is not whether there should be doctrinal parameters for fellowship in the church, but rather which doctrines should function in this defining way. Historically, Baptists have drafted confessions of faith to serve a twofold purpose—"the declaration of faith and the testing of its existence in others," as James Petigru Boyce put it. Such confessions, which are always subordinate to and revisable in the light of Holy Scripture, have been adopted by Baptist Christians at every level of church polity—local congregation, association, state, and national convention. They have been used primarily in the contexts of catechesis and worship, but they do serve a disciplinary function as well. Undoubtedly, the drawing of doctrinal boundaries is one of the most delicate tasks the church faces. We can err either by drawing the boundaries too tightly, or by refusing to draw them at all. On the one hand, we lapse into legalism, on the other, into relativism. Only spiritual discernment and theological vigilance can keep us from going astray.

Rather than engaging in a polemic against "fundamentalism," or posturing "doctrine" against "Christ," would it not be more helpful to stress those evangelical affirmations which most SBC conservatives and moderates share in common? Presumably this would cover a wide swath of doctrinal terrain extending even to biblical inerrancy which recent studies show most moderates embrace as their own view. (Consider the fact that the last time a self-confessed noninerrantist ran for the SBC presidency was in 1984.) Such a process could be a healthy exercise for conservatives and moderates alike. Conservatives could learn better to appreciate the rich fullness of historic Christian orthodoxy thus owning afresh vital doctrines such as the Trinity which have been unduly neglected in recent times. Moderates, on the other hand, might be led to recognize real theological dangers on their left and to distance themselves clearly from them. In the context of mutual affirmation, Bible-believing conservatives and Bible-believing moderates could together raise the question which much of our discussion has begged: What are the limits of acceptable diversity among the people of God called Southern Baptists?

2. Patterson's essay presents an overview of the historical-critical method of studying the Bible along with a catena of graphic examples illustrating the destructive potential inherent in this approach. This is followed by a series of eight guidelines intended to promote the "safe use" of this methodology by Baptist scholars within denominational institutions.

Patterson's depiction of the historical-critical method can be summarized in three affirmations: (1) Serious scholarly engagement with the text of Scripture is not to be prohibited but rather encouraged; (2) As defined by scholars such as Charles Talbert and George Ladd, biblical criticism can and should be embraced by conservative evangelicals no less than by more liberal theologians; (3) In point of fact, however, practitioners of this method frequently bring secular, antisupernaturalist presuppositions to their work which skew their conclusions and undermine their confidence in the veracity of the Scriptures. Drawing upon the example of Eta Linnemann, herself an evangelical convert from Bultmannian demythologization, he shows how far even well-meaning exegetes can be led astray by their uncritical assumption of postcritical presuppositions concerning the Bible.

The problem Patterson points to is absolutely critical if Southern Baptist conservatives and moderates are to work together toward a new consensus within the denomination. The question is not, nor has it ever been, whether the word *inerrancy* should be used to describe the Bible but rather to what extent one can appropriate the "advances" of modern biblical scholarship while still remaining faithful to the historic Baptist confidence in the Bible as the totally true and authoritative Word of God. Precisely this issue lies behind the now famous "four points" of the SBC Peace Committee Report (1988). In my judgment, these four statements are not the most important affirmations to be made about the Bible. Its inspiration, sufficiency, canonicity, and perspicuity are surely more primary qualities. Nonetheless, the four examples cited in the report do reflect a legitimate concern to affirm a wholly trustworthy Scripture which conveys literal truth, and not merely religious symbols or literary artifices, about God and His dealings with humankind.

Most Southern Baptists, moderates and conservatives alike, embrace a popular consensual understanding of biblical authority which can be expressed quite simply: What the Bible says, God says. What the Bible says happened, really happened. In the Bible, the history is historical (it has the character of having actually occurred), and the miracles are miraculous (God has intervened in space and time precisely as the text indicates). We might argue whether this view is an alien ideology imported from "scholastic evangelicalism," as James seems to believe, or whether it is a restatement of traditional Baptist beliefs, as Herschel Hobbs and others have claimed. In any event, the possibility of a new consensus among Southern Baptists based on anything less than full confidence in the total truthfulness or God's written Word is not a viable option, now or in the foreseeable future.

Does this mean that Southern Baptist scholars must bury their heads in the sand and parrot only Sunday School aphorisms? Not at all. The need for a reverent, believing biblical criticism is more urgent now than ever before. Southern Baptists can and should contribute to the evangelical renaissance in biblical scholarship in the worthy tradition of John A. Broadus, John R. Sampey, and A. T. Robertson, all of whom, I believe, could have signed in good conscience the *Chicago Statement on Biblical Inerrancy*. However, what is required, especially of those who are charged with preparing future ministers of the church, is the recognition that the historical-critical method of studying the Bible is not a neutral, value-free tool to be used with a facile nonchalance; it is rather a double-edged knife which can be used either as a scalpel to effect healing and renewal or as a switchblade to inflict destruction and death.

I have suggested that SBC conservatives should not be fixated so narrowly on inerrancy lest they miss the polyphonic harmony of a fully orbed, holistic Christian orthodoxy. As the danger from the left recedes within the denomination, this note may need to be sounded with increasing clarity. I agree with Carl Henry that inerrancy is a mark of evangelical consistency rather than evangelical identity. However, this is not to say that the question of inerrancy is trivial or unimportant. It is important because it undergirds the Reformation confession that Holy Scripture must be *"iudex, norma et regula* in the church and for the church" *(Formula of Concord,* 1577). Perhaps no one has understood this better than Immanuel Kant whose epochal contribution to philosophy stands at the headwaters of the Enlightenment. In arguing for the superiority of autonomous reason as a principle of authority, he described, in disparaging terms but quite accurately, the alternative Christian position.

> The theologian speaks according to statutory prescriptions for belief, which are contained in a book, preferably called the Bible, that is, in a codex containing the revelation of an old and a new covenant, . . . which was established many hundreds of years ago. . . . That a God exists is proved by the Biblical theologian from the fact that he has spoken in the Bible. *(Critique of Pure Reason)*

Sometimes our enemies understand us better than we understand ourselves!

3. Marshall offers a basically positive response to Newport's chapter on literary approaches to biblical hermeneutics, a more critical reaction to Mohler's proposal for theological renewal, followed by her own constructive application of the "theology of the cross" to the current Southern Baptist scene. She is to be commended for her creative engagement with the theological dimension of the controversy and also for the irenic way she has expressed her concerns. I wish to comment briefly on two themes in her essay which were also raised in different contexts by James and Patterson: first, the relation of hermeneutics and biblical authority; and second, what might be called the canonical imperative in theological method, that is, the issue of unity and diversity within the corpus of Holy Scripture.

Dennis Nineham *(The Use and Abuse of the Bible,* 1977) has characterized the basic hermeneutical problem as the difficulty of moving from "the meaning system of a relatively primitive cultural group" to the thoroughly enlightened assumptions of the modern world, a world in which the traditional understanding of a Bible which purveys infallible truths is both anachronistic and irresponsible. Recent hermeneutical theory has to a large extent been the outworking and nuancing of this fundamental conclusion. However, in a postmodern world the presumption and inadequacies of this approach are increasingly coming into view. Karl Barth was a prophet in this regard refusing to jump on the hermeneutical bandwagon of Ebeling, Fuchs, and others. As he saw it, the purpose of serious Scripture study was not to make the Bible "relevant" to the modern world, but rather to discover "the strange new world within the Bible" which in turn shows how irrelevant the modern world has become in its rebellion against God and His Word.

Reader-response hermeneutics of various ideological hues poses a major challenge to traditional interpretive principles. Significantly, the International Council on Biblical Inerrancy felt it necessary to produce a second Chicago statement (1982) which specifically addressed biblical hermeneutics. Article IX of this document highlights the dangers inherent in many contemporary schools of interpretation.

> We affirm that the term hermeneutics, which historically signified the rules of exegesis, may properly be extended to cover all that is involved in the process of perceiving what the biblical revelation means and how it bears on our lives. We deny that the message of Scripture derives from, or is dictated by, the interpreter's understanding. Thus we deny that the "horizons" of the biblical writer and the interpreter may rightly "fuse" in such a way that what the text communicates to the interpreter is not ultimately controlled by the expressed meaning of the Scripture.

Basic to this statement is the distinction between the *meaning* of the biblical text which is always single, definite, and fixed, and its *application* which may be multiple, fluid, and diverse.

On the basis of the new hermeneutics, feminist theologians of varying degrees of radicality have sought to depatriarchialize the Bible by insisting on gender-inclusive language for God, in some cases refusing to call God "Lord" as well as "Father" since both words are seen as terms of oppressive domination. Southern Baptist scholars who wish to join the ranks of evangelical feminism should

express with clarity their personal adherence to an unbroken doctrine of Holy Scripture while firmly repudiating the unbiblical soteriology and revisionist teaching about God which characterize most mainstream feminist thinking today. Few Southern Baptist moderates, including many who have little truck with the feminist agenda, have been willing to take this latter step lest they be accused of bridling Christian freedom. However, in refusing to say "no" to blatant forms of unbelieving theology, they confuse liberty with license and thus fall victim to a theological failure of nerve.

Both James and Marshall speak freely of the diversity and "pluriform character" of the Bible while Patterson warns against any interpretive scheme which would posit a "canon within the canon." Helmut Gollwitzer has pointed to the devastating impact which the disintegration of biblical unity has had on contemporary theology.

> The person who still speaks of *the* Bible, and *the* Holy Scriptures, seems to be hopelessly out of date, and the Bible can no longer be called 'the word of God' because its human character and historical conditioning is obvious, and because a voice of God which is broken up into so many divergent voices does not help us, but makes us perplexed.

Again, it was the penchant of liberal theology to look for the "essence of Christianity" in one distilled portion of the Bible, such as Jesus' teachings on the kingdom of God, which was then played off against other less palatable passages, such as Paul's "scholastic" doctrine of justification by faith.

What, then, is the proper evangelical response to such a method? It is not necessary to contrive a flat, homogeneous Bible. Clearly God has revealed His Word to us in a richly textured document written from various perspectives over several millennia of human history in at least three languages and containing numerous literary forms and genres. And yet the Christian church confesses that these diverse materials constitute not a small library of antique literature but rather one book with a single divine Author speaking through many human authors to make known His eternal purpose in creation and redemption. By placing itself under this canonical imperative Christian theology thus affirms the unity, harmony, and consistency of the Bible and rejects the notion that one passage corrects or militates against another. Thus, John and the Synoptics are equally reliable sources for understanding Jesus' life and ministry, although they addressed different audiences from diverse perspectives. Similarly, Elizabeth Schussler Fiorenza's "marginalization" of the later New Testament writings in the interests of her own ideology-driven concerns falls short of a proper respect for the *norma normans*-character of the biblical canon.

Still, Marshall is quite right to point us to the Christ-centeredness of Scripture. The *Chicago Statement on Biblical Hermeneutics* agrees: "We affirm that the Person and work of Jesus Christ are the central focus of the entire Bible." We can appreciate Luther's single-minded emphasis on this evangelical norm without agreeing with his near excision of the Epistle of James from the canon of the New Testament. Luther's *theologia crucis* was not developed as a contrasting principle to *sola Scriptura*; indeed, they emerged almost at the same time in his thought as twin concepts in his critique of medieval theology. The "theology of glory" referred to the exaltation of reason and speculation in scholasticism. To this Luther opposed his "theology of the cross" which focused on what God has *once and for all done* in the atoning death of His Son, and what He has *once and for all said* in His written Word, which Luther called "the Holy Spirit book" which was "written by men but was neither of men nor from men, but from God."

It is precisely because the Bible "preaches Christ," as Luther says, that we dare not impugn its character as an error-free Word from God. Perhaps no one has expressed more clearly what is so decisively at stake here than historian Mark Noll (*Between Faith and Criticism*, 200). While fully supportive of the genuine value of modern biblical scholarship, he declares:

> It is more important than words can express to maintain the belief that the Bible tells the truth about God, the world of nature, the human condition, and the course of human history. While different believing communities express such a conviction in different ways, traditionally evangelical ways of stating it—in terms of verbal inspiration, infallibility, and inerrancy—seem ever more valuable to me, if they are carefully defined and qualified. Such convictions, with all that they imply about finding the way to Truth and Life, remain especially important in the contemporary period when the skeptical fashions of the academy debunk, and the subjective practices of the church undermine, the authority of a truth-telling, life-giving Scripture.

CONCLUSION

Beyond the Impasse?
David S. Dockery

Most Baptists, as well as most other Christians, are longing for spiritual normalcy in the best sense of that word. In order to do so they seem willing to move beyond both denominational differences and denominational loyalties to follow new paths. Desiring for the people of God to be genuinely the people of God, they are prepared to follow biblical ways to move beyond the current impasse. A persuasive presentation will be needed for the people to hear and follow. Coercion, however, is not the way to move beyond the impasse.

A new vision must be put forward by trusted leaders. Creative directives must be offered. The contributors to this symposium have each put forward various descriptions of the issues that divide us. Honest dialogue has followed. A positive step has been taken. Differences are clear. Commonalities, however, must not be overlooked. In brief summary fashion we can describe these differences and common concerns and beliefs.

We all stand committed to the believers' church tradition, to the primacy of Scripture, and the regenerating reality of the Spirit of God who grants spiritual life to those who confess faith in the crucified, risen, and exalted Lord Jesus Christ. We agree on the need for the church to impact our secular world. Specifically we agree on the following:

1. We believe the Bible is Spirit-inspired and authoritative.
2. We concur that the Bible is a divine-human book.
3. We all pray that the Bible will have its way with us.
4. We believe historical-critical methodologies can help us interpret the Bible better.
5. We see value in literary-critical approaches.
6. We acknowledge the need for theological parameters.

7. We agree that the Christian faith is a confessional faith, grounded in the common confession, "Jesus is Lord."

8. We see the importance of an experiential faith and the need for genuine piety.

9. We realize the value of learning from those who have paved the way for us and thus see the importance of a historically informed faith.

10. We acknowledge the reality of diversity in the articulation of our faith and worship experiences.

11. We recognize some of our differences are due to cultural and regional differences, as well as personal preferences.

12. We are committed to world evangelization.

These common tenets are extremely important and provide hope for common ground on which we can build for the future. The differences, however, cannot be ignored.

1. We differ over the nature of biblical inspiration, the extent of biblical authority, and the importance of biblical inerrancy.

2. We differ regarding the Christological paradigm for understanding the divine and human aspects of Scripture.

3. We do not agree regarding presuppositions behind the historical-critical methodologies or the extent of their use.

4. We differ regarding the need for affirmations of history when employing literary-critical methodologies.

5. We cannot agree on the range or limits of our theological parameters.

6. We differ over what aspects of our theology are primary matters, what matters are secondary, and what matters are tertiary.

7. We differ over the priority of divine revelation or Christian experience.

8. We differ over the range of inclusiveness in our doctrinal differences.

9. We find little common ground regarding the value of tradition and historical confessions for informing our faith.

10. We struggle with the tensions of unity in diversity.

11. We differ over where the limits of diversity move into the realm of contradiction in our faith.

12. We wrestle with cultural differences, variety in worship practices, issues raised by modernity, the role of women in the church, and the challenges of secularization.

These vast differences cannot be ignored. We have tried to address them as honestly and irenically as we can. Some readers will be discouraged at the distance between us. Is it not true that the *lex orandi* is the *lex credendi*? How do we affirm the unity of the church (Eph. 4:1-16) in light of such differences?

Too much rhetoric and too little discussion has taken place regarding our differences in recent years. Some have even tried to dismiss the differences, denying they even exist. We, on the other hand, have acknowledged our differences as the first step to moving beyond the impasse. We pray our efforts are not too late.

As we noted in the preface much has changed in the SBC since this project was launched. With the development of the ''Fellowship,'' our differences have been magnified. Some key Baptist leaders are no longer on speaking terms, let alone on learning terms with each other. How do we speak to a watching world as a body whose members are necessary for each other when one member disowns another? Certainly the secular world, not to mention other Christians, is unimpressed by our continual infighting. Can we overcome the recent polarities of the recent past? Can a new denominational vision develop in these nondenominational times? Can moderates hear the concerns raised by conservatives regarding doctrinal integrity? Can conservatives continue to gain sensitivity concerning the need for cross-cultural contextualization? Can moderates and conservatives together recommit themselves to our Lord's commission regarding global outreach? These are just some of the new insights and directives needed for a new day.

Certainly we all need to repent before God for the way we have at times treated our brothers and sisters in Christ. We must be cautious that our desires for change are not simply desires for power and control. We need to hear Jesus' call for self-denial in a world of self-assertion. These are steps we must take together if we are to make progress while dealing with our differences. We have, perhaps, focused too much on our differences in this closing section. Perhaps the recognition of our common ground is the place to begin if we are to move forward.

We trust our discussions in this volume will prove valuable and move us in the right direction. We have talked to each other. We have heard each other. We have learned from each other. What does the future hold for Baptists? Though the answer remains unknown, we can join together in reaffirming our trust in the lordship of Jesus Christ as He providentially leads His church in days to come.

Moving on from Here
Robison B. James

I want to applaud the spirit of what my friend and coeditor has written in his conclusion. I believe I will best advance the purposes of this book, however, if I do not join him as coauthor in those words, constructive and irenic though they certainly are.

With most of what Dockery says in his narrative paragraphs I agree. My reservations begin to multiply with his enumerated lists. A number of Dockery's twelve "agreements" are helpfully stated. And others on his list could be stated satisfactorily also, if we could get all the parties sitting around a table for that purpose.

But I find Dockery's list of differences less helpful. Perhaps it is just harder, in the nature of the case, to state differences successfully. When you tell me what it is you and I disagree about, I am likely to say (since we disagree on this point), "Look, that is not what this disagreement is all about. That is not what our difference is."

And when we try jointly to define our difference, we may bog down, and that could tempt someone to say, "*Here* is what our difference is."

Obviously that is not what Dockery is doing. He is genuinely committed to *uncoerced* dialogue. To have it, however, I think we need to be rather reserved in defining differences. When we address that subject, perhaps we should speak often of a *subject* on which we disagree, rather than defining too precisely what the difference itself is.

Even then, we need to keep in mind that the minute we say, "Here is a remaining difference," that almost dictates an "agenda." It sounds for all the world like, "Here is something we've all got to agree on, somehow, once we get it stated so it gives everyone as little pain as possible."

Obviously that is not good dialogue, and not what Dockery intends. In good dialogue, we set our agenda *mutually*, while we discuss that question. And we may decide that some of the things we could talk about or agree on are not that important—a point Dockery himself makes when he says we do not agree over what matters are primary, secondary, and tertiary.

Also, I find that Dockery's lists may not cover the main concern of my two chapters—my concern that we do some written exchanges on the "paradigm questions" of our approach to the Bible.

That concern could be added to the list, true. Maybe it is already there in the statement that we should let the Bible have its way with us. But my concern is not really a "list" sort of thing. It is the question how important such lists are if we really let the Bible have its way with us—if we let it have its authority to the maximum "extent" (a word from Dockery's first difference).

And that leads to my final reservation. We editors can say some helpful things. But we should be humble. We should not upstage our talented, committed contributors. Since they need to make their own case, we should not stand too long in the spotlight saying where this book comes out. For we do not know where it comes out. That is in the hands of God.

FOR FURTHER STUDY

Scripture

Abraham, William J. *The Divine Inspiration of Holy Scripture*. New York: Oxford, 1981.

Achtemeier, Paul. *The Inspiration of Scripture*. Philadelphia: Westminster, 1980.

Barr, James, *Beyond Fundamentalism*. Philadelphia: Westminster, 1984.

Boone, Kathleen C. *The Bible Tells Them So*. Albany: SUNY, 1989.

Bush, L. Russ and Tom J. Nettles. *Baptists and the Bible*. Chicago: Moody, 1980.

Carroll, B. H. *Inspiration of the Bible*. New York: Revell, 1930.

Carson, D. A. and John D. Woodbridge, eds. *Scripture and Truth*. Grand Rapids: Zondervan, 1983.

Childs, Brevard S. *Old Testament Theology in a Canonical Context*, Philadelphia: Fortress, 1985.

Countryman, William. *Biblical Authority or Biblical Tyranny*. Philadelphia: Fortress, 1982.

Dagg, John L. *Origin and Authority of the Bible*. Charleston: Southern Baptist, 1853.

Dilday, Russell H., Jr., *The Doctrine of Biblical Authority*. Nashville: Convention, 1982.

Dockery, David S. *The Doctrine of the Bible*. Nashville: Convention, 1991.

Draper, James T. *Authority: The Critical Issue for Southern Baptists*. Old Tappan, N.J.: Revell, 1984.

Geisler, Norman, ed. *Inerrancy*. Grand Rapids: Zondervan, 1979.

Hanson, R. P. C. and A. T. Hanson. *The Bible Without Illusions*. Philadelphia: Trinity, 1989.

James, Robison B. "The Historical-Critical Study of the Bible: Dangerous or Helpful?" *The Theological Educator* 37 (Spring 1988): 62-74.

Knight, Douglas A. and Tucker, Gene M., eds. *The Hebrew Bible and Its Modern Interpreters*. Philadelphia: Fortress, 1985.

Knight, Douglas A. *Rediscovering the Traditions of Israel*. Missoula, Mont.: Scholars Press, 1975.

McKim, Donald K. *What Christians Believe About the Bible*. Nashville: Thomas Nelson, 1985.

Manly, Basil, Jr. *The Bible Doctrine of Inspiration*. New York: Armstrong, 1888.

Marshall, I. Howard. *Biblical Inspiration*. Grand Rapids: Eerdmans, 1982.

Miller, Patrick D., Jr., Hanson, Paul W. and McBride, S. Dean, eds. *Ancient Israelite Religion*. Philadelphia: Fortress, 1987.

Neusner, Jacob, Levine, Barush A. and Frerichs, Ernest S., eds. *Judaic Perspectives on Ancient Israel*. Philadelphia: Fortress, 1987.

Nicole, Roger and J. Ramsey Michaels, eds. *Inerrancy and Common Sense*. Grand Rapids: Baker, 1980.

Patterson, Paige. "The Historical-Critical Study of the Bible: Dangerous or Helpful? *The Theological Educator* 37 (Spring 1988): 45-61.

Pinnock, Clark H. *The Scripture Principle*. San Francisco: Harper and Row, 1984.

Reventlow, H. G. *The Authority of the Bible and the Rise of the Modern World*. Philadelphia: Fortress, 1985.

Ridderbos, Herman. *Studies in Scripture and Its Authority*. St. Catherines, Ontario: Padeia, 1978.

Rogers, Jack B. and Donald K. McKim. *The Authority and Interpretation of the Bible*. San Francisco: Harper and Row, 1979.

Smith, Michael A., ed. *The Proceedings of the 1987 Conference on Biblical Inerrancy*. Nashville: Broadman, 1987.

Tucker, G. M. and Douglas A. Knight. *Humanizing America's Iconic Book*. Chico, Calif.: Scholars, 1982.

Woodbridge, John D. *Biblical Authority*. Grand Rapids: Zondervan, 1982.

Interpretation

Ackroyd, P. R., et al. *Cambridge History of the Bible*. 3 vols. Cambridge: University Press, 1963-70.

Anderson, G. W., ed. *Tradition and Interpretation*. Oxford: Clarendon, 1979

Barr, James. *Holy Scripture: Canon, Authority, Criticism*. Philadelphia: Westminster, 1983.

Barton, John. *Reading the Old Testament*. Philadelphia: Westminster, 1984.

Black, David A., ed. *Scribes and Scriptures*. Winona Lake: Eisenbrauns, 1991

Black, David A. and David S. Dockery. *New Testament Criticism and Interpretation*. Grand Rapids: Zondervan, 1991.

Carson, D. A and John D. Woodbridge, eds. *Hermeneutics, Authority, and Canon*. Grand Rapids: Zondervan, 1986.

Cate, Robert L. *How to Interpret the Bible*. Nashville: Broadman, 1983.

Childs, Brevard S. *Introduction to the Old Testament as Scripture*. Philadelphia: Fortress, 1979.

―――. *The New Testament as Canon*. Philadelphia: Fortress, 1979.

Conn, Harvie M., ed. *Inerrancy and Hermeneutic*. Grand Rapids: Baker, 1988.

Cottrell, Peter and Max Turner. *Linguistics and Biblical Interpretation*. Downers Grove: InterVarsity, 1988.

Ellis, E. E. *Prophecy and Hermeneutic in Early Christianity*. Grand Rapids: Eerdmans, 1978.

Fee, Gordon D. and Douglas Stuart. *How to Read the Bible for All Its Worth*. Grand Rapids: Zondervan, 1982.

Fishbane, Michael, *Biblical Interpretation in Ancient Israel*. Oxford: Clarendon, 1988.

Garrett, Duane A. and Richard R. Melick, Jr., eds. *Authority and Interpretation: A Baptist Perspective*. Grand Rapids: Baker, 1987.

James, Robison B., ed. *The Unfettered Word*. Waco: Word, 1987.

Johnston, Robert K., ed. *The Use of the Bible in Theology*. Atlanta: John Knox, 1985.

Kelsey, David H. *The Use of Scripture in Recent Theology*. Philadelphia: Fortress, 1975.

Linnemann, Eta. *Historical Criticism of the Bible: Methodology or Ideology?* Trans. R. W. Yarbrough. Grand Rapids: Baker, 1990.

McKim, Donald K., ed. *A Guide to Contemporary Hermeneutics: Major Trends in Biblical Interpretation*. Grand Rapids: Eerdmans, 1986.

Noll, Mark A. *Between Faith and Criticism: Evangelicals, Scholarship, and Bible in America.* San Francisco: Harper and Row, 1986.

Osborne, Grant. *The Hermeneutical Spiral.* Downers Grove: InterVarsity, 1992.

Radmacher, Earl D. and Robert D. Pruess, eds. *Hermeneutics, Inerrancy, and the Bible.* Grand Rapids: Zondervan, 1984.

Ricoeur, Paul. *Essays on Biblical Interpretation.* Ed. L. S. Mudge. Philadelphia: Fortress, 1980.

Russell, Letty, ed. *Feminist Interpretation of the Bible.* Philadelphia: Westminster, 1975.

Silva, Moises. *Has the Church Misread the Bible? The History of Interpretation in Light of Current Issues.* Grand Rapids: Zondervan, 1987.

Smith, Michael A. *The Proceedings of the 1988 Conference on Biblical Interpretation.* Nashville: Broadman, 1988.

Soulen, Richard N. *Handbook of Biblical Criticism.* Atlanta: John Knox, 1981.

Thiselton, Anthony. *The Two Horizons.* Grand Rapids: Eerdmans, 1980.

Theology

Ashcraft, Morris A. *Christian Faith and Beliefs.* Nashville: Broadman, 1984.

Barr, James. *Beyond Fundamentalism.* Philadelphia: Westminster, 1984.

———. *Fundamentalism.* Philadelphia: Westminster, 1978.

Barth, Karl. *Church Dogmatics.* Trans. G. W. Bromiley and T. F. Torrance. 4 vols. Edinburgh: T & T Clark, 1936-77.

Bloesch, Donald G. *Essentials of Evangelical Theology.* 2 vols. San Francisco: Harper and Row, 1978-79.

Boyce, James P. *Abstract of Systematic Theology.* Philadelphia: American Baptist, 1887.

Calvin, John. *Institutes of the Christian Religion.* Ed. J. T. McNeil. 2 vols. Philadelphia: Westminster, 1960.

Carnell, E. J. *The Case for Orthodox Theology.* Philadelphia: Westminster, 1960.

Conner, W. T. *Christian Doctrine.* Nashville: Broadman, 1937.

Davis, John J. *Foundations of Evangelical Theology*. Grand Rapids: Baker, 1984.

Dockery, David S., ed. *Southern Baptists and American Evangelicals*. Nashville: Broadman, forthcoming.

Erickson, Millard J. *Christian Theology*. 3 vols. Grand Rapids: Baker, 1983-86.

————. ed. *The Living God*. 3 vols. Grand Rapids: Baker, 1973.

Fackre, Gabriel. *The Christian Story*. Grand Rapids: Eerdmans, 1987- .

Farley, Edward, *Ecclesial Reflection: An Anatomy of Theological Method*. Philadelphia: Fortress, 1982.

Garrett, James Leo, Jr. *Systematic Theology*. Grand Rapids: Eerdmans, 1990.

Garrett, James Leo, E. Glenn Hinson, and James E. Tull. *Are Southern Baptists "Evangelicals"?* Macon: Mercer, 1983.

George, Timothy and David S. Dockery, eds. *Baptist Theologians*. Nashville: Broadman, 1990.

Hampson, Daphne. *Theology and Feminism*. Oxford: Blackwell, 1990.

Henry, Carl F. H. *God, Revelation, and Authority*. 6 vols. Waco: Word, 1976-83.

Kliever, Lonnie D. *The Shattered Spectrum: A Survey of Contemporary Theology*. Atlanta: John Knox, 1981.

Leonard, Bill J. *God's Last and Only Hope: The Fragmentation of the Southern Baptist Convention*. Grand Rapids: Eerdmans, 1990.

Lewis, Gordon and Bruce Demarest. *Integrative Theology*. Grand Rapids: Zondervan, 1987.

Lindbeck, George. *The Nature of Doctrine*. Philadelphia: Westminster, 1984.

Moody, Dale. *The Word of Truth*. Grand Rapids: Eerdmans, 1981.

Mullins, E. Y. *The Christian Religion in Its Doctrinal Expression*. Philadelphia: Judson, 1917.

Newbigin, Lesslie. *The Gospel in a Pluralist Society*. Grand Rapids: Eerdmans, 1989.

Newport, John P. *Life's Ultimate Questions*. Waco: Word, 1989.

Pinnock, Clark. *Tracking the Maze: Finding Our Way Through Modern Theology from an Evangelical Perspective*. San Francisco: Harper and Row, 1990.

Strong, A. H. *Systematic Theology*. Old Tappan, NJ: Revell, 1907.